Your Undergraduate Dissertation in Health and Social Care

Your Undergraduate Dissertation in Health and Social Care

The Essential Guide for Success

Nicholas Walliman

Jane V. Appleton

Los Angeles | London | New Delhi
Singapore | Washington DC

SAGE Publications Ltd
1 Oliver's Yard
55 City Road
London EC1Y 1SP

SAGE Publications Inc.
2455 Teller Road
Thousand Oaks, California 91320

SAGE Publications India Pvt Ltd
B 1/I 1 Mohan Cooperative Industrial Area
Mathura Road, Post Bag 7
New Delhi 110 044

SAGE Publications Asia-Pacific Pte Ltd
33 Pekin Street #02-01
Far East Square
Singapore 048763

Library of Congress Control Number: 2009920279

British Library Cataloguing in Publication data

A catalogue record for this book is available from the
British Library

ISBN 978-1-84787-069-8
ISBN 978-1-84787-070-4 (pbk)

Typeset by C&M Digitals (P) Ltd, Chennai, India
Printed in Great Britain by TJ International, Padstow, Cornwall
Printed on paper from sustainable resources

Mixed Sources
Product group from well-managed
forests and other controlled sources
www.fsc.org   Cert no. SGS-COC-2482
© 1996 Forest Stewardship Council
FSC

To My Wife, Ursula (Nicholas Walliman)

To Howard and Thomas (Jane Appleton)

Summary of Contents

Acknowledgements

The authors would like to thank the many people who have provided their support in writing this book. In particular our discussions and debates with colleagues and students, past and present, at our respective institutions of Oxford Brookes University and the Open University have encouraged us in the book's development. We have been particularly inspired by the enthusiasm and determination displayed by our students. They have helped clarify for us some of the difficulties that students face as they tackle a major piece of academic work.

We have also greatly appreciated the guidance and help afforded by the editorial team at SAGE Publications: especially Patrick Brindle, Claire Lipscomb, Ian Antcliff, Anna Coatman and Lucy Do, and for the support and clear thinking of Jeremy Toynbee of Toynbee Editorial Services Ltd.

We could not have written this book without consulting the expertise of many other authors who are cited in the list of references and further reading sections and for the anonymous artists of the copyright-free illustrations used in this book.

Finally we would like to acknowledge the support of Ursula Walliman and Howard Appleton, who have provided the much needed impetus and encouragement at crucial times. A big thank you!

r interest, but also enables you to
eir best use. This will inevitably
uation of where your strongest
yourself shine in your best light!
ned 'research', as it is about find-
ew to you), making sense of these,
ed and well-argued way. As with
ims at the outset, and some kind
e increasing focus in health and
issertation component provides
clinical question for practice.
ots of opportunities, but also
uide you through the process
care, and to explain and dis-
age. It will help you to make
order to produce a successful
it will present some serious
derstanding of your subject
motivate yourself. However,
host satisfying processes to

le momentum in health
y 1990s. It is defined by
udicious use of current
e of individual patients'
ot only using the best
eds and preferences of
ent of the health and
s about ensuring that
ial care interventions
t effective and safe.
starts by identifying
raising and evaluat-
t evidence to under-

ing practice comes
h evidence. Indeed
esearch evidence is
here is no evidence
al [research] way'
ablished, evidence
periences, theory
clients, patients

Introduction

Starting work on a research dissertation for the first time can be quite scary and even overwhelming. The purpose of this book is to help make that process easier, by working through the stages of the dissertation research project in a straightforward and logical fashion. Reading this book should enable you to write your dissertation more quickly and easily and may even increase your likelihood of gaining a good grade. There is obviously a lot to learn when you are conducting a research-based project of this scale for the first time, whether it is an empirical study or audit, a literature based study or theoretical analyses. What's more, because of the relatively short timescale available to you, you have little room for making mistakes in the process as the deadline cannot be postponed. You will need to learn about how to set up a dissertation project successfully, find out what will get you good marks, organize and do all the work, and hopefully make the process as enjoyable as possible. That is where this book will be invaluable; it may even help you to avoid having to read lots of other textbooks to glean all the necessary information from; textbooks on research methods are generally a heavy read!

Your Undergraduate Dissertation in Health and Social Care is an updated version of the original, *Your Undergraduate Dissertation*, by Nicholas Walliman first published in 2004. I had often recommended the text to undergraduate students undertaking their dissertation projects, so it was great privilege to be given the opportunity to work with Nicholas to adapt this core text to meet the needs of health and social care students. The result, we hope, is a book that provides students with a really good grounding in what is involved in undertaking a successful undergraduate project. The chapters have been kept short (that is why there are so many of them) in order to focus on answering one particular question at a time. You should easily be able to pick out whichever question interests you at the moment. It is, therefore, not necessary to read through the whole book from beginning to end. However, we have tried to put the questions into the same general sequence as they appear when you progress through a research project, so you should find navigating the process easy enough. This also results in some elaboration later on in the book of topics that were raised earlier, consistent with your growing understanding of the issues.

Use this book as a guide, extract what you find useful (which we hope is most of it) and leave aside the parts that are not relevant. As you work through the relevant chapters, we urge you to constantly reflect on what you are reading, how this influences your thoughts in relation to your own dissertation topic, what you will do and how you will do it. In this way, you will be able to decide what is applicable to your own work and where you will need to follow up the issues in more detail in other literature. In order to prompt you to make some decisions at the end of each chapter, there is a section on 'What should I do next?'. We have also provided a short further reading list of books and web resources, at the end of each chapter, where you can find out more information on the topics discussed if you need to.

This book has been written as a basic introduction to producing research dissertation thesis in health and social care. Once you ha decided on your topic and the methods that you will use to explore research problem or answer the research question, you will be abl judge just what information you need to complete the work. Do not ex the book to provide you with all the answers. What this book will hel to do is to decide just what further information you require to comple research dissertation journey. Of course, background and specific mation about your subject will need to be gathered independently irrespective of which research approach you take.

Finally, we hope that you find doing your dissertation is not work, but also a useful and enjoyable experience, where you l about a subject in which you are interested and end up gettin marks you deserve. Good luck!

you a lot of freedom to pursue a particu put your own individual talents to th require some soul-searching and eval talents lie. It is really up to you to make

What you are required to do can be ter ing out new things (even if they are only n and presenting your findings in an organiz any research project, there must be stated a of achievement of these by the end. With th social care on evidence-based practice, the an ideal opportunity to consider a pertinent

This type of work obviously presents l some dangers. The point of this book is to g of doing a dissertation in health and social cuss the options you might have at each sta informed decisions that you can build on in outcome. It should not be all hard slog, but challenges in terms of your knowledge and u matter, and of your abilities to organize and undertaking a dissertation can be one of the go through – and come out of at the other sid

Evidence-based practice

Evidence-based practice has gained considerab and social care practice in the UK since the ear Straus et al. as 'the conscientious, explicit and best evidence in making decisions about the car (2005: 280). Evidence-based practice involves n available evidence, but combining this with the n the client, and the clinical expertise and judgem social care practitioner (Straus et al., 2005). It i finite resources are used for those health and so and care activities that are known to be the mo Evidence-based practice is a systematic process tha a clinical question, gathering relevant evidence, ap ing the quality of that evidence, and then using tha pin decision making and practice.

It is important to point out that evidence infor from a number of different sources, not just researc there is a substantial amount of practice for which r not available. 'This does not mean practice for which t is wrong, but that the evidence does not exist in a form (Coles, 2008: 19). Where research findings are not est might come from policy directives, experts, practice ex that is not research-based and from the experiences o and carers (Le May, 1999).

Introduction

Starting work on a research dissertation for the first time can be quite scary and even overwhelming. The purpose of this book is to help make that process easier, by working through the stages of the dissertation research project in a straightforward and logical fashion. Reading this book should enable you to write your dissertation more quickly and easily and may even increase your likelihood of gaining a good grade. There is obviously a lot to learn when you are conducting a research-based project of this scale for the first time, whether it is an empirical study or audit, a literature based study or theoretical analyses. What's more, because of the relatively short timescale available to you, you have little room for making mistakes in the process as the deadline cannot be postponed. You will need to learn about how to set up a dissertation project successfully, find out what will get you good marks, organize and do all the work, and hopefully make the process as enjoyable as possible. That is where this book will be invaluable; it may even help you to avoid having to read lots of other textbooks to glean all the necessary information from; textbooks on research methods are generally a heavy read!

Your Undergraduate Dissertation in Health and Social Care is an updated version of the original, *Your Undergraduate Dissertation*, by Nicholas Walliman first published in 2004. I had often recommended the text to undergraduate students undertaking their dissertation projects, so it was great privilege to be given the opportunity to work with Nicholas to adapt this core text to meet the needs of health and social care students. The result, we hope, is a book that provides students with a really good grounding in what is involved in undertaking a successful undergraduate project. The chapters have been kept short (that is why there are so many of them) in order to focus on answering one particular question at a time. You should easily be able to pick out whichever question interests you at the moment. It is, therefore, not necessary to read through the whole book from beginning to end. However, we have tried to put the questions into the same general sequence as they appear when you progress through a research project, so you should find navigating the process easy enough. This also results in some elaboration later on in the book of topics that were raised earlier, consistent with your growing understanding of the issues.

Use this book as a guide, extract what you find useful (which we hope is most of it) and leave aside the parts that are not relevant. As you work through the relevant chapters, we urge you to constantly reflect on what you are reading, how this influences your thoughts in relation to your own dissertation topic, what you will do and how you will do it. In this way, you will be able to decide what is applicable to your own work and where you will need to follow up the issues in more detail in other literature. In order to prompt you to make some decisions at the end of each chapter, there is a section on 'What should I do next?'. We have also provided a short further reading list of books and web resources, at the end of each chapter, where you can find out more information on the topics discussed if you need to.

This book has been written as a basic introduction to producing a research dissertation thesis in health and social care. Once you have decided on your topic and the methods that you will use to explore the research problem or answer the research question, you will be able to judge just what information you need to complete the work. Do not expect the book to provide you with all the answers. What this book will help you to do is to decide just what further information you require to complete the research dissertation journey. Of course, background and specific information about your subject will need to be gathered independently by you, irrespective of which research approach you take.

Finally, we hope that you find doing your dissertation is not just hard work, but also a useful and enjoyable experience, where you learn a lot about a subject in which you are interested and end up getting the good marks you deserve. Good luck!

Chapter 1
What Is a Dissertation?

Chapter contents

- Why do I have to do a dissertation? The point of independent study
- Evidence-based practice
- The main components of a dissertation
- What will impress? Seeing it from the examiner's point of view
- The marking criteria
- What should I do next?
- Where to find out more
- Further reading

Why do I have to do a dissertation? The point of independent study

The dissertation is commonly the last component of a degree course, or a module taken towards the end of the undergraduate course. After having, over the years, been fed with lots of information, guided step-by-step through various assignments and tested on your knowledge and understanding in examinations and during clinical or practice placements, you undertake the dissertation as an exercise in independent study. It tests your ability to educate yourself, to demonstrate your expertise in collecting and analysing information, and to come to conclusions based on solid argument. It also gives you an opportunity to show how well informed you are, how well organized you can be, and how you can make a clear presentation of your work for effective communication.

The big difference between this and your previous work is that you will be doing the dissertation on your own. Your dissertation supervisor will provide you with support and some general guidance, but most of the decisions about what you do and how you do it will be yours. This not only gives you a lot of freedom to pursue a particular interest, but also enables you to put your own individual talents to their best use. This will inevitably require some soul-searching and evaluation of where your strongest talents lie. It is really up to you to make yourself shine in your best light!

What you are required to do can be termed 'research', as it is about finding out new things (even if they are only new to you), making sense of these, and presenting your findings in an organized and well-argued way. As with any research project, there must be stated aims at the outset, and some kind of achievement of these by the end. With the increasing focus in health and social care on evidence-based practice, the dissertation component provides an ideal opportunity to consider a pertinent clinical question for practice.

This type of work obviously presents lots of opportunities, but also some dangers. The point of this book is to guide you through the process of doing a dissertation in health and social care, and to explain and discuss the options you might have at each stage. It will help you to make informed decisions that you can build on in order to produce a successful outcome. It should not be all hard slog, but it will present some serious challenges in terms of your knowledge and understanding of your subject matter, and of your abilities to organize and motivate yourself. However, undertaking a dissertation can be one of the most satisfying processes to go through – and come out of at the other side.

Evidence-based practice

Evidence-based practice has gained considerable momentum in health and social care practice in the UK since the early 1990s. It is defined by Straus et al. as 'the conscientious, explicit and judicious use of current best evidence in making decisions about the care of individual patients' (2005: 280). Evidence-based practice involves not only using the best available evidence, but combining this with the needs and preferences of the client, and the clinical expertise and judgement of the health and social care practitioner (Straus et al., 2005). It is about ensuring that finite resources are used for those health and social care interventions and care activities that are known to be the most effective and safe. Evidence-based practice is a systematic process that starts by identifying a clinical question, gathering relevant evidence, appraising and evaluating the quality of that evidence, and then using that evidence to underpin decision making and practice.

It is important to point out that evidence informing practice comes from a number of different sources, not just research evidence. Indeed there is a substantial amount of practice for which research evidence is not available. 'This does not mean practice for which there is no evidence is wrong, but that the evidence does not exist in a formal [research] way' (Coles, 2008: 19). Where research findings are not established, evidence might come from policy directives, experts, practice experiences, theory that is not research-based and from the experiences of clients, patients and carers (Le May, 1999).

So what relevance has evidence-based practice for the undergraduate dissertation? The concept is of central importance for a number of reasons. Over the course of your undergraduate studies, you will undoubtedly have become an informed consumer of evidence-based health or social care practice, developing skills in critically evaluating contemporary evidence in your subject area. You will have developed a questioning approach to your practice and studies and it is likely that you will have identified several practice questions that interest you and issues that have challenged your thinking. The undergraduate dissertation provides you with an opportunity to consolidate these skills and examine a practice issue that has really caught your interest. This might involve examining an area of practice through a comprehensive literature review, challenging an aspect of practice by examining the evidence in the area or generating new knowledge to increase understanding about health or social care practice. Evidence-based practice is a central feature of all these dissertation examples, it is about finding the evidence and then putting that evidence into current health and social care practice (Clare Taylor, 2000).

The main components of a dissertation

Although dissertations come in many types, shapes and sizes, there are some aspects that are shared by most of them. Of course, the subject and how it is dealt with will have an enormous influence on the form and appearance of the finished work. However, as all dissertations are an exercise in academic research, there will be certain components that are regarded as essential for them to have academic credibility. A standard type of dissertation in health and social care will probably have the following components.

Preambles

- A title – this provides the briefest summary of the dissertation.

- An abstract – a slightly longer summary of the dissertation outlining the main issues, the research question, methods of investigation and conclusions.

- Acknowledgements – an expression of thanks to all those people and organizations that have helped you in the funding of, or preparation and writing of the dissertation.

- A list of contents – the guide to the various sections of the work.

- A list of illustrations and figures – if this is appropriate.

The main section

This is usually a series of chapters or sections. A typical example contains separate sections consisting of:

- An introduction to the dissertation.

- Some background to the research that reveals the issues to be researched and the work already done on the subject.

- A statement of the research problem or question and an explanation of how the research work was carried out (i.e. the methods used).

- The results of data collection and analysis.

- A discussion of the results and what they mean.

- Some conclusions based on the results.

- Recommendations for health and social care practice, education and/or research.

The add-ons

At the end are sections that provide important information on aspects of the work:

- A list of references – fuller details about all the publications and other sources that you have cited in the text.

- A bibliography – other literature that is relevant to the study but has not been directly referred to in the text.

- Possibly some appendices (supplementary information such as letters of support, ethics committee review information, participant invitation letters, information sheets, consent forms, detailed literature search strategies, questionnaire schedules or data extraction forms, etc). These give examples of your methods of working and/or further background information about issues that are important to your work, but not so central as to warrant being included in the main text.

In addition we always like to see some kind of illustrations, diagrams or summary tables in things that we read. Not only do these enliven the appearance of the page by breaking up rows of solid text, but they also can encapsulate ideas or issues in an incredibly compact manner.

What will impress? Seeing it from the examiner's point of view

In order to be awarded a really good grade, it is obviously useful to understand exactly what the examiner will be looking for when giving marks. The following list will indicate the main areas that gain marks in any dissertation, regardless of topic. These areas will be discussed in detail in the following chapters of this book, with many handy hints to help you achieve the best possible result. The list is not presented in any order of priority, but focuses on three areas that the examiner is likely to focus on:

- first impressions of the thesis;
- quick review;
- detailed reading.

Then follows a list of the main assessment areas and the sorts of questions that the examiner will be asking him/herself.

First impressions

Presentation How does it look? A neat cover, practical binding and well-designed page layout all give a favourable impression to start with. Remember that your dissertation will be on a pile with all the rest, so comparisons can easily be drawn with the others. Your examiner will be naturally better disposed to the more attractive submissions.

Organization A brief scan through the dissertation should give an immediate impression of how the work is organized. This means clearly headed sections, page numbers, easily spotted chapter divisions and a logical arrangement of the sections of the study. The examiner will feel much more comfortable with work that is easy to navigate. A clear structure is a strong indication of clear thinking – a markable aspect of the work.

Length Should conform to the requirements. A dissertation that looks too thin or too thick immediately rings alarm bells for the marker. The former will be difficult to award sufficient marks and the latter will be a daunting task to wade through. Studies that are over the word limit are likely to attract a penalty. When submitting your thesis you should state the number of words used (excluding references and any appendices).

Figure 1.1 On the pile with all the rest

Quick review

Abstract   A very useful, brief introduction that should never be left out. Summarize your whole dissertation in 150–200 words, including main conclusions. Not an easy task but good practice, and again demonstrates clear thinking.

List of contents   Situated near the front of the dissertation, this gives a simple overview of not only what is in the text, but how it is organized. It will also provide a useful navigation tool for later finding the page numbers of the different sections.

Main conclusions   One of the main points for doing a dissertation is to come to some conclusions based on the research. The final chapter should spell out the conclusions extremely clearly so that they can be picked out by the examiner by simply scanning through the pages. He/she will check that the conclusions relate exactly to the research problem or question.

Reference list   This will be a measure of your background reading, both in depth and in scope. You will impress your examiner if the relevant journals and books are cited, but will not if your list is padded with numerous extraneous references.

Detailed reading

Relevance and quality of background literature   You will not be reinventing the wheel. Whatever the subject you are tackling, there will be numerous other writers and experts who have worked in the same area. The examiner will look to see if you have discovered the main ones relevant to your study and have understood what they have written. This will provide the context for your own research and will enable you to pinpoint the particular issue that you will tackle in your study. It will also provide precedents of how the research might be carried out.

Clarity of research problem or question   It is essential to be clear, not only in your own mind but also in your writing, about the exact problem or question that you are tackling. This is the foundation stone of your dissertation and produces the main aims of the research. The research problem or question will be elaborated and dissected during the course of your study, but it remains the linchpin of all your research efforts. It should be possible throughout the dissertation for the examiner to relate the writing to the stated aims derived from the research problem or question.

Selection of methods for data collection and analysis   One of the main reasons for doing a dissertation is to discover and implement basic research methods. The choice of methods is huge, so you will be marked both on the discussion about possible methods and on the appropriateness of your choice to answer your research question.

Use of research methods   Each method has its own rules and procedures, so you need to demonstrate that you have understood these and implemented them correctly. The methods selected should be appropriate to the particular question being asked and must be rigorous and sensitive.

Solidity of argument to support findings and conclusions   You could see the whole dissertation as a piece of detective work, with the report being the evidence and argument that leads to your conclusions. Do you have a watertight case? The examiner will dissect the logic of your argument and weigh the strength of your conclusions based on the evidence you bring forward.

Quality of referencing   Your work will inevitably be based on the research and writings of others; after all, that is how we learn about most things. It is therefore essential that you acknowledge the source of your information and ideas by consistent use of a citing and referencing system. Marks are specifically allotted to this aspect of the work.

Quality of writing   The main form of your communication is the written word. Correct spelling and grammar are basic requirements. Proper sentence and paragraph construction are also essential; these will be partly dependent on your personal style. You should aim for clarity throughout. The examiner will have limited time to read your work, so make it easy for him or her: you will be rewarded for this. If you are not writing in your first language, it is a good idea to find a native English speaker to read through your work and correct it as necessary.

The marking criteria

It will help you to understand the particular requirements of your own course if you read through the instructions for your dissertation extremely carefully. Make a note of the issues mentioned and compare these with the comments highlighted above. Do not hesitate to take any opportunity you may get to discuss the requirements with your tutor or dissertation supervisor. It is also really important that you familiarize yourself with the marking criteria for the dissertation, as this provides a very useful indication of how marks will be allotted or weighted to the various sections of the dissertation thesis. If there is no breakdown of the marks, try and read between the lines to see if there are any hints. Remember the marking criteria are there to help you and should be used as a guide on where to place most emphasis in your dissertation thesis.

What should I do next?

Even if you do not know yet exactly what you are going to choose as a topic for your dissertation, it is a good idea to go and look at the work of students from previous cohorts/years. Your department or your university/college library should keep copies of all the dissertations. Find out where they are. You will probably be impressed by the sheer number of them, so how do you start looking to find something useful? Here is a good way to do it.

Find out what order they are in on the shelves. If they are in some kind of subject order, then choose four or five on the subject area that you are interested in. If not, any recent dissertations from your course will do. If you can only get them by request from the library catalogue, then choose some from the list. Ideally, choose dissertations that have been completed according to the regulations and instructions that you have to follow.

Do not sit down and try to read them! First, compare the following features:

- format (size and shape);
- design of cover;
- type of binding;
- design of page layouts;
- printing fonts and styles, and text layout;
- number and type of illustrations and or figures.

Now that you have got a general impression of a range of designs (note how important these are in the initial impact), it is time to look more carefully at the different types of research dissertations, their components and structures. Check each for the following:

- Title – length and clarity. Can you understand what it is about just by reading the title? Is it too long and complicated? Is it too short and general? Can you determine whether the focus of the dissertation is a literature review, audit study or empirical piece of work?

- Preambles – are these clearly labelled and set out? Check what they consist of: title page, acknowledgements, abstract, list of contents with page numbers, lists of figures and tables, anything else (e.g. statement of individual work, dedication, etc.). Look at the layout and design of each of these.

- Chapters or sections – how many, how long and in what sequence? Does the sequence of chapter titles show you how the dissertation is structured? One example might be: introduction, background, research problem, research methods used, data collection, data analysis, and conclusions. There are, however, several different ways of structuring dissertations, depending on the type of research work undertaken. Compare those that you have selected.

Now go to the end of each and compare the add-on sections. Note:

- the length and format of the list of references;
- whether there is a bibliography;
- the number and type of appendices.

Now, if you want to, you can read a few sections of the text to see what the written style is like. Note the use of technical words, the method of citing references and the style of the writing. Check the length of paragraphs and sentence construction. Are they short and precise, or long and complex? Explore if and how the illustrations are used to complement the text. Whatever you do, do not try to read all the way through. Rather, if you have the time, pick a few more examples of dissertations and repeat the exercise. You will soon get a feel of the difference in quality and style, which will help you to form your preferences on which to base your own work.

The length and complexity of the dissertations might be rather daunting, particularly when you consider that you will have to produce something similar within a few months or even weeks. Do not get too worried. Although there will be a lot to learn and plenty to write, if you can choose a subject in which you are really interested, despite the hard work it should be a pleasurable and rewarding exercise, and something to be proud of when you have finished.

Where to find out more

As mentioned above, a good place to start is to look at previously completed health or social care dissertations in your subject area. This will not only provide you with instructions on how to proceed, but will give you plenty of food for thought, and help to stimulate your own critical faculties about the quality of the work presented. This will be important when it comes to reviewing your own work later on.

Most books on this subject cover the whole sequence of preparing and writing essays and dissertations, much like this one. But hardly any actually discuss why you should do a dissertation, and what the examiners will be looking for. Despite this it is interesting, if you have time, to compare the advice given at this stage of the process. The approaches vary, depending on the level of essay or dissertation aimed at, and in some, the specific subject area catered for. Only look at the preliminary advice given in the first few pages of the books and scan the contents page to see if there is anything else of interest further on. You can probably do this in the library without even taking the books out on loan.

Further reading

Here are a few books that we have found useful, and we have given notes on what to look for in them. Each gives a slightly different view of the issues, so refer to as many as possible. Consult your own library catalogue for these and any similar ones that are available. When you locate them on the shelves, look at the contents list of promising books for relevant chapters.

Blaxter, L., Hughes, C. and Tight, M. (2006) *How to Research,* 3rd edn. Maidenhead: Open University Press. The first chapter gives an entertaining review of what research is about.

Mounsey, C. (2002) *Essays and Dissertations*. Oxford: Oxford University Press. See Chapters 1 and 10.

Redman, P. (2005) *Good Essay Writing: A Social Sciences Guide,* 3rd edn. London: Sage/Open University. Chapter 2 discusses what tutors look for when marking essays.

Swetnam, D. (2000) *Writing Your Dissertation: How to Plan, Prepare and Present Successful Work*, 3rd edn. Oxford: How To Books. See Chapter 1.

For more information on evidence-based practice in general, visit:

Users' Guide to Evidence Based Practice: http://www.cche.net/usersguides/main.asp

For more information on Evidence-Based Medicine and resources, visit: http://www.cebm.net/

Chapter 2

What Types of Dissertation Are There?

Chapter contents

- Your choice
- Practical investigations versus theoretical analyses and literature reviews
- Practical/empirical investigations
- Theoretical studies
- Literature reviews
- Another way of looking at types of dissertation
- What should I do next?
- Further reading

Your choice

Undertaking a dissertation in health or social care offers a great deal of freedom about the subject you can choose to investigate. The subject matter of your choice will have a direct bearing on the type of study you will undertake and the type of dissertation that you will write. The character of possible studies range from highly scientific and technical through to abstract theoretical analysis, with a whole range of options in between.

One way of looking at different approaches to doing a dissertation is to list the five broad generic areas within whose boundaries almost all research falls (Leedy and Ormrod, 2005: 86–7). These headings concentrate on the objects of investigation and you can ask yourself whether you are particularly interested in any one of these:

- People – many aspects of health and social care research are concerned with how people exist, act, interact and behave, either individually, in groups and in society.

- Things – biological, physiological, chemical and all other subjects that look at the condition and behaviour of the things around us, including the scale of a microbe, the study of viruses and the effectiveness of a wound dressing.

- Records – studies of archives, written documents, reports, patient records, policies, recordings, biographies and even works of art, drama or literature.

- Thoughts and ideas – philosophy and religion, political theory, language and semantics, research problems concerned with concepts or theories and all other subjects that deal with the products of human intellectual argument.

- Dynamics and energy – studies of causes and effects relating to human activity, such as bionics, metabolism, human energy, hydrodynamics, where forces and reactions are present.

In fact, if you consider your degree subject, for example, physiotherapy, nursing or social work, it might even be based on dealing almost exclusively with one or two of these particular aspects of study.

Another way is to look at doing a dissertation from the point of view of the kind of approaches you might take. Investigation in any of the above areas requires different approaches, some of which you might be more attracted to than others. In order to give an indication of what may be involved in the different types, Figure 2.1 illustrates the three main dissertation types: theoretical analyses, literature review studies and practical/empirical approaches, and some of the offshoots of these. Following this diagram is a short account of the characteristics of some of the main activities and the skills you need to carry out these different types of dissertation. This might help you to decide what kind of research you will be interested in doing. In all the cases below, it is unlikely that you will be able to concentrate solely on one type, as there is invariably a cross-fertilization between one and another. You might also be limited in terms of the type of dissertation you are allowed to undertake as part of your undergraduate programme, so do check with supervisor and course regulations. For example, some universities may require you to develop a research proposal for the dissertation component (see Chapter 6 for information on how to write a research proposal).

Practical investigations versus theoretical analyses and literature reviews

Do you prefer to spend your time organizing and getting involved in real-life activities, or would you rather search through the library shelves and online databases, poring over the thoughts and theories of others? It is worth thinking about this carefully. There are elements of both activities involved in doing a dissertation; and what one chooses to research will influence the weighting to one or other activity. Any useful research must have a sound theoretical basis and most theories have a basis in reality: hence you will probably have to spend some time in both camps.

Figure 2.1 extrapolates beyond the simple descriptions outlined above to show some of the branches of investigation that might follow on from particular approaches. It is quite possible, indeed likely, that you will

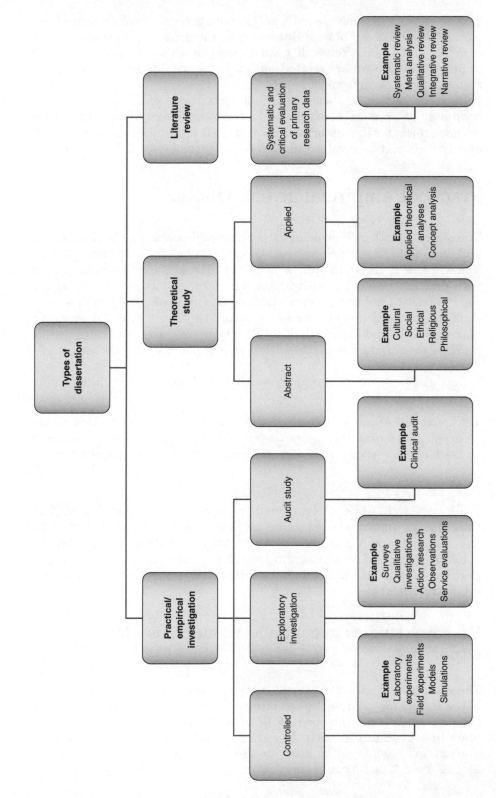

Figure 2.1 Types of dissertation

venture down more than one path, as it is usually very difficult to completely isolate aspects of a problem. But it will be important to limit yourself to a manageable task. You will need to keep a strong emphasis on one approach, with any other related aspects being considered only enough to feed into your main focus of effort.

In many health and social care subjects there will be an option of conducting a practical investigation, a theoretical analysis or a literature review project for the dissertation. Let us look in more detail at what sort of activities may be involved in each of the three types of dissertation

Practical/empirical investigations

The central focus here is on doing rather than philosophizing, though you will still have to do some thinking to make sure you are doing the right things. You will sometimes see the phrase 'empirical research' used interchangeably with practical research investigations. The term empirical investigation is used to refer to research studies where data is gathered using one's senses, through observation and experience according to an accepted scientific approach (Polit and Tatano Beck, 2004). There are three main categories of practical investigation work, these all involve primary data collection:

- research studies conducted in controlled conditions (such as a laboratory experiment or randomized controlled trial [RCT]);

- exploratory research studies and work conducted in uncontrolled conditions (such as surveys, interpretive or qualitative investigations) – this is often termed 'fieldwork' and might include service evaluation work;

- audit studies.

While research work is concerned with generating new knowledge, clinical audit compares performance against accepted standards of practice. In research, the emphasis may be on an attempt to verify or test an existing belief or theory, or an attempt to formulate a new theory. It is unlikely that you will be able to achieve the latter within the scope of an undergraduate dissertation.

Research studies in controlled conditions – the experiment

The essence of these is the control that you have over as many as possible of the factors (or, technically speaking, the variables) that are present in the process. It is not necessarily the case that experiments have to take place in a laboratory, or that they are limited to natural science subjects. For example, you might be interested in measuring reported stress levels among Year 1 and Year 3 social work students, to identify differences between the two groups using an experimental approach. The main point of experimentation is that you observe the influence of specific factors on a situation, so it is necessary to isolate the important elements in order that you can manipulate them and exclude as many extraneous influences as possible.

In order to do this successfully, you will have to be very clear about exactly what you want to test, and to devise or adopt a reliable way of doing this. In some cases you may need to have specific equipment in order to carry out the test, and you will have to be well organized in order to carry it through and record the results. It is also essential that you give yourself enough time to analyse the results of the experiments, as a long list of raw data is of no use to anyone.

You do not have to be a boffin in a white coat to do experiments. However, the personal attributes and enthusiasms needed for this are: a clear, logical thinking ability; practical DIY skills; good organization and timing skills; and, if you are dealing with human participants, good diplomacy and social skills.

Exploratory research studies

This usually involves getting out and about and possibly undertaking some kind of practical fieldwork, for example, in a GP's clinic, a local authority care home or voluntary setting. The main distinction is probably whether you are doing investigations that involve people or things. The techniques you use will be very different in each case, though even when investigating things, people are invariably involved in some way or another (e.g. in order to locate sites, to get access and ethics committee approvals, etc.). You might have to contend with unforeseen circumstances, people letting you down, practical and social difficulties and even dangers. The point about fieldwork is that you are entering into an existing situation (that you want to observe without changing it), so your control over events is intentionally weak.

As with experimentation, you will have to be well prepared as to exactly what you want to find out and how you are going to do so practically. For example, you might be interested in undertaking a small qualitative study to examine district nurses' perceptions of their role in relation to patients' nutritional needs. The methods you use should be tried and tested, and applied in an ethical and rigorous manner. It often requires some resourcefulness to get your own way, and persistence and patience are needed when everything does not go as planned, or if results are not immediately forthcoming. You will need to be clear about how you are going to carry out data collection and subsequent analysis.

To be successful in this type of field research you need to: be enthusiastic and to have a capacity for clear, logical thinking; practical organization skills; patience and resourcefulness to get over unexpected difficulties; methodical observation and recording skills; and as you are dealing with people, good diplomacy and social skills.

Audit studies

Audit is essentially a process of monitoring whether best evidence or agreed standards are being implemented in practice (Dawes, 1999). Within health and social care an audit is increasingly used to compare clinical performance against agreed standards of practice, e.g. nurses' documentation of care for patients with peripheral intravenous cannualae in comparison with local or national guidelines. Audit can be defined as 'a quality improvement process that seeks to improve patient care and outcomes through systematic review of care against explicit criteria and the implementation of change' (NICE, 2002: 1). Audit can be conducted through a process of self audit or through a system of peer audit and external review (McGovern, 2001).

While research and audit are different, 'research is concerned with discovering the right thing to do; audit with ensuring that it is done right' (Smith, 1992: 905), it is not always simple to discriminate between the two (Cave and Nicholls, 2007). Both approaches begin with a question, involve some form of data collection and may attempt to change or influence practice. However, it is important that a distinction is made between the two, to ensure that the correct approval processes are obtained for your study; as clinical audit does not require formal ethics committee review.

The clinical audit cycle is a systematic and cyclical process, which involves the following steps (see also Figure 2.2):

- selecting an audit topic;
- setting or establishing a standard;
- observing practice and collecting data;
- comparing practice to standards;
- implementing change (if needed).

Followed by a repeat of the audit cycle (Nursing Times, 2003).

If you choose to undertake an audit for your dissertation thesis, you will require many of the same personal attributes and skills highlighted under 'exploratory investigations' above. It is also worth considering that clinical audits are often conducted by those delivering a service to a local population, so you are more likely to gain approval if you are working as part of, or closely with the local team.

Theoretical studies

Ideal for bookworms and eggheads, you might think! Yes, but you could also be a revolutionary or a guru. Theoretical studies might be abstract,

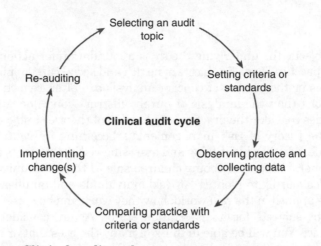

Figure 2.2 Clinical audit cycle

Source: 'First published in *Nursing Times,* www.nursingtimes.net'

but they are not always divorced from real life. After all, actions (apart from the most instinctive and animalistic) are based on theories, even if these are not overtly recognized. Also, our understanding of virtually everything is founded on concepts and theories: this is the way we make sense of the world around us.

Abstract concepts and theories

Whatever subject you are studying for your health or social care degree, you will have encountered abstract concepts and theories that underpin the thinking about the subject. Examples of these are feminism, wellness, empowerment, social capital, vulnerability, capitalism and so on. Spend a few moments thinking of the theoretical terms that appear over and over again in your subject. There is usually plenty of argument about the exact definition of these concepts and theories and about how they are relevant to the particular subject.

These arguments can be studied on an intellectual level, and conclusions can be drawn from the discourse arising. All subjects have theoretical base that is contentious and open to discussion and examination. Health care, social care, management and education – all subjects that have very practical applications – rely on theoretical foundations. For example, all of these require ethical issues to be addressed, economic priorities to be set, and equal rights to be considered, apart from theoretical matters uniquely connected with their individual characteristics.

You can define your study to examine these theoretical issues at an abstract level, weighing up arguments, contrasting positions, comparing approaches and verifying implications.

Applied

In most subjects, the underlying theory is a foundation for action. Certainly in the very practice-focused subjects of health and social care, applied theoretical analyses or the process of concept analysis are often regarded as more useful options than the analysis of purely abstract concepts. Applied theoretical studies consider the practical application of theories and concepts. For example, the theory of risk management is becoming influential in many aspects of life, whether identifying and assessing risks to patients and staff in an acute general hospital, keeping children safe in the community, or practitioners endeavouring to identify 'at risk' individuals and families. How such theories are applied in the real world, how they work and how useful they are, are excellent subjects for a dissertation study. Again, consider your own degree subject. You will be able to think of many theories that are influential in how the subject is studied and applied. Some theories may be strongly based on scientific evidence that would need expert knowledge to challenge, but others are more philosophical and institutional and thus more open to general critical examination. What their implications are and whether they deliver what is claimed can be studied by examining actual case studies. In this way, theoretical issues and their effects can be a focus for your dissertation e.g. Kübler-Ross's (1973) classic theory of death and dying.

Concepts are widely used in theory development and form the basic building blocks from which theories are constructed. It is essential that professionals define the attributes and meanings of concepts as these provide the basis for theoretical clarification and operational definitions for practice and research (Baldwin, 2008). One tool to use is the process of concept analysis, described by Walker and Avant as 'a formal linguistic exercise to determine [the key] ... defining attributes' (2005: 63) or characteristics of a concept. It is a strategy to facilitate critical thinking (Kemp, 1985), a rigorous and individual exercise which enables a practitioner to develop valid arguments to clarify a concept's purpose and dimensions for use in practice and research. Several authors have proposed methods of concept analysis which can be useful to examine concepts relevant to health and social care, for example, Wilson (1969), Walker and Avant (2005), who further developed Wilson's method, Rodgers (1989) and Chinn and Kramer (2008).

This kind of research combines investigation and understanding of theory – a literature-based activity, perhaps combined with consultations with influential thinkers – to study the application and effects of the theories, for example, self-esteem amongst teenage parents. This type of study will involve you with a really interesting and varied set of activities, particularly suitable if you are the type who wants to combine thinking with doing.

Literature reviews

A literature review is a comprehensive summary of research literature on a particular topic of interest (Polit and Tatano Beck, 2004). It involves a systematic process: identifying a research question, searching for and appraising relevant research evidence to answer that question and then synthesizing the material to develop new insights into the topic of interest. As literature reviews collate and summarize research evidence from a diverse range of sources on a particular topic area, they have an important role to play in promoting evidence-based practice, as busy professionals can apply evidence from a well conducted literature review to their practice (McGovern, 2001; Aveyard, 2007).

There are a number of different approaches to reviewing the literature, including systematic reviews, meta-analysis, narrative reviews and integrative reviews. The term systematic review refers to 'concise summaries of the best available evidence that address sharply defined clinical questions' (Mulrow et al., 1997: 389) and which are conducted according to rigorous and explicit methods. The most popular approach for undertaking systematic reviews to examine clinical effectiveness of health care interventions is the standardized method used by the Cochrane Collaboration. The Cochrane Collaboration undertakes and reports reviews according to a strict pre-defined protocol (Mulrow, 1994; Deeks, 1998; CRD, 2009). Systematic reviews in the Cochrane library have traditionally focused on clinical research, synthesizing the results from RCTs and quantitative evidence, but increasingly systematic reviews of qualitative research are being undertaken (Dixon-Woods and Fitzpatrick, 2001; Dixon-Woods et al., 2001; Kane et al., 2007). A meta-analysis 'is the mathematical sum of the results of more than one primary study, all of which have used similar methods to address the same question' (McGovern, 2001: 20). The intention is to examine the efficacy of a particular intervention (Taylor, 2000).

A narrative review is a literature review that does not adhere to a systematic approach and is therefore open to a number of weaknesses and biases (Greenhalgh, 1997). The integrative review as described by Whittemore and Knafl (2005) is an approach that combines diverse methodologies such as experimental and non-experimental designs within the same review. Aveyard (2007: 13) helpfully clarifies that all literature reviews undertaken for undergraduate research projects, should adopt 'systematic' and rigorous methods using the general principles of the Cochrane approach, but that they are not required to 'reach the same exacting standards.'

If your research question lends itself to a literature review study, this will usually involve you spending a lot of time in the library and/or searching online heath and social care databases to collate the relevant data. You will be examining the primary data of other researchers, appraising that data and critically synthesizing the evidence to provide new insights relevant to your research question and topic of interest. This type of study will interest those who enjoy considering the work of others, bringing together diverse scholarly and cross-disciplinary perspectives, and reflecting on how these might impact on current health or social care practice.

Another way of looking at types of dissertation

Another way to review the choice of dissertation types is to consider what is the main technique of enquiry that you will use when doing the research. Here are seven that are commonly used in health and social care research.

Tracking through time

This is the study of the history of events or people. The actual time element can be anything from a few months to more than a hundred years, depending on what you are studying, for example, the introduction of new ways of working, or the history of the midwife's role in childbirth.

Describing

Finding out what things are like. This involves identifying particular features, classifying, measuring sizes and quantities, examining constituents and organizations. The things can be objects, people, organizations, systems, or even ideas, such as the types of patients (including their medical condition, age, gender, ethnic origin) seen in one A&E department.

Comparing

This can be comparing like with like, or like with unlike. In both cases the aim is to identify differences and similarities. Aspects studied might be performance, organization, methods of health service delivery, approaches to care, appearance, attitude, and so on.

Correlating

Searching for relationships between objects and events, and sometimes tracking influences and causes. This technique often uses statistics to record the behaviour of two or more phenomena and judges the likelihood and strength of relationships. Other non-statistical methods can be used in some cases, for example, in-depth case study examination.

Evaluating

This is examining something and judging it against a set of criteria. Questions such as how successful, effective, quick, efficient, profitable, etc. are answered. It is necessary to set up a basis for a judgement before you start the evaluation, for example, as in an audit study.

Intervening

By making changes to a care system or health delivery approach, evaluations can be made as to whether the change is beneficial or not, or to gauge other effects on the system's performance. It is often difficult to predict in theory what will happen when changes are made, so this technique is used, often on a small scale at first, to help development efforts.

Simulating

This is the technique of making a controllable microcosm of the phenomena that you want to study. It always involves simplification of the real-life situation, sometimes miniaturization or expansion, and possibly abstraction. Experiments and models are the typical medium for this kind of study.

Of course, these techniques can and often must be combined. The introduction to a dissertation will commonly give some historical background and contextual information; description is normally the necessary first step in carrying out the other techniques. It is, however, useful to be aware of these different techniques, as one or more can be used as the basis for your study.

What should I do next?

Consider what you have read in this chapter and think about what sort of activities, interests and possible research questions attract you the most. Do you like the company of people and are you comfortable with talking to strangers, or are you more retiring and do you prefer to observe from the background or to manipulate inanimate things? Are you interested in abstract ideas, or do you only see the point in something if you can go out and do it? Are you more fascinated by how things became what they are, or would you prefer to explore how things might be changed in the future? Are you interested in developing new knowledge or analysing best evidence to improve current clinical practice? Are you a specialist, better at concentrating on a narrow field of study and in great depth and detail, or are you more of a generalist, who likes studying the wider context and is adept at making cross-disciplinary connections?

Use the answers to these questions to help you decide the direction your study should take and the activities that you will enjoy doing. Keep in mind that you will write a much better dissertation if you enjoy the activities involved. It will not all be easy-going and entertaining, but it will take much less effort to motivate yourself if you actually quite like doing the main tasks.

Make a list of the activities you will enjoy doing best and relate them to the dissertation types above. This will give you an indication of the sort of dissertation that you want to write. You could draw up a sort of specification for the work. Now you can go on to the next chapter to consider how this can be used to focus on the actual title and topic of your dissertation.

Further reading

There are lots of books on 'doing research' that have sections on the different types of theses or dissertations. If you want to add to what is given here, it would be a good idea to do a search in your library catalogue to find subject specific resources. Do be careful though that you do not get bogged down in books that are all about specific research methods. Look for books and resources that are aimed at doing undergraduate dissertations. Here are a few examples that we found of books in this genre. Generally, as in this book, the issue of what choices you have in your research will appear near the beginning of the book.

Aveyard, H. (2007) *Doing a Literature Review in Health and Social Care: A Practical Guide.* Maidenhead: Open University Press. A very useful and readable text and an excellent guide for beginners.

Bell, J. (2005) *Doing your Research Project: A Guide for First-time Researchers in Education, Health and Social Science,* 4th edn. Maidenhead: Open University Press. A very useful introductory book.

Blaxter, L., Hughes, C. and Tight, M. (2006) *How to Research,* 3rd edn. Maidenhead: Open University Press.

Boden, R., Kenway, J. and Epstein, D. (2005) *Getting Started on Research.* London: Sage Publications.

Brett Davies, M. (2007) *Doing a Successful Project: Using Qualitative or Quantitative Methods.* Basingstoke: Palgrave MacMillan.

Fink, A. (2005) *Conducting Research Literature Reviews: From the Internet to Paper,* 2nd edn. London: Sage Publications.

Gilbert, N. (ed.) (2008) *Researching Social Life,* 3rd edn. London: Sage Publications.

Hart, C. (1998) *Doing a Literature Review: Releasing the Social Science Research Imagination.* London: Sage Publications.

Hart, C. (2001) *Doing a Literature Search: A Comprehensive Guide for the Social Sciences.* London: Sage Publications.

Leedy, P. and Ormrod, J.E. (2005) *Practical Research: Planning and Design,* 8th edn. Upper Saddle River, NJ: Pearson, Merrill Prentice Hall.

Robson, C. (2002) *Real World Research: A Resource for Social Scientists and Practitioner-Researchers, 2nd edn.* Oxford: Blackwell Publishers. A very good resource book, which should be used to find out more about different methods of data collection and analysis. See the guide at the front 'Ways of Using the Book'.

Ridley, D. (2008) *The Literature Review: A Step-by-Step Guide for Students*. London: Sage Publications.

Saks, M., Williams, M. and Hancock, B. (2000) *Developing Research in Primary Care*. Oxford: Radcliffe Medical Press. See Chapter 1 'Starting a research project and applying for funding'.

Sharp, J.A., Peters, J. and Howard, K. (2002) *The Management of a Student Research Project*, 3rd edn. Aldershot: Gower Publishing.

Chapter 3

What Will it Be About?

Chapter contents

- What really interests you?
- Regulations and supervision
- Previous examples
- Getting background information
- Starting a research diary
- What should I do next?
- Further reading

What really interests you?

In health and social care, it is usual for students to choose the subject that they will write about for their dissertation. Sometimes, this amounts to so much freedom that it is really difficult to know where to begin. If you are in this situation, or if you do not know how to make a choice between suggested titles or themes, the following thoughts will help.

As mentioned in Chapter 2, it is always easier to write an extended piece of work if you are interested in the subject and when the research involves activities that you enjoy doing. Moreover, greater interest inevitably means a greater thirst for knowledge, and this enthusiasm is bound to show in the final product. So, how can you weave your favourite topic or pastime into the dissertation? You might need to indulge in some creative thinking to achieve this, depending on the subject you are studying.

Most dissertation subjects are a combination of a background subject discipline, for example, nursing, social work, occupational therapy, physiotherapy, public health, etc., and a particular situation, activity or phenomenon, for example, A&E department, pre-operative care, poverty, etc.

You will have to take the subject discipline you are studying as a given, as that is presumably what you are studying for your degree. The freedom lies in what you choose to investigate within this context.

A few examples of subjects and study titles are given below:

- Paediatric nursing and end of life care. 'End of life care for young people in the community – a critical review of policy and research evidence.'

- Social work and self-harming behaviours – 'Psychosocial interventions with teenagers who self harm: a literature review.'

- Occupational therapy and falls prevention. 'What evidence underpins occupational therapy involvement in fall prevention programmes with older people?'

- Physiotherapy and reflective practice – 'Physiotherapy students' perceptions of reflective practice – a qualitative study.'

- Mental health nursing and needs assessment. 'A concept analysis of needs assessment related to mental health nursing.'

- Paramedic science and ambulance response times – 'A comparative study to review ambulance response times across three inner city and three rural areas.'

- Health visiting and child accident prevention – 'Do home visiting interventions by health visitors reduce the incidence of accidental childhood injury in the under fives?'

You might come up with a list of several interests and favoured approaches. Try to devise a connection between each interest and your main study subject and to formulate titles such as we have done above. You will need to be aware of the diversity inherent in your main subject in order to spot promising connections: for example, nursing covers pretty well all aspects of patient care and involves a range of different patient groups, while social work which is concerned with a range of vulnerable client groups from infants to older citizens. Almost all disciplines have a history, and provide pointers to the future. Even purely technical subjects such as pharmacology have a range of applications that affect everyday life.

If you find it difficult to pin down what your main interests are, you could try answering the following questions:

(1) What do you do when you are not 'working'? You may be doing something very useful, but you regard it as an enjoyable activity rather than 'work'. If it is something as general as watching the television, what programmes do you watch most? Wherein lies this fascination?

(2) If you are together with like-minded friends, what do you enjoy talking about most?

(3) Is there any activity, subject or skill that you have always wanted to find out more about, but have never had the time or incentive? This may just be the opportunity to get to grips with it.

(4) What do you like reading? Newspapers, professional journals, romantic fiction, crime or historical novels, etc.? Analyse what it is that fascinates you and drives you to read these.

(5) Where do you like to go when you have time off? What do you like to see? Are you an avid gallery visitor, or would you rather scale the highest peaks? Even foreign holidays and travel have potential research value in relation to health and social care and in particular public health.

(6) What do you like about things? Are you design conscious? Are you fascinated by miniaturization or by mega-projects? Do you look for simplicity or thrive on complexity? Do you prefer artificial or natural materials? Are you the type that likes to think about things as abstract concepts or are you a nuts and bolts practical type and keen to identify the evidence underpinning practice?

When you have devised one or perhaps several promising dissertation subjects, discuss these with colleagues, friends, fellow students or even a potential research supervisor. It is then time to look more carefully at the practical implications of these. At this stage you will not be able to go into details, but you will definitely be able to make a preliminary assessment so that really impractical ideas are rejected. Several issues need to be examined.

Scope of the subject

You will need to limit the 'width' and 'depth' of your study to keep it manageable. There is so much information on every subject, and so many implications can be followed up that link to a wider field, that it is easy to lose your direction and end up with an unfocused piece of work. Think about where you will draw the line, where you will say 'this goes beyond my field of study'. Delineation can be achieved, for example, by stipulating a time frame (e.g. in a literature review you could examine the research evidence published over a particular 10-year period), location, size, type (e.g. of public health intervention, drug treatment, social group, etc.) and level of detail.

Individuality

Is what you are planning just a repeat of what has been done before, or is there something different or new that can be learned from the outcomes?

You do not have to achieve a scientific breakthrough or a new direction in thought. What is needed is an individual stamp on the work, some personal contribution that makes your project unique. This is gained by adding your own perspective to the study, your own collection of data (perhaps surveys or research papers) and your own interpretation of some data, yours or from elsewhere. At this stage it is worth assessing your own capabilities in relation to the task: can you see yourself being able to do it?

Timing

You will only have a limited time in which to complete your work. How fast a worker are you, and how much do you already know about the topic, and how much time will you be able to dedicate to the project? If you are planning to travel as part of the work, or need to observe particular events, make sure that these can be reliably programmed into your allotted time. At this stage it will be difficult to devise a reliable programme of work, but you will be able to get a feel for how much time might be involved in getting prepared, seeking ethics committee review, research governance and or other approvals, accessing data, collecting information, evidence and data, sorting and analysing it, and writing it all up and presenting it.

Resources

Many dissertation projects involve getting specific information and/or using particular pieces of equipment, or even meeting certain people. Does your subject imply the necessity for these? If so, what is the likelihood of you gaining the required access? Is ethical approval and research governance approval required? You will need to establish alternatives if things do not work out as expected. There is also the question of money. Calculate the likely cost implications of pursuing your topic(s), and whether you can afford it. You will incur basic costs anyway in the production of your dissertation thesis (printing, photocopying, binding, etc.)

Regulations and supervision

Important aspects of your dissertation are bound to be governed by the regulations of your university or college, and also by more detailed instructions issued by your course administration. The principal matters covered are the maximum and minimum length (word count), format and presentation, dissertation type, quality of work, marking criteria and expected outcomes, approvals for subject choice and supervision arrangements, deadlines, extent of group or individual working, and so forth.

It is essential that you are fully informed about these issues, so if you do not have a copy of both the general regulations issued by the university or college, and the course-specific instructions, get hold of them now and read them carefully. Your work will be judged on the basis of compliance with these, so you can save yourself a lot of time and grief by getting it right from the beginning!

Although the point of doing a dissertation is to challenge you to produce a piece of work devised and organized by yourself, you are not really expected to do this without any help. You should be allocated a tutor or dissertation supervisor whose duty it is to guide and advise you during the project. Do make use of him or her, both to check on your progress and as a source of ideas and advice. Ask what format has been arranged for consultations: is there a regular prearranged meeting, or do you have to book a slot when they become available? The onus will probably be on you to ensure that you get regular tutorials.

The regulations are likely to be quite specific about the type of dissertation you may conduct and the approval required for the choice of your dissertation topic, so early consultation with your supervisor is essential. He or she will quickly be able to comment on the suitability of your title(s), research question and planned approach. It is best if you can give a short explanation of how your topic relates to your main area of study (your dissertation supervisor might not be familiar with your particular interest) and how it will develop your knowledge and skills in the subject. Once you get the initial approval of the title and subject, you will be able to start to develop a greater understanding of the tasks ahead. A good way to get a feel for the requirements of the whole project is to look at examples of completed dissertations.

Previous examples

As already mentioned in Chapter 1, most courses will keep copies of all their previous dissertations and they should be available for you to consult. They might be held in the central library or in your own department: you should know by now where they are. You should look at them rather differently now from the last time. One of the really useful aspects of looking at completed dissertations is to be able to gauge the size and content of the finished works. The risk, however, is that you become intimidated by the scale and detail provided, especially if they deal with subjects unfamiliar to you. Do not worry, they managed and so will you.

It is best to look at several dissertations. Perhaps you will find one or two that deal with similar subjects to your own. What should you look for when reviewing these dissertations? Just as the last time, you will certainly not want to read them all. Here are a few points to consider:

- Visually compare the different styles of presentation, that is, the use of fonts, illustrations and graphs, colour, chapters and headings, indexes and lists of references, etc. Which do you find more attractive and immediately informative?

- Look to see how the subject title is broken down into different aspects to make it easier to investigate. A clue to how this is done is to look at the chapter headings.

- Scan through the whole collection to get an idea of the range of topics covered. Are there any similar to your chosen title? If so, have a quick look at them to get an idea of the dissertation type, approach taken and content. Again, chapter headings will be revealing. Spot the differences and similarities to your own thoughts about your approach. Again, make a note of those that might serve as a model. If there are no titles remotely similar to the one you have devised, you might be either way off the mark or brilliantly innovative.

- Compare the scope of the work in several examples. Some will look at a wide subject but not in much depth; others will concentrate on one narrow aspect but delve deeply; and others will fall somewhere in between. Observe how the styles differ. Reflect on where your subject lies within this spectrum.

- Examine how the work was done. Did it involve careful measurement and calculation on a scientific basis, or was it more an interpretation of events or opinions that could not be accurately measured? Consider your own subject and ponder what sort of approach might be suitable. Sometimes a combination of both is required.

You will probably want to refer to previous examples later in your work, when you are faced with specific problems of method, organization or presentation. So do make a note of those that you think could serve as good examples so that you will easily be able to find them again.

If you cannot get to see previous examples from your course, then you will have to look elsewhere, perhaps at those from a different course. But be aware that the course, and therefore dissertation requirements may have been different, and you will not gather any relevant information from the range of subject choices. Even so, issues of organization and presentation will still be worth investigating.

Getting background information

A title is only a germ of an idea. In order really to understand the implications of it, you need to investigate what has been done on the subject already, what information is available to inform your study, and what gaps in your knowledge need to be filled. This is called doing a background study and is important in producing a clear research problem.

The main aim of doing this background study is to make sure that your subject idea is not just 'pie in the sky'. We are sure that you based your selection on some considerable knowledge of both your main subject and your enthusiasm. But what you probably are not so informed about is what other people have done in this field, and how they have done it. When, shortly, you will devise the research proposal that gives a rationale for your project, you will need to argue that the subject is relevant to your studies and fits within the remit of the main subject. There is no better way of doing this than to cite work that has already been done in this field and to identify the gaps that still need to be filled.

Figure 3.1

Your title will give indications of where to look for information. Take for example the first on the list given earlier: 'End of life care for young people in the community – a critical review of policy and research evidence.' Data will be required on end of life care and how it is defined in both policy and practice terms. The age ranges of the young people to be involved in the study's review should be clearly stated. End of life care will need to be studied by examining research evidence and existing literature, health and social care policy documents, government statistics and health care practices (both past and present). The practical knowledge of paediatric nurses is likely to be a valuable guide to how end of life care is delivered in the community. The perspectives of the young people themselves will be important in considering what really matters to them.

Every title will have a series of connections to related information and research. Greater familiarity with the issues will in turn lead on to further relevant fields. There is a danger here of getting overwhelmed by the amount of information available and there is the problem of sorting out what is useful. A quick way to check that you have not missed anything important after you have done some initial investigation is to talk with experts in the field – those in your department or in other parts of the university or college, or those working in practice. Just a few words will suffice, so do not be shy to contact them by Email or letter.

Where will you find the required information? The first step is your university library. You should be pretty good at doing searches by now.

atthorn, A.A. and Joyner R.L. (2005) *Writing the Winning Dissertation: A Step-by-Step Guide*, 2nd edn. Thousand Oaks, CA: Corwin and Sage Publications.

urray, R. (2006) *How to Write a Thesis*, 2nd edn. Maidenhead: Open University Press, McGraw-Hill Education.

idestam, K.E. and Newton, R.R. (2007) *Surviving Your Dissertation: A Comprehensive Guide to Content and Process*, 3rd edn. Thousand Oaks, CA: Sage. See Chapter 2 on selecting a suitable topic.

Try using some selected key words to search library catalogue. For more specialist issues, a vant health and social care databases of journa ductive. Ask your librarian for help or attend a li you get stuck, or do not seem to be finding the ri Then there is the Internet, again doing a search to get bogged down or waylaid by the sheer vol advice on searching for secondary (published and given in Chapter 8, and on how to organize your 9. The secret is to know when to stop. At this sta the feasibility of your suggested title and getting the project.

These first steps in collecting information will tion for your work, and help you to decide on the your study. Now is the time to change your mind i are not working out how you wish. Explore altern if you develop a real distaste for the prospect of v abandon it and choose an alternative. In the latte to move quickly to establish a new direction and g new subject; it is important not to lose too much ti the project.

Just remember that your best work will be done v interested in what you are doing. But also rememben things is always tough: there is no really easy way.

Starting a research diary

Whatever stage you have reached in your research proj early to start keeping a research diary (in paper or in a A research diary should be a log or record of everything tl research project, for example, recording ideas about poss ics, database searches you undertake, your contacts wit sites, access and approval processes and difficulties yo overcome, etc. The research diary is the place where you sl your thoughts, personal reflections and insights into the r You will find your research diary invaluable when you st methods chapter of your dissertation thesis. The diary will reference when you critically review the strengths and lim research approach.

What should I do next?

If you have followed the advice above, you will already have you are still dithering, now is the time to examine your o

Chapter 4

How Do I Get Started?

Chapter contents

- What's the problem?
- Second review of the literature
- What are the main concepts?
- What about indicators?
- What are the main variables and values?
- Ways of stating your research problem
- Definition of research objectives
- What should I do next?
- Further reading

What's the problem?

Writing a dissertation is not like writing a novel: you cannot just sit down and start writing from out of your head. You need to do some preparation work first; you have already begun this if you have followed the book to this stage. By now you will have decided the subject area and done some background reading to get information and explore aspects of the subject. Now it is time to build on this and to focus more clearly on the direction of your intended study. To start with, it is best to define your research problem as clearly as possible in order to provide a focus for all your subsequent work. It sounds easier than it actually is, so do not worry if you agonize over it for a few days and alter your ideas several times over. Only by grappling with the issues can you forge some clarity in your thinking.

The purpose of the dissertation task is to get you to do some individual research. To do research you need to identify a problem or an issue that you will focus on in your investigations. After selecting your subject area and deciding on the issues that are of the greatest interest to you, the next step is to define the research more closely so that it can be expressed as a specific *research problem*. You will get to the point, when you are clear and decided, that you can explain the nature of your research problem in one or two sentences.

It can be quite difficult to decide on and to define your research problem. So what should you look for in your subject in order to generate a focus for your dissertation? It is not as if problems are hard to find: in fact, we are surrounded by problems.

Many problems are connected with society, health and social care services, education and so forth, and can readily be seen and read about. Take for example social problems such as poverty, crime, poor housing, health inequalities and social exclusion; or organizational problems such as managerial failures, infection control issues and bureaucratic bungles. In many subjects there may be a lack of knowledge that prevents improvements from being made, for example, the effectiveness of different treatment interventions for adolescent heroin users, or the influence of parents on a child's progress at school.

But do not think that real-life problems are the only subjects to choose. Many issues are worthy of investigation but present no threat to anyone. How about critically examining a nursing or social care theory, undertaking a concept analysis, or conducting a historical study of a custom or ritual of health care practice, or study the use of language in particular contexts? The possibilities are endless. The difficulty lies more in identifying a specific research problem that will be suitable in scale and character as the subject of a dissertation.

So, what are the necessary features of a dissertation research problem?

- It should be of great interest to you. You will have to spend many weeks or even months investigating the problem. A real interest in the subject is a great incentive to keep you going. If you have some choice in the subject you choose, then do yourself a favour and investigate something you want to find out about anyway.

- The problem should be significant. It is a waste of time and effort investigating a trivial problem or repeating work that someone has already done. Although you are not obliged to break new ground and extend the boundaries of knowledge, you will at least be expected to throw some new light on existing knowledge and evidence.

- It should be delineated. You do not have much time, even if it seems that you do at first. As you have to learn so many things in order to complete a good dissertation, you will take longer than you might think to do the necessary tasks. Hence the topic must be kept manageable, with restricted aims. Work out how much time you have got to complete the study, taking into account all the other commitments you have. How much detail do you need to go into? You can cover a wide field only superficially, and the more you restrict the field, the more detailed the study can be. Also consider the cost of any necessary travel and other expenses.

Try using some selected key words to search for books on the main library catalogue. For more specialist issues, a search through the relevant health and social care databases of journal articles should be productive. Ask your librarian for help or attend a library training session if you get stuck, or do not seem to be finding the right kind of information. Then there is the Internet, again doing a search using key words; try not to get bogged down or waylaid by the sheer volume of material. More advice on searching for secondary (published and stored) information is given in Chapter 8, and on how to organize your note taking in Chapter 9. The secret is to know when to stop. At this stage you are only testing the feasibility of your suggested title and getting a feel of the nature of the project.

These first steps in collecting information will form a useful foundation for your work, and help you to decide on the nature and scope of your study. Now is the time to change your mind if you see that things are not working out how you wish. Explore alternative approaches, or if you develop a real distaste for the prospect of work in that subject, abandon it and choose an alternative. In the latter case, you will have to move quickly to establish a new direction and get approval for your new subject; it is important not to lose too much time at the outset of the project.

Just remember that your best work will be done when you are really interested in what you are doing. But also remember that learning new things is always tough: there is no really easy way.

Starting a research diary

Whatever stage you have reached in your research project, it is never too early to start keeping a research diary (in paper or in an electronic form). A research diary should be a log or record of everything that you do in your research project, for example, recording ideas about possible research topics, database searches you undertake, your contacts with research study sites, access and approval processes and difficulties you encounter and overcome, etc. The research diary is the place where you should also record your thoughts, personal reflections and insights into the research process. You will find your research diary invaluable when you start to write the methods chapter of your dissertation thesis. The diary will also be a useful reference when you critically review the strengths and limitations of your research approach.

What should I do next?

If you have followed the advice above, you will already have done a lot. If you are still dithering, now is the time to examine your options and to make decisions. If you do not make your mind up about your subject, it is impossible to make any real progress in your work, as you cannot know where to focus your research.

Here is a checklist of things that have been suggested so far in this chapter:

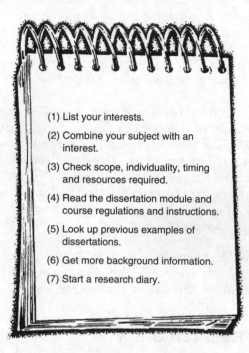

(1) List your interests.

(2) Combine your subject with an interest.

(3) Check scope, individuality, timing and resources required.

(4) Read the dissertation module and course regulations and instructions.

(5) Look up previous examples of dissertations.

(6) Get more background information.

(7) Start a research diary.

If you are really lost for ideas, or have got hopelessly bogged down, make an appointment with your supervisor and explain what you have done so far and ask for advice. If you have taken any of the steps recommended above, you will be some way to getting started, and will probably be aware of where your problem lies. This may be because, for instance, you are daunted by the complexity of the task, you cannot decide between several options or you are not confident that your choice is feasible. It will be best if you can identify specific problems before seeing your supervisor, rather than turning up and saying simply 'I don't know what to do!'.

To get yourself well organized, make a list of the sources of background material that you have found useful. Then write a short text in the form of bullet points indicating the main issues that this material has raised. This text should indicate:

- The sort of information that you will be likely to need, and where you might obtain it.

- The sort of techniques you might need to use or to learn in order to obtain the information and to analyse it.

- The equipment and/or resources that might be needed.

- The people and places you might need to see.

- Any timing considerations that need to be taken into account (e.g. ethics committee review processes, research governance approvals, waiting for special events).

When you are clear about these, and they seem achievable, it will give you confidence that the project is 'doable' and free you to proceed with defining and planning the project in greater detail.

Further reading

The guidance given above should be sufficient to put you on the right road (your road) to working out what your dissertation will be about. However, if you have time and want to compare advice, or need further inspiration, there are other books like this one that have a section with advice on how to decide what to do as a dissertation, or in many cases, a postgraduate thesis. It may help you to compare the different approaches. Explore your own library catalogue for both general and health and social care-related guides to dissertation writing. But do be careful not to get bogged down in technicalities: peck like a bird at the juicy pieces of use to you now, and leave the rest.

Ajuga, G. (2002) *The Student Assignment and Dissertation Survival Guide: Answering the Question Behind the Question!* Thornton Heath: GKA Publishing. See pp. 46–55. Do you want to become the teacher's pet?

Bell, J. (2005) *Doing your Research Project: a Guide for First-time Researchers in Education, Health and Social Science*, 4th edn. Maidenhead: Open University Press.

Blaxter, L., Hughes, C. and Tight, M. (2006) *How to Research*, 3rd edn. Maidenhead: Open University Press. See Chapter 2 on how to get started.

Mounsey, C. (2002) *Essays and Dissertations*. Oxford: Oxford University Press. Chapter 2 looks at ways to develop research questions.

Swetnam, D. (2004) *Writing Your Dissertation: The Bestselling Guide to Planning, Preparing and Presenting First-Class Work*. Oxford: How To Books Ltd. See Chapters 1 and 3 for simple guidance on how to get started.

The following books are aimed more at postgraduate research, but again, selective reading of the preliminary chapters will provide further hints about getting started.

Glatthorn, A.A. and Joyner R.L. (2005) *Writing the Winning Dissertation: A Step-by-Step Guide*, 2nd edn. Thousand Oaks, CA: Corwin and Sage Publications.

Murray, R. (2006) *How to Write a Thesis*, 2nd edn. Maidenhead: Open University Press, McGraw-Hill Education.

Rudestam, K.E. and Newton, R.R. (2007) *Surviving Your Dissertation: A Comprehensive Guide to Content and Process*, 3rd edn. Thousand Oaks, CA: Sage. See Chapter 2 on selecting a suitable topic.

Chapter 4
How Do I Get Started?

Chapter contents

- What's the problem?
- Second review of the literature
- What are the main concepts?
- What about indicators?
- What are the main variables and values?
- Ways of stating your research problem
- Definition of research objectives
- What should I do next?
- Further reading

What's the problem?

Writing a dissertation is not like writing a novel: you cannot just sit down and start writing from out of your head. You need to do some preparation work first; you have already begun this if you have followed the book to this stage. By now you will have decided the subject area and done some background reading to get information and explore aspects of the subject. Now it is time to build on this and to focus more clearly on the direction of your intended study. To start with, it is best to define your research problem as clearly as possible in order to provide a focus for all your subsequent work. It sounds easier than it actually is, so do not worry if you agonize over it for a few days and alter your ideas several times over. Only by grappling with the issues can you forge some clarity in your thinking.

The purpose of the dissertation task is to get you to do some individual research. To do research you need to identify a problem or an issue that you will focus on in your investigations. After selecting your subject area and deciding on the issues that are of the greatest interest to you, the next step is to define the research more closely so that it can be expressed as a specific *research problem*. You will get to the point, when you are clear and decided, that you can explain the nature of your research problem in one or two sentences.

It can be quite difficult to decide on and to define your research problem. So what should you look for in your subject in order to generate a focus for your dissertation? It is not as if problems are hard to find: in fact, we are surrounded by problems.

Many problems are connected with society, health and social care services, education and so forth, and can readily be seen and read about. Take for example social problems such as poverty, crime, poor housing, health inequalities and social exclusion; or organizational problems such as managerial failures, infection control issues and bureaucratic bungles. In many subjects there may be a lack of knowledge that prevents improvements from being made, for example, the effectiveness of different treatment interventions for adolescent heroin users, or the influence of parents on a child's progress at school.

But do not think that real-life problems are the only subjects to choose. Many issues are worthy of investigation but present no threat to anyone. How about critically examining a nursing or social care theory, undertaking a concept analysis, or conducting a historical study of a custom or ritual of health care practice, or study the use of language in particular contexts? The possibilities are endless. The difficulty lies more in identifying a specific research problem that will be suitable in scale and character as the subject of a dissertation.

So, what are the necessary features of a dissertation research problem?

- It should be of great interest to you. You will have to spend many weeks or even months investigating the problem. A real interest in the subject is a great incentive to keep you going. If you have some choice in the subject you choose, then do yourself a favour and investigate something you want to find out about anyway.

- The problem should be significant. It is a waste of time and effort investigating a trivial problem or repeating work that someone has already done. Although you are not obliged to break new ground and extend the boundaries of knowledge, you will at least be expected to throw some new light on existing knowledge and evidence.

- It should be delineated. You do not have much time, even if it seems that you do at first. As you have to learn so many things in order to complete a good dissertation, you will take longer than you might think to do the necessary tasks. Hence the topic must be kept manageable, with restricted aims. Work out how much time you have got to complete the study, taking into account all the other commitments you have. How much detail do you need to go into? You can cover a wide field only superficially, and the more you restrict the field, the more detailed the study can be. Also consider the cost of any necessary travel and other expenses.

- You should be able to obtain the information required. Obviously, you cannot carry out research if you cannot collect the relevant information needed to address your problem. Can you get access to relevant documents or other sources, and/or can you obtain the co-operation of individuals or organizations, such as local authorities, NHS trusts or voluntary agencies essential to your project?

- You should be able to draw conclusions related to the problem. The point of asking a question is to find an answer. The problem should be one to which the research can offer some solution, or at least the elimination of some false 'solutions'.

- You should be able to state the problem clearly and concisely. Aim for a precise, well-thought-out and fully articulated sentence, that is understandable by anyone and clearly explains just what the problem is.

When searching for a research problem, you need to have an enquiring mind, an eye for inconsistencies and inadequacies in current ideas and practice, and also a measure of imagination. It often helps to pose a simple question, for example, 'What support is available to women diagnosed with breast cancer?', 'Does attendance at a parenting programme increase parental confidence and self-esteem?', 'How can prevention measures reduce adolescent substance misuse?' or 'What makes a successful young children's play area in an acute hospital setting?' At this stage, the nature of the question will give some indication of the type of research approach (or approaches) that could be appropriate. Will it be a literature review, a descriptive inquiry, an analysis of correlations or an experimental exercise, or a combination of more than one of these? (See Chapter 2.)

Note, though, that seemingly simple questions are riddled with ambiguities that must be cleared up by careful definition. For example, in the above questions, what does 'support' mean, what sort of 'prevention measures' are envisaged, and are all types of 'young children's play area' included? A few additional questions posed against each word can help to delineate the problem: where, who, what, which, when? Break the problem down into short sentences, not worrying at this stage about the overall length of the problem statement. It is a useful trick to put each sentence on a separate slip of paper, so that they can be ordered in different sequences. When the best logical progression from sentence to sentence is achieved, the statement can be edited into a more elegant form.

Most research problems are difficult, or even impossible, to solve without breaking them down into smaller problems. The words used during the problem formulation period can give a clue to the presence of *subproblems*. Does one aspect have to be researched before another aspect can be begun? For example, in one of the research questions asked above, the kinds of prevention measures that can be used to reduce adolescent substance misuse, how they can be implemented and for what types of substance misuse will all have to be examined. By defining the subproblems, you will be able to delineate the scope of the work.

Second review of literature

Once you have defined a research problem, you will be able to make a much more focused review of the literature. You will be able to learn more about existing research on aspects of your research problem, and how it has been carried out. You will also be able to make more in-depth investigations into the factors that are important in your subject. Look for the following information in order to help you get started on your own research:

- results of previous research, which can form a springboard for your own investigations;

- concepts, indicators and variables used (see below for details of these);

- ideas on how to gather data;

- data presentation techniques;

- methods of data analysis;

- instrumentation which has been used;

- methods of argument and the drawing of conclusions;

- success of the various research designs of the studies already undertaken.

This exercise should not take too long, as you will be able to hone in on the relevant research quite quickly using the key words from your research problem and question(s). Do reference everything relevant that you find, and make notes with comments about how the information relates to what you are intending to do (see Chapter 9 for specific instructions on note taking and Chapter 17 for referencing). This will be really useful material to put into your research proposal and the introduction and background section of your dissertation, in order to demonstrate that you have really investigated the current evidence base of your particular topic.

The words you use in your problem statement are loaded with meaning. You must have carefully chosen them from many other words to precisely indicate the main components of your investigation. Let us now look more closely at these words, or concepts, and how they are used.

What are the main concepts?

First, what is a concept? It is a general expression of a particular phenomenon, e.g. cat, human, anger, fear, alienation, social exclusion, etc. Each one of these represents an idea, and the word is a label for this idea.

We use concepts all the time as they are an essential part of understanding the world and communicating with other people. Many common concepts are shared by everyone in a society, though there are variations in meaning between different cultures and languages. There are also other concepts that are only understood by certain people such as experts, professionals and specialists, for example dermatoglyphics, parachronism, anticipatory socialization, etc. Sometimes, common phenomena can be labelled in an exotic fashion, often in order to impress or confuse, for example, a 'domestic feline mammal' instead of a 'cat'. This is called jargon, and should be avoided.

Any kind of enquiry requires a set of concepts that communicate the elements being studied. It is important to define concepts in such a way that everyone reading the work has got the same idea of what is meant. This is relatively easy in the natural sciences where precise definition is usually possible, e.g. acceleration, radio waves, elements. In health and social care and the social sciences this may be much more difficult. Human concepts such as spirtuality, vulnerability, empowerment and dignity are difficult to pin down accurately, as their meanings are often based on opinions, emotions, values and traditions. Hence the importance of carefully formulating definitions when using concepts that are not precise in normal usage.

You will be able to find definitions of the concepts that you are planning to use in your investigations from your background reading. Because definitions for non-scientific and non-technical concepts can vary in different health and social care contexts, for example, 'child care' has different meanings internationally across different countries, you may have to decide on which meaning you want to give to those concepts. Rarely, you might even have to devise your own definition for a particular word.

What about indicators?

As you can see, many concepts are rather abstract in nature, and difficult or even impossible to evaluate or measure. Take 'anger' as an example. How will you detect this in a person? The answer is to look for indicators – those perceivable phenomena that give an indication that the concept is present. What might these be? Think of the signs that might indicate anger: clenched fists, agitated demeanour, spluttering, shouting, wide-open eyes, stamping, reddened face, increased heart rate, increased adrenaline production, and many others. Again, you can see what indicators are used in previous studies – which is much easier and more reliable than trying to work them out for yourself. For more technical subjects, indicators are usually well defined and universally accepted, for example changes of state like condensation, freezing and magnetism. For many medical conditions, indicators can also be well defined such as hypothermia, anaemia and hypertension.

What are the main variables and values?

If you want to gauge the extent or degree of an indicator, you will need to find a measurable component. In the case of anger as above, it would be very difficult to measure the redness of a face or the degree of stamping, but you could easily measure a person's heart rate. You could even ask the subject how angry he or she feels. The values used are the units of measurement. In the case of heart rate, it would be beats per minute; level of anger felt could be declared on a scale from 1 to 10. Obviously the precision possible will be different depending on the nature of the variable and the type of values that can possibly be used. Certain scientific experiments require incredibly accurate measurement, while some social phenomena, for example, opinions, might only be gauged on a three-point scale such as 'against', 'neutral' and 'for'.

To summarize then, there is a hierarchy of expressions, going from the general to the particular, from abstract to concrete, that make it possible to investigate research problems. The briefest statement of the research problem will be the most general and abstract, while the detailed analysis of components of the research will be particular and concrete. The terms introduced are linked as follows:

- **Concepts** – the building blocks of the research problem which are usually abstract and cannot be directly measured.

- **Indicators** – the phenomena which point to the existence of the concepts.

- **Variables** – the components of the indicators which can be measured.

- **Values** – the actual units or methods of measurement of the variables.

Note that each concept may have several indicators, each indicator several variables and each variable several values. To clarify these terms consider the following, which gives only one example of each term:

- Concept – poverty.

- Indicator – poor living conditions.

- Variable – provision of sanitary facilities.

- Values – numbers of people per WC.

Try to think of more indicators, variables and values related to the concept of poverty.

Being aware of these levels of expression will help you to break down your investigations into manageable tasks. This will enable you to come to overall conclusions about the abstract concepts in your research problem based on evidence rooted in detailed data at a more concrete level.

Ways of stating your research problem

You have a choice of how to state your research problem. How you state it will provide some indication of how you will go about your investigation. Here are some of the most common ways of presenting the research problem with examples to show how they work.

Research question or questions

The formulation of a research question is a commonly used approach for expressing the research problem in health and social care and is particularly favoured by those conducting randomized controlled trials and systematic reviews. The method of investigating the problem may be expressed through asking a question or a series of questions, the answers to which require scrutiny of the problem from one or more directions. This is a very direct and open-ended way of formulating your investigations. Your aim is to provide some answers to the questions. It is your judgement, and that of the examiner's, whether your answers are sufficient and based on enough evidence. Here is an example of this form of presentation:

- The subject of this dissertation is 'Representations of social work in the media'.

- The main research question is 'How is contemporary social work represented in the media?'.

- Three interrelated research subquestions are raised:

  1 What are the characteristics of the representation of contemporary social work in the media?

  2 How does this representation differ in coverage presented in different types of media, e.g. television, magazines, newspapers?

  3 What role do specialist journalists, and specifically health and social care correspondents, play in shaping this representation?

Obviously, the question or questions should be derived directly from the research problem, give a clear indication of the subject to be investigated and imply the methods that will be used. As above, the form of the questions can be a main question, divided into subquestions that explore aspects of the main question. The main question is very general: you could probably devise other subquestions to explore different aspects of this question. But by being so specific in your choice, you can limit your research to only those issues that you think are important, or that you have interest in pursuing.

Hypothesis

The use of hypotheses is the foundation of the hypothetico-deductive approach to research, so it is important to know what makes good hypotheses and how they can be formulated. When used in a rigorous scientific fashion, there are quite strict rules to follow. Important qualities distinguish hypotheses from other forms of statement.

According to Kerlinger (2000) a hypothesis:

1   is an assertion (not a suggestion);

2   is limited in scope;

3   is a statement about the relationships between certain variables;

4   contains clear implications for testing the relationships;

5   is compatible with current knowledge;

6   is expressed as economically as possible using correct terminology.

The objective of the method is either to reject the hypothesis by finding evidence that contradicts it, or to support it (you will not be able to prove it) by presenting evidence that underlines it. It might also be possible to modify the hypothesis in the light of what you have found out.

Actually, hypotheses are nothing unusual: we make them all the time. They are hunches or reasonable guesses made in the form of statements about a cause or situation. If something happens in our everyday life, we tend to suggest a reason for its occurrence by making rational guesses. For example, if the car does not start in the morning, we might hypothesize that the petrol tank was empty, or that the battery was flat. For each hypothesis, a particular action taken could support or reject it. If the petrol gauge indicated 'full', then the hypothesis of an empty petrol tank could be rejected, and so on. When a particular hypothesis is found to be supported, we have got a good chance that we can take the right action to remedy the situation. If, for example, we hypothesized that a wire to the starter motor had become loose, and then we find such a loose wire, fixing the wire back might result in the car starting again. If this were not the result, further hypotheses would be needed to suggest additional faults. Although these examples may seem banal, many of the greatest discoveries in science were based on hypotheses: Newton's theory of gravity, Einstein's general theory of relativity and a host of others.

In order to formulate a useful researchable hypothesis, you need to have a good knowledge of the background to the subject and the nature of the problem or issue that you are addressing. A good hypothesis is a very useful aid to organizing the research effort. It specifically limits the enquiry to the interaction of certain variables; it suggests the methods appropriate for collecting, analysing and interpreting the data; and the resultant confirmation or rejection of the hypothesis through empirical or experimental testing gives a clear indication of the extent of knowledge gained.

You need to formulate the general hypothesis on a conceptual level, in order to enable the results of the research to be generalized beyond the specific conditions of the particular study. This is equivalent to the general research question. Then, you normally need to break down the main hypothesis into two or more subhypotheses. These represent components or aspects of the main hypothesis and together should add up to its totality and are equivalent to the subquestions. It is one of the fundamental criteria of a hypothesis that it is testable. However, a hypothesis formulated on a conceptual level cannot be directly tested: it is too abstract. It is therefore necessary to convert it to an operational level. This is called operationalization. The operationalization of the subhypotheses follows four steps in the progression from the most abstract to the most concrete expressions by defining in turn the concepts, indicators, variables and values. Each subhypothesis will suggest a different method of testing and therefore implies different research methods that might be appropriate. The various research methods for collecting and analysing data are explained in some detail later in this book.

Although the term 'hypothesis' is used with many different meanings in everyday and even academic situations, it is advisable to use it in your research only in its strictest scientific sense. This will avoid you being criticized for sloppy, imprecise use of terminology. If your research problem does not lend itself to being formulated in a hypothesis, do not worry: there are plenty of alternatives, many of which involve a completely different research approach to that of the hypothetico-deductive method.

Proposition

Focusing a research study on a proposition, rather than on a hypothesis, allows the study to concentrate on particular relationships between events, without having to comply with the rigorous characteristics required of hypotheses. Consider this example:

- The title of the research is 'Caring for patients' nutritional needs in hospital'.

- The main research problem is formulated in the form of three interrelated propositions:

1   Caring for patients' nutritional needs is an important aspect of the nursing role in a district general hospital.

2   Organization of patient meals at ward level is greatly influenced by hospital catering policies and systems.

3   From these two propositions follows the third: there is a mismatch between ward organization systems for meal delivery and nursing care to address patients' nutritional requirements.

Statement of intent to critically investigate and evaluate

Not all research needs to answer a question or to test a hypothesis. Especially in undergraduate dissertations or in smaller research studies, a more exploratory approach may be used. You can express the subject and scope of the exploration in a statement of intent. Again, this must be derived from the research problem, imply a method of approach and indicate the outcome. Here are four examples of this form of research definition:

(1) The intention of this study is to identify the main drivers in UK government policy to engage young people in the development of local authority services and then to assess the extent to which systems and processes adopted from the USA can be applied to the UK to increase and improve young people's engagement.

(2) This study examines the problems in career development of black and ethnic minority (BME) female nurses in the British National Health Service (NHS). It focuses on the identification of specific barriers (established conventions, prejudices, procedures, career paths) and explores the effectiveness of specific initiatives that have been aimed at breaking down these barriers.

(3) In this study it is intended to consider whether relevant UK standards for food safety as applied to hotels and restaurants could be transferred to hotels and restaurants in Nigeria.

(4) This thesis provides a re-examination of the concept of reflective practice. It aims to explore the foundations of reflective practice and critically analyse its application in contemporary occupational therapy practice.

Definition of research objectives

When you have successfully formulated the various detailed research problems, questions and statements, you will need to indicate what measures you will take to do the investigation. You can do this by defining the research objectives and indicating how the research objectives will be achieved. This is a first step to planning your project and will enable you to check back to see if the objectives fall in line with your preferences for the type of research that you were interested in doing.

In a national study conducted by one of the authors to examine the problem of safeguarding children in primary care trusts (PCTs), the following research question was identified: 'How do designated child protection nurses in England perceive the new primary care organizations are managing, organising and delivering services to meet their child protection responsibilities in the context of increased interdisciplinary and multi-agency working?' Three measurable research objectives were then stated:

Objectives:

(1) To identify what organizational arrangements have been put in place by primary care organizations to meet their child protection responsibilities since the Commission for Health Improvement (CHI) child protection audit in 2003 from the perspective of designated child protection nurses.

(2) To assess the extent to which those arrangements meet evidence-based guidance and recommendations.

(3) To discover novel approaches towards meeting child protection responsibilities not identified in the literature as reported by designated child protection nurses.

Notice how there is an argument behind the build-up of the research problem and the definition of objectives. Briefly, it goes like this:

- According to the background research there is a problem, or a lack of information, or an unanswered question about such-and-such.
- The important aspects to be studied are this, this, etc.
- In order to investigate these it is necessary to do such-and-such.

Pretty obvious really, but it is important that it makes logical sense. In fact, there is usually a choice of things you could do, so it may be necessary to limit the scope of the problem or question to make the necessary investigations more inevitable. Once you have got this far, you will have a good idea of what you are planning to undertake. Do you think you will be able to manage it?

What should I do next?

Now is the time to make some decisions about how you will formulate your research problem(s) so that you can make the first steps in embarking on planning your dissertation. If you take the following steps, this will provide you with a good foundation for all the work ahead:

- Once you have decided on the particular research problem you will focus on, test it against the list of necessary features given previously. If it conforms to all of these you can be assured that you have got a good one.
- Consult the notes you have made during your background reading, or delve back into the books that are relevant to your research focus. Now

search for what has already been done in this field, how it was carried out, and what were the main components of the work. Look at what terminology has been used, what factors have been studied and what methods have been used. This will help you enormously in deciding on what you could do, and in expressing your intentions in the appropriate language.

- In order to do this you should decide how you will state your research problem. Will you pose a question, formulate a hypothesis, suggest a proposition or make a statement of intent? Perhaps try out more than one way to see which works the best. Formulate it as succinctly as possible.

Now you should be in the situation where you will be able to put down in writing just how you will tackle the research problem. Break it down into 'doable' components, and clarify just what your objectives will be. Check that you will actually be able to reach the objectives; be practical, as it is you that has to do it! Check also, when you have written it down, that the argument you make is sound (read more about argument in Chapter 10).

Further reading

Again, most books that provide an introduction to research and advise how to do dissertations have a section on how you get started. Apart from the ones that have been listed in the previous chapters, here are a few more in case you want to check them out. To decide which might be useful to you, take a quick look through the contents list and perhaps the index at the end of the book and just look at the relevant bits. Identifying those books which are going to be the most relevant to your needs depends on what aspects you are particularly interested in.

Allison, B. and Race, P. (2004) *The Student's Guide to Preparing Dissertations and Theses*. Milton Park: RoutledgeFalmer.

Bell, J. (2005) *Doing Your Research Project: a Guide for First-time Researchers in Education, Health and Social Science*, 4th edn. Maidenhead: Open University Press.

Mounsey, C. (2002) *Essays and Dissertations*. Oxford: Oxford University Press.

McNiff, J., Lomax, P. and Whitehead, J. (2003) *You and Your Action Research Project*. 2nd edn. London: RoutledgeFalmer.

Neale, J. (ed.) (2008) *Research Methods for Health and Social Care*. Basingstoke, Palgrave Macmillan. See Chapter 2. Starting a new research project.

Polgar, S. and Thomas S.A. (2007) *Introduction to Research in the Health Sciences*, 5th edn. Edinburgh: Churchill Livingstone.

Swetnam, D. (2004) *Writing Your Dissertation: The Bestselling Guide to Planning, Preparing and Presenting First-Class Work*, 3rd edn. Oxford: How To Books Ltd. See Chapters 1 and 3 for simple guidance on how to get started.

Chapter 5

What's All This About Philosophy?

Chapter contents

- Can I believe what I see? Do I see what I believe?
- Positivism
- Relativism (or interpretivism)
- Alternative philosophical viewpoints
- How do these attitudes affect your dissertation?
- Two opposite approaches to enquiry: induction and deduction
- What should I do next?
- Further reading

Can I believe what I see? Do I see what I believe?

You might well ask, 'Why a chapter about philosophy? After all, I'm doing a degree in physiotherapy, health sciences, social care, nursing?' The simple answer is that your whole life is determined by your philosophical approach, whether you realize it or not. Everyone is a philosopher – everyone has his or her own concept of the world.

> The alternative to philosophy is not *no* philosophy but *bad* philosophy. The 'un-philosophical' person has an unconscious philosophy, which they apply to their practice – whether of science, politics or daily life. (Collier, 1994: 16)

The research work involved in doing your dissertation requires you to take a conscious stance with regard to the nature of knowledge, its acquisition and analysis, and the quality and certainty of the conclusions that can be reached from it. You cannot assume that your position will necessarily be shared by your reader, so you will have to make clear to the reader what your philosophical approach is.

So, what is it that makes up this philosophical approach, and how can one recognize its nature? The best way is to look at some of the debate about different approaches to knowledge and enquiry – the sorts of issues that are inherent in the process of producing a dissertation. There is a wide spectrum of attitudes in the debate about research, with two opposing camps, the positivists (sometimes referred to as realists) and the relativists (sometimes called interpretivists) at the extremes and a range of intermediate stances. This chapter will compare these divergent attitudes and briefly describe a range of alternative positions including postpositivism, constructivism, critical realism and participatory inquiry.

Positivism

On the one hand, the positivist viewpoint maintains that in order to know something it should be observable and measurable. The observer must stand apart and take a detached and neutral view of the phenomenon. For example, in Diggle's (2006) RCT examining the effect of needle size on the immunogenicity and reactogenicity of vaccines in infants. The research team measured local and general reactions as recorded by parents for three days after each immunization dose and also 'the geometric mean titres of serogroup C meningococcal glycoconjugate antibodies and geometric mean concentrations of diphtheria, tetanus and *Haemophilus influenzae* type b antibodies 28–42 days after the third vaccine dose' (2006: 2).

Examination of venous blood samples revealed that non-inferiority of the immune response was shown for diphtheria and serogroup C meningococcal glycoconjugate vaccine, but not for *H. influenzae* type b and tetanus although there was no evidence of a decrease. The study found that local reactions following pertussis, diphtheria, tetanus and *H. influenzae* type b immunisations decreased significantly when administered using wide gauge, long needles, compared to narrow gauge, short needles. In this RCT the researchers took a detached and objective view. Any other researchers undertaking the same serological analyses would come up with identical results and knowledge about those samples.

This is simple enough to understand when dealing with controllable inanimate material and forces. But extreme positivists would go further. They would say that any observable phenomenon can be understood and explained in a logical way, if only enough was known about all the complexities of the situation. Hence, for example, the development of life on earth will be fully explained when enough information is gained and enough experiments are carried out to successfully test the theories about the process.

Inherent to this way of thinking is a set of assumptions. It is these that underpin the positivist approach and form the basis of scientific method that has brought us so many advances in science, medicine and technology. The main assumptions are as follows.

Order

There is a conviction that the universe has some kind of order, and because of this, it is possible that we should be able to achieve some kind of understanding of it. Consequently, we can find out the links between events and their causes and thus understand 'the rules of the game'. This then allows us to make predictions, for example, the researchers in Diggle et al.'s (2006) study predicted that using a wide gauge, long (25 mm) needle for infant vaccination can significantly reduce local reactions following each dose rather than the use of a narrow, short (16 mm) needle. Admittedly, some phenomena are so complicated that it is very difficult to possess enough information and understanding to make reliable predictions (e.g. long-range weather forecasting).

External reality

This maintains that everyone shares the same reality and that we do not all live in different worlds that follow different rules. Although there is much philosophical debate about the nature of reality, positivists rely on the assumption that knowledge is shareable and verifiable: that is, you see the same as we do when, say, looking down a microscope. A theory built upon observations can therefore be tested by any observer to see if it is reliable, in order that the theory can achieve general acceptance.

Reliability

Human intellect and perceptions are reliable. You can depend on your senses and methods of thinking. Despite the dangers of deception and muddled thinking, careful observation and logical thought can be depended on. The accuracy of memory is also an important feature of this assumption.

Parsimony

Parsimony maintains that the simplest possible explanation is the best. Needless complexity should be avoided. Einstein's formula $E = mc^2$ that sums up his momentous theory of relativity, is a good example of this.

Generality

It is no good if the results of one experiment are only relevant to that one case, at that particular time, in that particular place. It must be possible to generalize from particular instances to others, for example, in Diggle et al.'s (2006) study comparing infants' immune responses to vaccines using different needle lengths, the data support the delivery of infant vaccinations to similar population groups using the longer needle size. It is impossible to see every instance of a phenomenon, for example, water boiling when it is heated, but it is possible to maintain that any water will boil if heated sufficiently.

The underlying thrust of this understanding of reality is based on the human capacity to think logically and mathematically. When society is organized in a 'scientific' way, logical methods can be applied to all aspects of life, so as to share all the increasing benefits equally and to ensure that people themselves act rationally. This approach is often labelled *modernism*, and promotes the fundamental interrelated ideas of reason, science, objectivity and happiness. Wouldn't you be happy if you won the lottery and could afford all the latest equipment and facilities? If you think not, perhaps you tend to the relativist point of view.

Relativism (or interpretivism)

On the other hand, relativists adopt the position that we humans are inextricably bound up with the events of the world, and that it is impossible for anyone to stand aside and observe it impartially, as it were, 'from on high'. We are all encumbered by our own experiences and viewpoints, and are enmeshed in our society. However well established they are, facts are human interpretations of reality, and may well change with time or be understood quite differently by different cultures.

This approach is particularly relevant when studying anything to do with the human aspects of health and social care. The scientific method is poorly equipped to track the inconsistencies, conflicts and subtleties of beliefs, ideals and feelings that form such an important part of human life.

> The world is not an object such that I have in my possession the law of its making; it is the natural setting of, and field for, all my thought and all my explicit perceptions. (Husserl, 1964: 11)

But even in what is regarded as pure scientific research, for example, astronomy, physics and biology, the mindset of society, referred to as the current paradigm, is an enormously powerful force that distorts thinking away from idealistic detachment and channels it into socially (and sometimes religiously) 'acceptable' routes. A striking example of this in the past was the complicated solutions devised to explain the movement of the heavenly bodies to conform to the belief that the Earth was the centre of the universe. A more modern situation is the enormous momentum that political and economic favour gives to a particular direction in scientific enquiry to the virtual exclusion of exploration of alternative theories, for example, in research into climate change. Commercial pressure can also distort scientific efforts, for example, in the development of particular drug treatments where heavy investment almost 'requires' that it be shown that the treatment works.

In order to understand this basically different approach to understanding reality it is revealing to compare the relativists' attitudes to the previously listed assumptions that underlie the positivist position.

Order

Relativists maintain that the creation of some kind of order in our understanding of the world is based on our own human perceptions of the world. As time passes, our ordering of the world changes, not because the world has changed but because our attitudes to life, society and beliefs have changed. However much knowledge is gained, we will never reach a definitive understanding of the world order. The 'rules of the game' are constructed by our intellect, which is irrevocably bound up in our society and individuality.

External reality

Relativists believe that our perceptions of the world are uniquely individual. The world we actually perceive does not exist of a series of stimuli that we interpret through our senses and make sense of logically in a void. Rather, we already have a picture of the world, and what we perceive is interpreted in relation to our feelings and understanding – our reality. Admittedly, we might share reality by using the same meanings of words in language (even that is debatable), but this sharing is only a tiny part of our individual experience. We look on the world from within it, and from within ourselves.

Reliability

Can we believe our senses? Does our memory always fool us? We will answer 'not always' to the first and 'quite often' to the second, if we believe that human nature is inevitably bound up in its culture and past experiences. These lead us to a personal interpretation of our perception and memorizing of events in our surroundings. Our senses can be tricked in many ways, and our memory is far from perfect, so researchers cannot rely on these to give a definitive record and measurement of the work. However, our skills of reasoning must be taken as a reliable method of organizing data and ideas, even though there may be several ways of interpreting data.

Parsimony

Life and society are not so simple and uniform that a simple explanation is possible. Hence simplification usually implies oversimplification. Although needless complexity should be avoided, it is rarely possible to sum any situation up in the form of a neat formula.

Generality

Relativists tend to reject the importance, or even possibility, of categorizing individuals and events into classes. Owing to the uniqueness of each person and the uniqueness of each event and situation, it is very difficult to predict what may happen in the future under similar conditions; it is dangerous and inappropriate to generalize from studied cases.

The function of language becomes an important issue in this debate. Actually, this issue is widened into the subject of communication, which goes beyond just the spoken and written message. We communicate by all sorts of gestures; we assume roles and follow conventions. Consider how difficult it is to gauge people's meanings and feelings when you are in a strange country where different social rules apply, even if you understand the language. This subject of communication is called discourse. How things are communicated is often as important as what is communicated. Discourse analysis recognizes these important factors and stresses that there is no 'neutral' way of communication.

Alternative philosophical viewpoints

Increasingly in health and social care research, positivist and relativist viewpoints are being challenged with postpositivism, constructivism, critical realism and participatory inquiry approaches increasing in popularity in health and social care research (see Appleton and King [2002] for a more detailed discussion). Postpositivism is often described as a modified form of positivism (Guba, 1990). It still assumes that there is a single, tangible, objective reality, which is at least partly apprehendable. However, while researchers strive to be as neutral as possible, postpositivists recognize that it is impossible to take a totally objective stance (Guba, 1990). Adopting a similar view, critical realism suggests that the world is created by 'structures, mechanisms and causal powers', which can be explained but are not necessarily observed (Wainwright, 1997:

1265). These researchers are concerned with how social structures impact on peoples' perceptions about reality (Pawson and Tilley, 1997).

In contrast to these viewpoints constructivists adopt the belief that multiple and intangible realities exist, which are not influenced by natural laws. Reality is regarded as pluralistic. These 'researchers believe that social reality exists as individuals experience it and assign meaning to it' (Appleton and King, 2002: 643). Constructivists therefore focus on attempting to understand the beliefs which people possess trying to achieve some consensus of meaning, yet always being ready to acknowledge new explanations with the benefit of experience and/or further information. Interaction between researcher and participants is regarded as a crucial and central part of data collection.

Participatory inquiry, which includes approaches such as participatory action research action science and inquiry and co-operative inquiry, shares a close alignment to a relativist ontology (Reason, 1994a, 1998). These researchers stress the importance of undertaking collaborative research '*with* people rather than *on* people' (Reason, 1994b: 11) and view 'human beings as cocreating their reality through participation' (Reason, 1994a: 324). Participatory research is action focused and the primary outcome of research adopting this philosophical stance is some form of change in the experiences of study participants (Reason, 1998).

How do these attitudes affect your dissertation?

You will need to think about this. Your own personal philosophy about how we can see and understand the world around us will be a fundamental factor in your attitude to your investigations. There are many ways in which any situation in health and social care can be analysed. Each approach will have a tendency to be based on a particular philosophical view that influences what you look at, the data you collect and the types of conclusions that you aim at. This is best explained using an example.

Suppose that you have decided to carry out some research into preventing obesity in children living in cities. You could base your research on official statistics about children who are overweight and obese using data from the National Child Measurement programme which was launched in 2005. Children in Reception (age 4–5) and Year 6 (age 10–11) have their weight and height measured and these data are used to help inform local planning and services. You could examine statistics on the proportion of school children who spend a minimum of two hours each week on sport activities, or look at how many playgrounds there are in relationship to population figures, their sizes, facilities and locations. You could look at healthy eating options in schools through an observation study or school survey. Or you could arrange interviews with children and parents to find out what they felt about healthy eating strategies and interventions to increase physical activity as part of school based programmes. You could even undertake a literature review to examine the type of interventions conducted with children to reduce overweight and obesity in adults and children. Each of these approaches involves basic theoretical as well as methodological decisions.

So, for example, if you wanted to establish correlations between 'social facts', you would favour collecting official statistics. However, if you were concerned with finding 'social meanings', then interview studies would be more appropriate. If you were more interested in theories of interactionism or ethnomethodology, you would make a close observation of what people did, either as a whole or in detail. Finally, if you were interested in the technical performance of blood pressure measurement equipment, then tests and experiments according to scientific method would produce the relevant answers.

Accordingly, you will have to decide which philosophical standpoint(s) to adopt when carrying out your research. This is not to say that any approach is better or truer than any other. Your research approach will depend on the characteristics of your research problem, your research question and your own convictions about the nature of research. The decision will help you to determine the nature of your enquiry, the choice of appropriate research methods, and the characteristics of the outcomes that you can expect.

Two opposite approaches to enquiry: induction and deduction

While we are discussing the issue of philosophy in research, it is appropriate to consider the two different approaches to enquiry: induction and deduction. These are the methods of structured thinking expressed as opposite approaches. Explained simply, they describe opposing extremes, which are actually equally impossible to carry out in a pure form. However, it is always easier to explain things when they are compared as being as different as black and white. There is nothing weird about these ways of thinking: you do it like this all the time, sometimes more one way, sometimes more the other. So what are we talking about?

Induction

In one phrase, induction is 'going from the particular to the general'; or, if you prefer the *Oxford English Dictionary* definition, 'the process of inferring or verifying a general law or principle from the observation of particular instances' (2002: 1361). If, like the Moravian monk Gregor Mendel (1822–84), you observed over many years the occurrence of red and white blossoms on the peas that you carefully cultivated from generations of seeds derived from these plants, you might have come to the same conclusions about the exact ratios of inherited characteristics with regard to blossom colour. You might even have been able to formulate some basic general rules about dominant and recessive genes. This would have been the result of inductive thinking – observing many particular instances (of pea blossoms in this case) to derive a general rule applicable to many other situations. You start with observations and then work out a theory that fits the phenomena you have recorded.

This approach can be traced back to Aristotle, whose empirical scientific observations particularly in the field of biology (for example, the development of the chick embryo) were unparalleled in the ancient world and laid the foundations for both Islamic and later western scientific thought. Galileo (1564–1642), Newton (1642–1727) and other scientists of that time heralded the scientific revolution with this method of enquiry. As the philosopher Francis Bacon (1561–1626) summed up: in order to understand nature, one should consult nature, rather than the writings of ancient philosophers and the Bible.

There are three conditions that must be satisfied in order to make generalizations from observations legitimate:

Take note

- There must be a large number of observations.
- The observations must be repeated under a large range of circumstances and conditions.
- No observations must contradict the derived generalization.

Despite the undisputed success of this approach, there are several inherent problems. The 18th-century philosopher Hume pointed out that the logic on which the justification for this form of argument is based is circular, that is, it uses its own argument to justify itself. Notice the same method of deriving a general rule from numerous observations:

Induction worked successfully on one occasion.
Induction worked successfully on a second occasion.
And so on.
Therefore the principle of induction always works.

The other problems are about the number of observations and conditions required in order to come to reliable conclusions. How many times do you have to put your hand in the fire to conclude that fire burns? How many cigarette smokers do you have to observe to conclude that smoking can cause cancer? How can you avoid missing the possible exceptions to the rule? You cannot review every possible case in the universe.

These problems have led to the attitude that, although there may be overwhelming evidence for a certain theory, it can never be claimed to be irrevocably true. The greater the number of observations under the greater number of conditions, the greater is the probability of the truth of the generalization.

Deduction

Deduction starts from the other end. In one phrase again, deduction is 'going from the general to the particular'; or again, if you prefer the *Oxford English Dictionary* definition, 'the process of deducting a conclusion from what is known or assumed; inference from the general to the particular' (2002: 621). For example, medieval astronomers were convinced that the Earth was the centre of the universe. All their calculations about the movement of the heavenly bodies were based on this theory. Despite this erroneous 'law' they managed to predict the positions of the planets and stars at different times in the future with considerable accuracy. The calculations for their predictions were based on deductive thinking founded on the general idea of the Earth-centred solar system.

This approach is often associated with the ancient Greek philosopher Plato, who relied on our powers of reason to make sense of the world. He developed the doctrine that the material things that we handle and see around us, and abstract concepts such as 'justice', are ephemeral and imperfect copies of ideal and perfect entities that exist outside the physical world. He called these 'ideas' or 'forms'. This kind of knowledge puts theory before observation. Reality was interpreted in terms of these theories, and any observations that appeared to contradict them must automatically be wrong.

This may seem to be a silly way to do research. You could invent any kind of theory, for example that cars have personalities and feelings, and argue that evidence to the contrary must be mistaken (though you might even be able to make a good case for this). But this approach has its uses. After all, you cannot really begin to do research with a completely unstructured idea of what you are looking for. There are so many things to observe around us: where will you begin? It is essential to have some theoretical basis for your investigations. What if you had strong feelings (i.e. had a theory) that trying to teach health and social care professionals to ignore their intuition is counter-productive?

After all, Einstein's theory of relativity could not be tested until long after it was formulated. Since Einstein's theory was formulated, scientists have struggled to find ways in which the theory could be tested. Despite this, relativity theory has been useful in developing scientific thought. It is only recently that technology has provided the means to produce equipment that could investigate the forces that are the subject of the theory. This issue of testing theories brings us to the main approach to modern scientific investigation.

Hypothetico-deductive method

This approach combines the focusing power of deductive thinking with the observative power of inductive thinking. It was formulated by Karl Popper in the 1930s, and consists of a basically simple process of four steps. These are:

(1) identification of a problem;

(2) formulation of a hypothesis or tentative solution (synonymous with a theory in deductive thinking);

(3) practical or theoretical testing of the hypothesis or solution (synonymous with observations in inductive thinking);

(4) elimination or adjustment of an unsuccessful hypothesis or solution (this is the significant step in this process).

How does this work in practice? Let's take a simple example:

- Problem – to what temperature do you have to heat water in a kettle in order for it to boil?

- Hypothesis – water boils in an open vessel at 100°C.

- Testing – heat up water and measure the temperature at which it boils in as many situations as possible.

- Results – it is found that water boils at 100°C at sea level, but at lower temperatures at altitude.

- Adjustment of hypothesis – water at 1 atmosphere pressure boils in an open vessel at 100°C.

You can even develop a new hypothesis on the basis of this work, i.e. that the temperature at which water boils is affected by the surrounding pressure.

This method is often referred to as 'scientific method'. In practice, problems are rarely as simply defined as this; nor can one straightforward practical hypothesis sufficient to set up a testing regime be formulated. Generally, the hypothesis to a research problem is more abstract in nature, and from it subhypotheses can be derived. These are at a more concrete level, enabling them to be subjected to practical testing. You read about this in the previous chapter.

What should I do next?

In the light of what you have read in this chapter, how does your thinking about your dissertation topic fit in with the different philosophical approaches? Are the assumptions of positivist thought acceptable in your research approach, or is a more relativist basis appropriate?

In order to examine what might be an appropriate philosophical stance to the issues of your research, first look carefully at the subject of your dissertation. Now ask yourself the following rather general questions, and consider the comments we have made in response to the different options you may be offered.

- Is your study concerned with things or people, or does it include a study of both, perhaps of their interrelationships?

The study of things can usually be carried out using scientific method. Are you going to look at the things themselves and their properties and performance, e.g. the performance of emollients in treating atopic eczema in children in the UK, or will you look at how emollients are applied and used in practice? A positivist approach is quite suitable for either option, as the uncertainties of human interaction, feelings and habits are not an issue.

If it is people that you are going to study, will you look at trends in society, i.e. taking an overview of large groups or classes of people, or will you investigate personal relationships within small groups or between individuals?

The large amounts of quantitative data involved in the former also imply that taking a positivist approach is possible if you think that there are 'natural' or inevitable forces and laws that determine social events on a large scale. If you believe that the uncertainties of human reactions and beliefs operate even at this large scale, then a more relativist stance is appropriate. Scientific method could be used to examine the data.

The latter, examining individuals and small groups, is more likely to be approached in a relativist manner as your own background and attitudes make it difficult to see the situation from a purely neutral stance. Even so, if you were a psychologist or neurologist, you might disagree: there might be a purely scientific biological basis for all our actions.

If you are examining the relationships between people and things, at what scale will you be working? You could be using a large scale via general principles, for example, the design of hospital buildings; on an operational scale in systems studies, for example, nursing workforce organization at a hospital ward level; or a small scale in practical studies, for example, the design of individual aids for disabled people.

In every case, the technical and organizational aspects will be influenced by the human aspects. Hard science will need to be adapted to cater for the abilities, feelings and habits of people. You will need to adapt your approaches to these different aspects.

- Can your problem be analysed and explained in terms of forces or inner physical processes, or rather in terms of meanings and subjective forces?

Clearly in the case of the former, a positivist approach is appropriate here, with the use of scientific method being a strong contender as a way ahead.

- Are notions of causation an important aspect, or are you seeking to find explanations in order to reach an understanding of a situation?

Causation has a sort of inevitability about it, as if it followed certain rules: 'If these certain events take place, then they will cause this other event to happen.' In the natural sciences the role of human relative values plays little part, for example, the rules of aerodynamics can be harnessed to make a plane fly even without a pilot. A positivist approach is appropriate here. When the issues have a more human perspective, then certainties are more elusive, for example, what are the causes of poor behaviour? In this case, understanding and explanations will be more subjective and relativistic.

- Will knowledge be gained through impartial observation and/or experimentation, or will you have to immerse yourself in the situation and make subjective interpretations or value-laden observations?

Here is a clear distinction between a positivist approach and a relativist approach. The very assumption that you can observe impartially implies a belief in the possibility of detachment and neutrality, while experimentation rests on assumptions that you can really control certain selected variables. Subjective interpretations and value-laden observations can only make sense when you recognize the partiality of the researcher.

- Are you trying to find solutions to a perceived problem, explain reasons for events, investigate to discover new knowledge, or compare and critique the work of others?

How you approach these tasks depends on what the problem, events, type of knowledge or work of others comprise.

Do remember though, when thinking about the philosophical attitude you develop to study your research question, that the positivist and relativist stances are crude formulations of the range of approaches one could take. Increasingly in health and social care research positivist and relativist paradigms are being challenged, with postpositivism, constructivism, critical realism and participatory approaches playing more dominant roles in knowledge generation. What may be appropriate for one aspect of your study might be inappropriate for another. The main thing is to be aware of your attitudes, and to question your own assumptions when you formulate the design of your research activities. It is a good exercise to explain your motivations for choosing your particular topic: this might quite clearly reveal your attitudes towards the subject and your particular research question.

Further reading

You could spend an awful lot of time reading about philosophy and its impact on enquiry and research. If you get interested in this subject, beware of getting bogged down and spending too much time exploring. You could carry on for a lifetime. Still, you can follow up all the interesting aspects after you have finished your dissertation.

If you are doing a topic that involves social research, that is, with people and society, then it might be worth having a look at the following for more detail:

Hughes, J.A. and Sharrock, W. (1997) *The Philosophy of Social Research*, 3rd edn. Harlow: Longman.
Seale, C. (ed.) (2004) *Researching Society and Culture*, 2nd edn. London: Sage Publications.

For an interesting text on the scientific method see:

Chalmers, A. (1999) *What is this Thing Called Science?* 3rd edn. Maidenhead: Open University Press.

For a simple general introduction to philosophy, seek this one out. This approachable book explains the main terminology and outlines the principal streams of thought:

Thompson, M. (2006) *Teach Yourself Philosophy*. London: Hodder.

And here are books that deal in more detail with some aspects of philosophy – really for the enthusiast!

Collier, A. (1994) *Critical Realism: An Introduction to Roy Bhaskhar's Philosophy*. London: Verso.
Husserl, E. (1999) *The Idea of Phenomenology: A Translation of Die Idee Der Phänomenologie; Husserliana II* trans. L. Hardy. Springer.
Matthews, E. (1996) *Twentieth-Century French Philosophy*. Oxford: Oxford University Press.

And these we have selected which are more focused on the research process – mostly in great detail. They could provide inspiration and a few enlightening revelations, but you will have to work at it. If you do delve into these, seek out the bits on the philosophical approach(es) – not always clearly stated!

Booth, W., Colomb, G. and William, J.M. (2003) *The Craft of Research*, 2nd edn. Chicago, IL: University of Chicago Press.

May, T. (2001) *Social Research: Issues, Methods and Process*, 3rd edn. Buckingham: Open University Press.

Neale, J.M., Liebert, R.M. and Liebert, L.L. (1995) *Science and Behaviour: An Introduction to Methods of Research*, 3rd edn. New York: Prentice-Hall.

Chapter 6

How Do I Write a Proposal?

Chapter contents

- What is a proposal?
- The subject title
- The aims or objectives
- The background
- Defining the research problem and question
- The main concepts and variables
- Methods
- Expected outcomes
- Programme of work
- What should I do next?
- Further reading

What is a proposal?

A proposal is a careful description of what your dissertation will be about and how you intend to carry out the work involved to achieve its completion. Whatever type of research study you are intending to embark on whether it be an empirical study, a literature review or an audit project, you will be required to write a research proposal. The proposal is a really useful document that challenges you to think very carefully about what you are going to do, how you will do it and why. It will be required in order to inform your supervisor of your intentions so that he or she can judge whether:

(1) The subject and suggested format conform to the requirements of the course.

(2) It is a feasible project in respect of scope and practicality.

Table 6.1 (Continued)

Research proposal headings	Theoretical Study	Literature Review	Empirical Study/Audit Study
	• Why are these methods suitable and appropriate? • Which search terms will you use? • Select and justify the computerized databases you will search. *Data analysis methods* • Outline your intended approach to reading about, reviewing and analysing a concept or theories. *Validity, reliability and rigour* • Consider the validity and reliability of the methods you intend to use.	• Which search terms will you use? • Select and justify the computerized databases you will search. Any hand searching or consultation with experts. *Data analysis methods* • Describe the critical appraisal framework to be used. • Outline how you will analyse the research findings, e.g. summarize the research papers, identify themes and compare and contrast the themes across the research studies. *Validity, reliability and rigour* • Consider the validity and reliability of the methods you intend to use.	• Why are these methods suitable and appropriate? • Describe proposed pilot work. • Consider the validity and reliability of research instruments, or ways in which rigour and credibility will be addressed *Data analysis methods* • Proposed methods of data analysis. • Any statistical techniques and software tools to be used. • Ensure proposed analysis techniques suit approach selected. *Validity, reliability and rigour* • Consider the validity and reliability of research instruments, or ways in which rigour and credibility will be addressed.
Ethical issues	• Consider any ethical issues associated with using and	• Consider any ethical issues associated with	• Discuss/outline potential ethical dilemmas,

(Continued)

(3) You have identified some questions or issues that are worth investigating.

(4) Your suggested methods for information collection and analysis are appropriate.

(5) The expected outcomes relate to the aims of the project.

In addition, many grant funding bodies will ask to see a research proposal in order to decide whether a study is worth supporting. It is also a requirement of research governance and research ethics committee application procedures.

So, not only is the proposal the main opportunity to crystallize your thoughts before you embark on the project, it is also a sober consideration of how much you will be able to actually achieve within the few weeks or months allowed. You will not be able to sit down and write your proposal without referring to your background research. A good proposal will indicate how your chosen topic emerges from issues that are being debated within your subject field, and how your work will produce a useful contribution to the debate. At this level of research you do not have to make any earth-shattering discoveries, but it is necessary to produce some useful insights by the appropriate application of research theory and methods.

Because the proposal must be quite short (usually not more than two–three sides of paper for an undergraduate dissertation), a lot of thought needs to be put into its production in order to cover all the matter to be conveyed in an elegantly dense manner. Several redrafts will be needed in order to pare it down to the limited length allowed, so don't panic if you cannot get it all together first time. A really informative proposal will not only impress your supervisor, but also give you a good guide to the work, and help to get you focused back on the important issues if (probably, when) you get diverted on other paths of investigation later on in the project.

There is a fairly standardized format for writing research proposals which, if followed, ensures that you cover all the important aspects that must be included. The advice under the following headings will help you to focus on the essential matters and to make the hard choices required at this early stage in the project. Table 6.1 provides a suggested structure for the different dissertation approaches and some key headings to consider when writing your research proposal.

The subject title

The subject title summarizes in a few words the entire project. You will probably not be able to formulate this finally until you have completed the proposal, but you will need a working title in order to focus your thinking.

A title should contain the key words of the dissertation subject, that is, the main subjects, concepts or situations. Added to these are normally a few words that delineate the scope of the study. For example:

Table 6.1 Dissertation structure by approach and key headings

Research proposal headings	Theoretical Study	Literature Review	Empirical Study/Audit Study
Study title	• Make it explicit and concise. • Focus on what you are intending to do.	• Make it explicit and concise. • Focus on what you are intending to do.	• Make it explicit and concise. • Focus on what you are intending to do.
Introduction	• A short summary stating what you are going to do and why. • Provide a clear rationale and justification for your proposed study.	• A short summary stating what you are going to do and why. • Provide a clear rationale and justification for your proposed study.	• A short summary stating what you are going to do and why. • Provide a clear rationale and justification for your proposed study.
Background	• Preliminary brief and focused literature review summarizing the key theories and main points in the existing literature. • Outline the theoretical or conceptual basis for the research.	• Brief and focused preliminary literature review summarizing the accepted position in the subject area. • Refer to existing research evidence, relevant policy (national and international), statistical evidence and theory.	• Preliminary brief and focused literature review summarizing the key issues in the existing research evidence, relevant policy and theory. • Outline the limited evidence on your topic and set the scene for your proposed research and the problem you will tackle
Research problem	• A precise research problem. • Clear, concise and achievable research question(s).	• A precise research problem. • Clear, concise and achievable research question(s).	• A precise research problem. • Clear, concise and achievable research question(s).
Aims or objectives	• Must be clear, specific and measurable.	• Must be clear, specific and measurable.	• Must be clear, specific and measurable.

(Continued)

Table 6.1 (Continued)

Research proposal headings	Theoretical Study	Literature Review	Empirical Study/Audit Study
Why chosen approach?	• Justify briefly why a theoretical study is suitable to answer the research question.	• Justify briefly why a review of existing research literature and evidence is appropriate to answer the research question.	• Justify briefly why your chosen research design, or an audit study is appropriate.
Research methods (1) Access (2) Sample (3) Data collection methods (4) Data analysis methods (5) Validity, reliability/rigour	*Access* • Describe your plans to access and acquire the relevant data – literature. *Sample* • Describe how you will select a sample of literature. • Outline the inclusion and exclusion criteria. *Data collection methods* • Outline and justify which theoretical method you are adopting, e.g. concept analysis. • Describe the methods that you will use to collect the relevant theoretical work	*Access* • Describe plans to obtain the existing research literature and articles. • Library access, Internet access and other sources, etc. *Sample* • Describe how you will select a sample of research articles. • Outline the inclusion and exclusion criteria. *Data collection methods* • Describe and justify the literature review approach you will use. • Outline the methods that you will use to obtain the research literature.	*Access and recruitment* • Describe plans to access the study site and recruit the sample. • Outline any collaborators or existing practice links. *Sample/population* • Describe the study population from which you will select a sample and the planned sampling strategy. • Outline the inclusion and exclusion criteria. *Data collection methods* • Methods of data collection: what data/information do you intend to collect and/or measure.

(Continued)

Table 6.1 (Continued)

Research proposal headings	Theoretical Study	Literature Review	Empirical Study/Audit Study
	examining existing concepts and theories.	using existing research literature. • Reflect on how and whether the research papers you use in your study addressed ethical issues and concerns.	i.e. confidentiality, informed consent, any potential risk of harm. • Plans for seeking ethics committee review and research governance approval.
Expected outcomes	• Specify the planned outcomes of the theoretical study. • What are the possible benefits of the proposed theoretical study for health or social care practice/ management and/or education – locally, nationally and internationally? • Explain what you will do with the results when the study is completed.	• Specify the planned outcomes of the literature review. • What are the possible benefits of the proposed literature review for health or social care practice/management and/or education – locally, nationally and internationally? • Explain what you will do with the literature review when the study is completed.	• Specify the planned outcomes of the research. • What are the possible benefits of the proposed research for health or social care practice/management and/or education – locally, nationally and internationally? • Explain what you will do with the results when the research or audit study is completed.
Programme of work/timetable	• Provide a clear outline of the steps you intend to undertake in this theoretical study.	• Provide a clear outline of the steps you intend to undertake in this literature review.	• Include a timeline or Gantt chart detailing the research study milestones and your plan of work.

(Continued)

Table 6.1 (Continued)

Research proposal headings	Theoretical Study	Literature Review	Empirical Study/Audit Study
	• Include a timeline or Gantt chart detailing the stages of the theoretical study and how long each will take.	• Include a timeline or Gantt chart detailing the steps of the literature review and how long each will take.	• Is the research/audit study feasible in the time available? • Consider all the resources that you will require to complete the research. • List the project costs in a table.
References	• Within the proposal references must be pertinent, up to date and correctly presented. • Include a complete and accurately formatted final reference list.	• Within the proposal references must be pertinent, up to date and correctly presented. • Include a complete and accurately formatted final reference list.	• Within the proposal references must be pertinent, up to date and correctly presented. • Include a complete and accurately formatted final reference list.
Appendices	Unlikely to be relevant for a theoretical study.	*If relevant include:* • Critical appraisal framework or checklist. • Data extraction tool. • A worked example of your critical appraisal of a research paper using a critical appraisal framework or checklist.	*If relevant include:* • Letters of support for research. • Participant invitation letter. • Participant information sheet. • Consent form. • Interview schedule/questionnaire.

Health promotion activity in British schools: the impact of the National Healthy Schools Programme (NHSP).

Start, therefore, by summing up the core of your chosen subject by its principal concepts. To find these, refer to the background reading you have done. What words are mentioned in the book titles, the chapter headings/content lists and the journal papers and research abstracts you have read? These may be quite esoteric, but should represent the very heart of your interest. This part of the title will, by its nature, be rather general and even abstract. In order to describe the nature of the project itself, more detail will be required that states limitations such as the location, time and extent. Locations can be countries or towns, types of place or situations. Time might be historical periods, the present or during specific events.

The previous delineations help to define the extent of the project, but further factors can be added, such as under certain conditions or in particular contexts. A few examples here will give you the general idea:

- In Sub-Saharan Africa.

- In inner city schools.

- In one-to-one teaching sessions.

- In the 19th century.

- Contemporary trends.

The title may be made more explicit and focused by clearly describing the type of study approach you are intending to undertake:

- a qualitative study;

- a critical review of the research evidence;

- a literature review;

- a concept analysis.

The aims or objectives

The aims or objectives of the project should be summarized in three or four bullet points. This then provides a very succinct summary of the focus of the research, and an introduction to the rationale that follows. If you find this difficult to write, then you have probably not thought sufficiently about what you are actually going to do. Some useful indicative words you can use are: to explore, to test, to investigate, to explain, to compare, to predict. Ensure that there is an indication of the limits of the project by mentioning place, time, extent and so forth. Here is an example:

Resilience in childhood as represented in the literature

Objectives:

- To explore the concept of resilience and its application to children's well-being.
- To contrast the ways that policymakers, researchers and other writers have examined and applied resilience factors.
- To compare and seek connections between these different sources of evidence.
- To consider the relevance of childhood resilience to social care practice.

The background

Anyone reading your proposal for the first time needs to be informed about the context of the project and where it fits in with current thinking. Do not assume that the reader knows anything about the subject, so introduce it in such a way that any lay person can understand the main issues surrounding your work. That is one function of the background section. The other function is to convince your supervisor that you have done the necessary reading into the subject, and that you have reviewed the literature sufficiently. This is why it is necessary to have plenty of references in this section.

The references should refer to policy, theories, relevant statistics, accepted practices in health and social care, contentious issues, and empirical research publications dealing with your subject of study. It requires quite an effort to get a lot of information across in a succinct manner. Use the notes you have made from your reading. Check that the key theories, writers and researchers have been mentioned. You will find these in the main publications about your subject. Expect to cite about 10–20 references in this section.

You could spend an enormous time doing this, as the amount of previous work in the field could be extensive. Alternatively, you could worry that you have missed out on essential references, especially if your searches are not very productive. Just remember that at undergraduate level you are not expected to already know everything in your chosen subject. One of the points of doing a dissertation is to widen your knowledge and understanding. So stop as soon as you can provide enough background material to give a context to your project. Your supervisor should be able to tell you if you have missed out any crucial references.

Defining the research problem and question

Based on the issues explained and discussed in the background section, you should be able to identify the particular part of the subject that you

(3) You have identified some questions or issues that are worth investigating.

(4) Your suggested methods for information collection and analysis are appropriate.

(5) The expected outcomes relate to the aims of the project.

In addition, many grant funding bodies will ask to see a research proposal in order to decide whether a study is worth supporting. It is also a requirement of research governance and research ethics committee application procedures.

So, not only is the proposal the main opportunity to crystallize your thoughts before you embark on the project, it is also a sober consideration of how much you will be able to actually achieve within the few weeks or months allowed. You will not be able to sit down and write your proposal without referring to your background research. A good proposal will indicate how your chosen topic emerges from issues that are being debated within your subject field, and how your work will produce a useful contribution to the debate. At this level of research you do not have to make any earth-shattering discoveries, but it is necessary to produce some useful insights by the appropriate application of research theory and methods.

Because the proposal must be quite short (usually not more than two–three sides of paper for an undergraduate dissertation), a lot of thought needs to be put into its production in order to cover all the matter to be conveyed in an elegantly dense manner. Several redrafts will be needed in order to pare it down to the limited length allowed, so don't panic if you cannot get it all together first time. A really informative proposal will not only impress your supervisor, but also give you a good guide to the work, and help to get you focused back on the important issues if (probably, when) you get diverted on other paths of investigation later on in the project.

There is a fairly standardized format for writing research proposals which, if followed, ensures that you cover all the important aspects that must be included. The advice under the following headings will help you to focus on the essential matters and to make the hard choices required at this early stage in the project. Table 6.1 provides a suggested structure for the different dissertation approaches and some key headings to consider when writing your research proposal.

The subject title

The subject title summarizes in a few words the entire project. You will probably not be able to formulate this finally until you have completed the proposal, but you will need a working title in order to focus your thinking.

A title should contain the key words of the dissertation subject, that is, the main subjects, concepts or situations. Added to these are normally a few words that delineate the scope of the study. For example:

Table 6.1   Dissertation structure by approach and key headings

Research proposal headings	Theoretical Study	Literature Review	Empirical Study/Audit Study
Study title	• Make it explicit and concise. • Focus on what you are intending to do.	• Make it explicit and concise. • Focus on what you are intending to do.	• Make it explicit and concise. • Focus on what you are intending to do.
Introduction	• A short summary stating what you are going to do and why. • Provide a clear rationale and justification for your proposed study.	• A short summary stating what you are going to do and why. • Provide a clear rationale and justification for your proposed study.	• A short summary stating what you are going to do and why. • Provide a clear rationale and justification for your proposed study.
Background	• Preliminary brief and focused literature review summarizing the key theories and main points in the existing literature. • Outline the theoretical or conceptual basis for the research.	• Brief and focused preliminary literature review summarizing the accepted position in the subject area. • Refer to existing research evidence, relevant policy (national and international), statistical evidence and theory.	• Preliminary brief and focused literature review summarizing the key issues in the existing research evidence, relevant policy and theory. • Outline the limited evidence on your topic and set the scene for your proposed research and the problem you will tackle
Research problem	• A precise research problem. • Clear, concise and achievable research question(s).	• A precise research problem. • Clear, concise and achievable research question(s).	• A precise research problem. • Clear, concise and achievable research question(s).
Aims or objectives	• Must be clear, specific and measurable.	• Must be clear, specific and measurable.	• Must be clear, specific and measurable.

(Continued)

Table 6.1 (Continued)

Research proposal headings	Theoretical Study	Literature Review	Empirical Study/Audit Study
Why chosen approach?	• Justify briefly why a theoretical study is suitable to answer the research question.	• Justify briefly why a review of existing research literature and evidence is appropriate to answer the research question.	• Justify briefly why your chosen research design, or an audit study is appropriate.
Research methods (1) Access (2) Sample (3) Data collection methods (4) Data analysis methods (5) Validity, reliability/rigour	*Access* • Describe your plans to access and acquire the relevant data – literature. *Sample* • Describe how you will select a sample of literature. • Outline the inclusion and exclusion criteria. *Data collection methods* • Outline and justify which theoretical method you are adopting, e.g. concept analysis. • Describe the methods that you will use to collect the relevant theoretical work and literature.	*Access* • Describe plans to obtain the existing research literature and articles. • Library access, Internet access and other sources, etc. *Sample* • Describe how you will select a sample of research articles. • Outline the inclusion and exclusion criteria. *Data collection methods* • Describe and justify the literature review approach you will use. • Outline the methods that you will use to obtain the research literature.	*Access and recruitment* • Describe plans to access the study site and recruit the sample. • Outline any collaborators or existing practice links. *Sample/population* • Describe the study population from which you will select a sample and the planned sampling strategy. • Outline the inclusion and exclusion criteria. *Data collection methods* • Methods of data collection: what data/information do you intend to collect and/or measure.

(Continued)

Table 6.1 (Continued)

Research proposal headings	Theoretical Study	Literature Review	Empirical Study/Audit Study
	• Why are these methods suitable and appropriate? • Which search terms will you use? • Select and justify the computerized databases you will search. *Data analysis methods* • Outline your intended approach to reading about, reviewing and analysing a concept or theories. *Validity, reliability and rigour* • Consider the validity and reliability of the methods you intend to use.	• Which search terms will you use? • Select and justify the computerized databases you will search. Any hand searching or consultation with experts. *Data analysis methods* • Describe the critical appraisal framework to be used. • Outline how you will analyse the research findings, e.g. summarize the research papers, identify themes and compare and contrast the themes across the research studies. *Validity, reliability and rigour* • Consider the validity and reliability of the methods you intend to use.	• Why are these methods suitable and appropriate? • Describe proposed pilot work. • Consider the validity and reliability of research instruments, or ways in which rigour and credibility will be addressed *Data analysis methods* • Proposed methods of data analysis. • Any statistical techniques and software tools to be used. • Ensure proposed analysis techniques suit approach selected. *Validity, reliability and rigour* • Consider the validity and reliability of research instruments, or ways in which rigour and credibility will be addressed.
Ethical issues	• Consider any ethical issues associated with using and	• Consider any ethical issues associated with	• Discuss/outline potential ethical dilemmas,

(Continued)

Table 6.1 (Continued)

Research proposal headings	Theoretical Study	Literature Review	Empirical Study/Audit Study
	examining existing concepts and theories.	using existing research literature. • Reflect on how and whether the research papers you use in your study addressed ethical issues and concerns.	i.e. confidentiality, informed consent, any potential risk of harm. • Plans for seeking ethics committee review and research governance approval.
Expected outcomes	• Specify the planned outcomes of the theoretical study. • What are the possible benefits of the proposed theoretical study for health or social care practice/ management and/or education – locally, nationally and internationally? • Explain what you will do with the results when the study is completed.	• Specify the planned outcomes of the literature review. • What are the possible benefits of the proposed literature review for health or social care practice/management and/or education – locally, nationally and internationally? • Explain what you will do with the literature review when the study is completed.	• Specify the planned outcomes of the research. • What are the possible benefits of the proposed research for health or social care practice/management and/or education – locally, nationally and internationally? • Explain what you will do with the results when the research or audit study is completed.
Programme of work/timetable	• Provide a clear outline of the steps you intend to undertake in this theoretical study.	• Provide a clear outline of the steps you intend to undertake in this literature review.	• Include a timeline or Gantt chart detailing the research study milestones and your plan of work.

(Continued)

Table 6.1 (Continued)

Research proposal headings	Theoretical Study	Literature Review	Empirical Study/Audit Study
	• Include a timeline or Gantt chart detailing the stages of the theoretical study and how long each will take.	• Include a timeline or Gantt chart detailing the steps of the literature review and how long each will take.	• Is the research/audit study feasible in the time available? • Consider all the resources that you will require to complete the research. • List the project costs in a table.
References	• Within the proposal references must be pertinent, up to date and correctly presented. • Include a complete and accurately formatted final reference list.	• Within the proposal references must be pertinent, up to date and correctly presented. • Include a complete and accurately formatted final reference list.	• Within the proposal references must be pertinent, up to date and correctly presented. • Include a complete and accurately formatted final reference list.
Appendices	Unlikely to be relevant for a theoretical study.	*If relevant include:* • Critical appraisal framework or checklist. • Data extraction tool. • A worked example of your critical appraisal of a research paper using a critical appraisal framework or checklist.	*If relevant include:* • Letters of support for research. • Participant invitation letter. • Participant information sheet. • Consent form. • Interview schedule/ questionnaire.

Health promotion activity in British schools: the impact of the National Healthy Schools Programme (NHSP).

Start, therefore, by summing up the core of your chosen subject by its principal concepts. To find these, refer to the background reading you have done. What words are mentioned in the book titles, the chapter headings/content lists and the journal papers and research abstracts you have read? These may be quite esoteric, but should represent the very heart of your interest. This part of the title will, by its nature, be rather general and even abstract. In order to describe the nature of the project itself, more detail will be required that states limitations such as the location, time and extent. Locations can be countries or towns, types of place or situations. Time might be historical periods, the present or during specific events.

The previous delineations help to define the extent of the project, but further factors can be added, such as under certain conditions or in particular contexts. A few examples here will give you the general idea:

- In Sub-Saharan Africa.

- In inner city schools.

- In one-to-one teaching sessions.

- In the 19th century.

- Contemporary trends.

The title may be made more explicit and focused by clearly describing the type of study approach you are intending to undertake:

- a qualitative study;

- a critical review of the research evidence;

- a literature review;

- a concept analysis.

The aims or objectives

The aims or objectives of the project should be summarized in three or four bullet points. This then provides a very succinct summary of the focus of the research, and an introduction to the rationale that follows. If you find this difficult to write, then you have probably not thought sufficiently about what you are actually going to do. Some useful indicative words you can use are: to explore, to test, to investigate, to explain, to compare, to predict. Ensure that there is an indication of the limits of the project by mentioning place, time, extent and so forth. Here is an example:

Resilience in childhood as represented in the literature

Objectives:

- To explore the concept of resilience and its application to children's well-being.
- To contrast the ways that policymakers, researchers and other writers have examined and applied resilience factors.
- To compare and seek connections between these different sources of evidence.
- To consider the relevance of childhood resilience to social care practice.

The background

Anyone reading your proposal for the first time needs to be informed about the context of the project and where it fits in with current thinking. Do not assume that the reader knows anything about the subject, so introduce it in such a way that any lay person can understand the main issues surrounding your work. That is one function of the background section. The other function is to convince your supervisor that you have done the necessary reading into the subject, and that you have reviewed the literature sufficiently. This is why it is necessary to have plenty of references in this section.

The references should refer to policy, theories, relevant statistics, accepted practices in health and social care, contentious issues, and empirical research publications dealing with your subject of study. It requires quite an effort to get a lot of information across in a succinct manner. Use the notes you have made from your reading. Check that the key theories, writers and researchers have been mentioned. You will find these in the main publications about your subject. Expect to cite about 10–20 references in this section.

You could spend an enormous time doing this, as the amount of previous work in the field could be extensive. Alternatively, you could worry that you have missed out on essential references, especially if your searches are not very productive. Just remember that at undergraduate level you are not expected to already know everything in your chosen subject. One of the points of doing a dissertation is to widen your knowledge and understanding. So stop as soon as you can provide enough background material to give a context to your project. Your supervisor should be able to tell you if you have missed out any crucial references.

Defining the research problem and question

Based on the issues explained and discussed in the background section, you should be able to identify the particular part of the subject that you want to investigate. Every subject could be studied for a lifetime, so it is important that you isolate just one small facet of the subject that you can manageably deal with in the short amount of time that you are given. Once you have explained the topic of your study, and argued why it is necessary to do work in this area, it is a good idea to briefly state the research problem in one or two clear sentences. This will be a direct reflection of your title, and will sum up the central question or problem that you will be investigating.

A clear definition of the research problem is an essential ingredient of a proposal; after all, the whole project hinges on this. The nature of the problem also determines the issues that you will explore, the kind of information that you will collect, and the types of analysis that you will use. The main research problem should grow naturally and inevitably out of your discussion of the background. You can state it clearly as a question, a hypothesis etc., as explained in Chapter 4. Then explain briefly how it will be broken down into subproblems and subhypotheses in order to make it practicable to research. There should be a connection between these and the aims or objectives of the project: everything should link up neatly.

The main concepts and variables

Every subject has its own way of looking at things, its own terminology and its own methods of measuring. Consider the differences between analysing the narrative of a patient interview and the research evidence collated during a systematic literature review. You will certainly be familiar with some of the concepts that are important in your subject: just look at the title you have chosen for examples of these. It will probably be necessary to define the main concepts in order to dispel any doubts as to their exact meaning. There might even be some dispute in the literature about terminology: if so, highlight the nature of the discussion.

A mention of the indicators that are used to make the concepts recognizable will be the first step to breaking down the abstract nature of most concepts. Then a description of the variables that are the measurable components of the indicators can be used to demonstrate how you will actually be able to collect and analyse the relevant data to come to conclusions about the concepts and their nature (see Chapter 4 if you have forgotten what indicators and variables are).

You do not need to write much here, just enough to convince the reader that you are are aware of how to investigate any abstract concepts that you might be dealing with, for example, effectiveness, pain, quality of life and so forth. Even well-known terms might need to be broken down to ensure that the reader understands just how you will study them, for example, evidence-based practice.

Methods

What exactly will you do in order to collect and analyse the necessary information? This is the practical part of the proposal where you explain what you will do, how you will do it, and why. It is important to demonstrate the way that your research activities relate to the research question and aims or objectives of your project and thus will enable you to come to conclusions relevant to the research problem. Different methods will be required for different parts of the research. Scan through Chapters 12 and 14–16 in order to get an idea of the range of research methods that are available. At this stage you need not know in detail just how you will implement them, but you should quite easily be able to choose those that seem appropriate to answer your research question. Consider the following actions that you might need to take:

- Do a literature search and critical analysis of sources.

- Consult with friends, peers and experts.

- Identify research population(s), situations, possible case studies.

- Select samples – size of sample(s), location of sample(s), number of case studies.

- Seek ethical approval and/or research governance approval.

- Collect data: literature sources and research evidence; quantitative data, qualitative data or a combination of both, that is, questionnaires, interviews, study of documents and observations.

- Set up experiments or models and run them.

- Analyse data – critical appraisal; quantitative analysis using statistical tests, enumerating and classifying; qualitative analysis involving data reduction, data display and conclusion drawing.

- Evaluate results of analysis – summarizing and coming to conclusions.

It is best to spell out what you intend to do in relation to each subproblem or subquestion when they require different methods of data collection and analysis. Try to be precise and add reasons for what you are planning to do, that is, add the phrase 'in order to …'. This methods section of the proposal can be in the form of a list of actions.

This whole process will need quite a lot of thought and preparation, especially as you will not be familiar with some of the research methods. But time spent now to make informed decisions is time well spent. It will make you much more confident that you can plan your project, that you have not overreached yourself, and that you have decided on activities that you will quite enjoy doing.

Expected outcomes

It is a good idea to spell out to the reader, and to yourself, just what you hope will be achieved by doing all this work. Since the proposal is a type of contract to deliver certain results, it is a mistake to 'promise mountains and deliver molehills'. Although you cannot predict exactly what the outcomes will be (if you could, there would be little point in carrying out the research), you should try to be quite precise as to the nature and scope of the outcomes and as to who might benefit from the information. Obviously you should make sure that the outcomes relate directly to the aims of the research that you described at the beginning of the proposal. The outcomes may be a contribution at a practical and/or a theoretical level.

Programme of work

Chapter 7 addresses in detail how to plan your time, but you could even now, before reading it, provisionally allocate your major future activities into your available timeframe. A simple bar chart showing the available time in weeks, and the list of tasks and their sequence and duration, will be sufficient. Do not forget to give yourself plenty of time to actually write up and present your dissertation. You will quickly spot if you have been too ambitious in your intentions, because the tasks just will not fit realistically into the time. If you see problems ahead, now is the time to adjust your proposal to make it more feasible. Reduce the scope of the investigations by narrowing the problem still further (you can do this by becoming more specific and by reducing the number of subproblems or subquestions), by being less ambitious with the amount of data to collect, and by simplifying the analytical stages.

What should I do next?

Write your proposal. Just follow the above recommendations and it should not be too difficult. The biggest risk is that you agonize for ages over what to do before you even write anything down. This is a mistake, for if you try to work out everything in your head you cannot realistically review it. Committing yourself to paper or computer screen not only relieves your memory from having to retain all your decisions, but also forces you to construct an argument to structure your intentions. Once you have something written down, you can review it, build on it, add detail to it and alter it as required.

Using a computer gives you the opportunity to sketch out your ideas, perhaps as a series of headings or points. You do not have to worry too much about what you write down, as it can so easily be altered,

Figure 6.1

moved, expanded or even deleted. You can work like a painter who first sketches out a few indicative lines, then builds on these to produce, stage by stage, a finished picture. Assuming you have a good idea about the sort of problem you wish to address, you do not even have to start at the beginning. You could work back from the desired outcomes and create a rationale on how you would get there. Or you could select the activities that you enjoy doing most and explore how you could exploit these to devise a project. Once you have a framework that looks feasible, you can add the detail – work that will require rather more reflection and reference to further information.

The final version should be set out following the structure outlined above. You will also need to add a list of references that give the details about the publications cited in your text. Check with any coursework instructions you have been given to make sure that you are fulfilling the requirements. When you have finished, even if you are not formally obliged to do so, give a copy to your supervisor and request his or her comments. Be prepared to alter your proposal in response to any comments you receive, but first think carefully about the implications of these changes. The comments should help to make life easier for you, or clarify the implications of your proposal. It is also in the interest of your supervisor that you do well and enjoy the experience of writing your dissertation.

The proposal will form a firm foundation for your research work. You should refer to it from time to time during the next weeks when you get into the detail of your work, in order to check that you are not going astray, getting too bogged down on one particular aspect, or missing out on an essential detail.

Further reading

There are books that are solely dedicated to writing academic proposals of all kinds. The principles are the same for all of them; it is the extent and detail that vary. All are reasoned arguments to support a plan of action. If you want to read more, or find different approaches to proposal writing, you can explore some of these books. Some will be rather too detailed for your purposes, but you will undoubtedly find something useful. We have put them in order of complexity, simplest first. The first two provide detailed information on writing effective research proposals, including some very helpful worked examples using different research approaches.

Locke, L.F, Spirduso, W.W. and Silverman S.J. (2007) *Proposals That Work: A Guide for Planning Dissertations and Grant Proposals*, 5th edn. London: Sage Publications.

Punch, K.F. (2006) *Developing Effective Research Proposals*, 2nd edn. London: Sage Publications.

The following two books are also worth looking at:

Coley, S.M. and Scheinberg, C.A. (2007) *Proposal Writing: Effective Grantmanship*, 3rd edn. London: Sage Publications.

Jay, R. (1999) *How to Write Proposals and Reports That Get Results*. London: Prentice Hall.

Most books on how to do dissertations will also have a section on writing a proposal. Several have been mentioned in previous chapters. See also the example below for a good starting point:

Appleton, J.V. (2008) 'Starting a new research project', in J. Neale (ed.), *Research Methods for Health and Social Care*. Basingstoke: Palgrave Macmillan. Chapter 2.

Chapter 7

What About Working and Planning My Time?

Chapter contents

- Motivation and discipline
- Moods
- Being creative
- All the things you need to do
- Setting up a work timetable
- Starting to write
- What should I do next?
- Further reading

Motivation and discipline

This chapter is in danger of sounding patronizing in places, partly because it sometimes states the obvious, and partly because the idea of discipline evokes the picture of someone talking from on high and wagging a finger at you. But we know only too well (from writing this book) that motivation and discipline are two factors that play an important part in helping to actually get the work done. It is after all *self*-motivation and *self*-discipline that are the issue, not something imposed by a higher authority. So, to become aware of a few techniques which help to make life easier is no bad thing.

Ideally, if you have enough motivation, you are unlikely to need to impose much onerous discipline on yourself. In order to be motivated, it is pretty important that the project you have chosen really interests you. When you think of it, this is probably the first opportunity you have had since beginning your education to choose yourself what you will study for the next few months, so you should seize the opportunity to select something that will make this exercise enjoyable and rewarding. This point has already been more fully made in Chapter 3.

Even so, not every task can be interesting, and there are so many other enjoyable things to do and other deadlines to meet. There will also be several new skills to learn and others to develop, both of which require energy and dedication. You are only human, so it is worth considering how your efforts can be optimized by being in tune with your personality and mental and physical characteristics. Below are some ideas of how you can achieve this.

Moods

No one can be upbeat and raring to go all of the time. We are all subject to moods that have an important influence on our ability to concentrate and be creative. Philippa Davies (2001: 15) mentions two sets of opposite conditions – energetic/tired and calm/tense – which can be understood to contain a range of moods from mild to extreme. One cannot simply equate one or other state with being conducive to hard work or concentrated effort. It depends on your personality how you react to these moods. What is useful though is to be aware of how you are feeling, and also what sort of activities you can do best in which mood. For instance, some people need the tension of working to a deadline to get going, while others are only productive when they can mull over their work in a peaceful setting.

It is well known that people's mood varies during the course of the day. But they are not all the same: some are 'morning people', others 'evening people', while some fall between the two, or are even 'night people'. Take note of how you feel during the day. Do you find working easiest during the morning, or do you only get going in the evening hours? This is not just a psychological phenomenon, but also a physiological one (something to do with body temperature at different times of the day). If you can detect a pattern, then plan your activities to suit. Not all that you need to do requires intense concentration, so you can reserve the less demanding tasks for your 'weaker' periods.

Moods are also a form of information or feedback about your biomedical condition. Healthy living in the form of plenty of exercise, a balanced diet, and regular and sufficient rest promotes an upbeat mood. Conversely, a lack of sleep, poor diet, too much drink and smoking, and lack of exercise will tend to depress your mood. We know that these often feature large in student life, but it is just as well to be aware of it, and know that a good meal and a night's sleep will actually make working easier.

You can also do things to influence your mood. To avoid getting stuck in a boring and depressing routine, why not organize a shift of scene? Work somewhere different, visit different libraries, choose case studies or conduct practical research in different locations. Although you might not be in a position to make a study of an aspect of health or social care outside the UK, visits to new places can be a stimulating experience.

Ruminating about a subject for a long time can be a 'downer'. There is only so much that one can resolve in one's head. Thinking too long around a problem, without getting it down on paper or discussing it with someone, tends to lead to circular thinking and the feeling of being stuck. Only when the problem gets clearly laid out can you find ways to grapple with it, or even to let your subconscious work on it.

Make the best of when you are feeling great. At these times you will feel inspired, ideas will tumble into your head, you will see connections and have insights and have a strong urge to get it all down onto paper. Avoid getting interrupted, as it is difficult to pick up from where you left off. Put off other commitments and savour the moments: this is when you will be at your most productive. There are other times when you feel that you are running at half speed. Make use of these times for more menial tasks, such as tidying up, sorting out notes, drawing or scanning illustrations, making graphs and figures. You can also catch up on your reading.

Sometimes, having worked for some time you can get stuck, fed up or just tired. Peter Woods (2006: 17–20) has collected a few ploys that he and other well-known writers have used to reinvigorate themselves. Spend some time gazing out of the window (at a panoramic vista if there is one), drink lots of cups of coffee, pace the room, listen to the birds singing or to a piece of music, examine what is going on in the neighbourhood with a pair of binoculars, give an imaginary speech or hold a conversation with yourself, take a walk or go for a run, play the violin or a computer game or a game of snooker, go out and do some sport.

Being creative

One of the main purposes of getting you to do a dissertation is to force you to work independently, and this requires a certain creativity. Although you will get a certain level of support, it is really up to you to work things out and find solutions, and even to discover problems that need solving. Understanding complex situations also needs an open-minded approach. Creative thinking helps you to break out from habitual thought patterns and to explore a wider range of possibilities. There are several easy-to-use techniques that can help you to think creatively. Here are a few exercises you might find useful.

Brainstorming

You need a group of people for this (though you can do it on your own; it is then called brainwriting or a thought shower). First, clearly define a particular problem you want to solve. List the ideas as they come into your heads. In a group, you can also feed off other people's suggestions, combine ideas and extrapolate or modify them. The main rule is not to criticize, however bizarre or ridiculous the suggestions may be. The evaluation of the ideas comes later. A typical brainstorming may produce about 50 different ideas (probably rather less for brainwriting) for solutions to a particular problem. These can then be classified and evaluated.

Checklists

A bit like a shopping list or to-do list. Make lists of things you need to consider, difficulties you might encounter, tasks you need to do, information you need to collect and so forth. Again, you need to focus on one aspect of your project for useful results. You can also use checklists to look at alternative ways of doing things by using trigger words, for example, combine solutions, reverse the problem (see it from a different perspective). Other trigger words are adapt, rearrange, substitute, magnify, minify, modify, put to other uses.

Analogies

You can often draw parallels between two different problems or situations, where knowledge about one can help to explain or solve the other. This is quite a natural process, a way of learning from experience. Put to more deliberate use, it can help to obtain new insights and perspectives. For example, the techniques your favourite chat show hosts use to prise information out of their guests could be used in your own interviews; or analysis of dynamics amongst a group of people could be compared with that of an extended family or a small business.

Immersion in the problem

This takes time, and is a good reason for defining a problem at an early stage. Once you are aware of the problem, be it of a practical or a theoretical nature, think about it for a bit, make a note of it in your research diary and then just 'forget' it for a few days and allow your subconscious to work on it. You might just jump out of the bath shouting 'eureka' as a solution presents itself out of the blue.

Discussion

A problem shared is a problem halved, so they say. It is best if you talk with people who share similar problems, and especially those who have found good solutions. Discuss your research ideas with friends, peers, health and social care professionals and university lecturers. This will help to clarify and focus your thinking on your research ideas or topic.

Systems thinking

There is a range of ways of looking at systems, that is, a complex of inter-related things or events such as machines, organizations, social groups or natural phenomena. You can draw a diagram to explore the sequences of cause and effect, or of the influence that factors have on one another. Other types of diagram are organization diagrams, cognitive maps, flow-charts and decision trees. A simple example of a systems map is illustrated in Figure 7.1. See Chapter 16 for examples of other diagrams.

You will probably find it necessary to spend plenty of time by yourself in order to get yourself going. Having the television on in the background is a real concentration killer. Often even having music on is a distraction – one keeps wanting to listen.

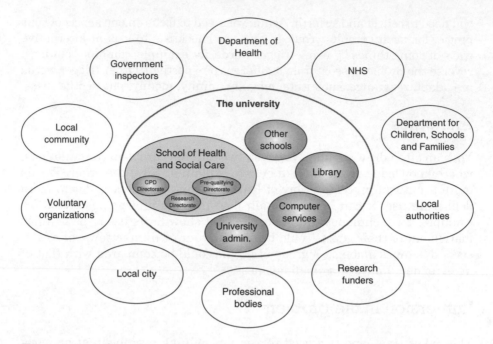

Figure 7.1   Systems map of the university (very simplified)

All the things you need to do

A dissertation is probably the biggest academic project that you have ever undertaken. The worst aspect of this is not that the task seems impossibly complex and lengthy, but that there are so many unknown factors that it will become very difficult to plan for a successful and timely completion.

In order to remove some of the mystique, here is a list of the tasks that you will (or in some cases, might) need to undertake, in a typical order. This list, tailored to the requirements of your type of study, will help you to work out a sequence of activities, make an estimate of how long each activity might take, and thus give you the information to set up a programme of work. You can then use this both to assure yourself that you can complete on time, and to check that you are not falling behind too much in your rate of work. It will also ensure that you do not spend too long on any aspect of the work, thus avoiding last minute panics. You can get some idea of what is involved in each task by scanning through the chapters mentioned.

- *Decide on a subject and type of investigation* and, if possible, get it provisionally approved by your supervisor (see Chapters 2 and 3).

- *Investigate the subject* so that you have enough information to write the proposal (see Chapter 4).

- *Write a research proposal* explaining the subject of your research and giving some indication of how you will do it i.e. through a systematic literature review or primary data collection study (see Chapter 6). It is a good idea to discuss your proposal with your supervisor, as it represents the foundation of your efforts over the next months.

- *Organize your note taking* and your archiving system (see Chapter 9).

- *Carry out background research* through study of the literature to determine what has been done already in the subject (see Chapter 8) in order to see where your study fits into current and past work.

- *Investigate methods of data collection and analysis* which have been used for similar studies to your own, and the practical aspects of doing them, for example, experiments, observations, surveys and literature reviews (see Chapters 2, 12, 14, 15 and 16). This will help you to decide just how you do your investigation and enable you to make estimates of what will be involved in time, expense, organization and perhaps getting permissions and access to sources of information.

- *Consider ethical concerns and research governance*. If you are planning to undertake primary data collection methods in health and social care and other settings, you will need to allow sufficient time to obtain the necessary approvals/permissions (see Chapter 13).

- *Work out a structure* for the dissertation (chapter headings and short lists of contents for each) and write a draft of your preliminary chapter(s) (see Chapters 10 and 18).

- *Start writing*. It is a good idea to start writing the introductory chapter(s) quite early on while you are immersed in the literature review. Do not try to perfect it – even blocks of notes will be a useful start.

- *Plan your project work*, that is, the part of the research that will generate new information (for example, fieldwork or primary data collection, experiments, qualitative interviews, electronic database searches, textual analyses, etc.). This might entail getting permissions for access to institutions, selecting study sites, obtaining documents for analysis and setting up questionnaires (see Chapters 11 and 13).

- *Carry out the project work* as planned above. Take into account time required for ethical review and research governance approval, travel, waiting for responses to questionnaires and getting appointments with people (see Chapters 13 and 14).

- *Sort and analyse the collected information*. In some cases, you may need to take some time to learn computer programs to help with the analysis (see Chapters 12, 15 and 16).

- *Write up the results* of your analysis, devising graphs, diagrams, summary tables and illustrations to help explain the data.

- *Write up how you did the research* (easier to do this after you have done it, though it should appear earlier in the dissertation), and write conclusions based on what you have found out (see Chapter 18).

- *Prepare a final draft.* This is the time to pull all the written work together in a structured form. Check that the length complies with the requirements, ensure that chapters or sections follow a good sequence, and assess the need for illustrations, graphs and diagrams. You can experiment with layout designs at this stage (see Chapter 19).

- *Write up the final version* based on the final draft. This will also involve inserting illustrations, graphs, summary tables and diagrams, lists of references, contents and finally setting out the layout and page numberings.

Setting up a work timetable

At the beginning of a project, when there seems to be loads of time to complete it, it is easy to sit back and believe that planning can be done later, when time starts to run out. After all, there is no need to be all organized when time is not an issue, is there? The trouble is, until you actually assess how much work is involved in writing your dissertation, it is quite difficult to judge whether there actually is loads of time. For this reason, it is a good idea to devise a simple timetable early on so that you can reassure yourself that you will not get into a desperate panic later.

In order to be of any real use, a timetable should be realistic in its aims. It is easy to plan out a timetable of work that *should* be done, ignoring all the obstacles that might get in the way. For this reason it is important to include in your timing any other commitments you may have, for example, holidays, sport, other assignments and examination dates. If the objectives are realistic, then you may actually keep referring to the programme that you have spent time devising in order to check on your progress and to plan your next moves.

It helps to break up your project into stages. Give yourself deadlines to complete aspects of the work. This is a common requirement of professional research projects, where intermediate reports are required to check up on the progress of the work. You are unlikely to have to submit your work in stages like this, but the satisfaction and comfort of consciously getting parts of the project out of the way are worth the effort. The other advantage of splitting the work into sections is that you set limited goals, ones that you can see that you can achieve without being daunted. In addition, having some intermediate deadlines will stop you getting carried away or dithering on any one aspect of the work and spending far too much time on it.

The easiest way to devise a timetable is to set up a table, with a list of tasks on the left-hand side and the time in weeks along the top. See Figure 7.2. It is best to use the table facility in your word processor or a spreadsheet program for ease of adjustment and neat presentation. If you like, you can include your other activities to make sure that there are

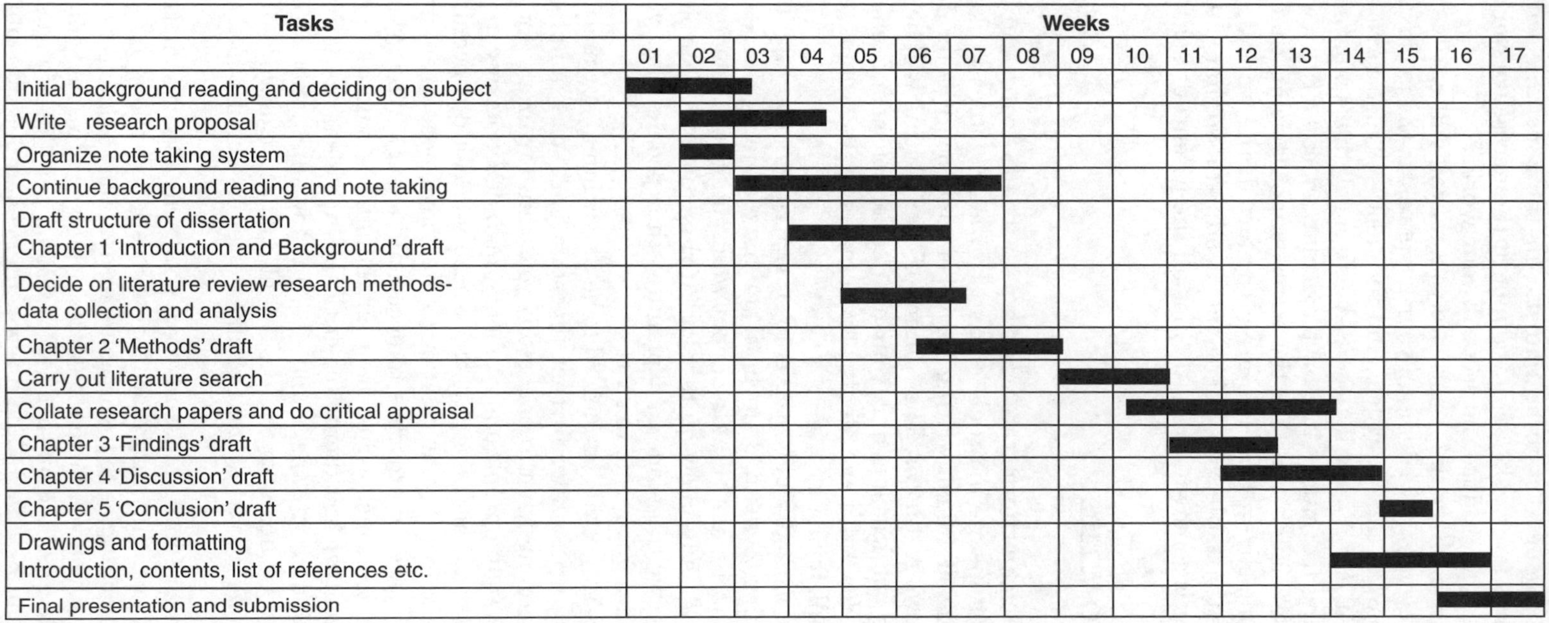

Tasks							Weeks										
	01	02	03	04	05	06	07	08	09	10	11	12	13	14	15	16	17
Initial background reading and deciding on subject	■																
Write research proposal			■	■													
Organize note taking system		■															
Continue background reading and note taking					■	■	■										
Draft structure of dissertation						■											
Chapter 1 'Introduction and Background' draft						■											
Decide on literature review research methods- data collection and analysis					■												
Chapter 2 'Methods' draft						■	■										
Carry out literature search								■	■								
Collate research papers and do critical appraisal										■							
Chapter 3 'Findings' draft											■	■					
Chapter 4 'Discussion' draft												■	■				
Chapter 5 'Conclusion' draft														■			
Drawings and formatting														■	■		
Introduction, contents, list of references etc.																■	
Final presentation and submission																■	■

Figure 7.2 Work timetable for a literature review

no clashes in timing. Try to be realistic, or the timetable will become obsolete within a few weeks. If you cannot fit the necessary work into the time available, then reduce the scope of your work.

Your timetable will help to motivate you, as you will easily be able to see that whatever you are doing in your list of tasks, the job is useful and a necessary part of the sequence. And the task will also have a defined and meaningful end. You will also be able to check that you are not drifting by spending too much time on particular aspects of the work, and that you allow enough time for the latter stages. Seeing that you will manage to complete on time is a great comfort. If the work does slip in relation to the timetable, you will be able to adjust it so that you still find time (even if it is somewhat reduced) for all the essential tasks.

Starting to write

Even professional writers state what a pain it is to write, and how they need to be a bit insane in order to do it. However, you can take comfort in the fact that you are not writing a novel or some poetry – totally dependent on your own resources. The content of your writing will be based on other people's publications and your own collection of information and observations. You will have plenty of raw materials, so the page will not need to be blank for long.

Perhaps the most difficult step is to start writing. You might feel that you have nothing to write about until you have done all the reading and research. In fact, by just thinking about what you want to do for your dissertation you already know quite a lot. At the start of any project, there has to be some writing done to explain to other people what you intend to do. So this is a good time to start.

At this early stage, you can afford to be uncertain about matters; raise them anyway as points for further investigation. For example, you can start with describing what area of study you want to pursue (for example, end of life care, young people and resilience, high dependency care nursing), and exploring some of the situations where you could concentrate your investigation (for example, in relation to the above, hospice environments, local authority care, approaches to decision making). What you write is not chiselled into stone, so just let your thoughts get onto paper (or the computer screen) without being too critical. Once ideas are written, then you can play around with them, and add, cut, and adjust them. You cannot do this all in your head, so the process of writing it down will actually help you to think about it, and to make decisions about what you really want to do.

As you get more into your subject, a good way to get something onto paper without even having to form sentences is to make a list. This can be of things to do, topics to investigate, or headings of subjects you want to write about. Once you have a basic list, you can add some subheadings to the items that expand on these. Before long, perhaps after doing some reading, you will be able to add a few sentences under the subheadings.

You can first concentrate on the bits that are easy. Later, when you already have a body of text, you will be more confident to tackle the harder aspects that require more thought and knowledge.

Later on in the project, when the real bulk of writing needs to be done, the pressure and difficulty will be at their greatest. This is where the creative and original work is produced. Peter Woods (2006: 14–17) describes how he needs to 'crank himself up' before he starts writing up his research. Analysis and presentation of the information you have collected is a multifaceted task that is quite painful and demanding work. A few tentative starts are to be expected as you 'psych yourself up'. People often remark on how they become unsociable when they are involved in creative work: you need to concentrate on yourself and your own thinking in quite a selfish way. However, do switch off in between your working sessions. If you are quite strict with your timing and set yourself realistic goals (for example, so many words per day), then you can feel you have really earned your time off. Most professional writers work regular office hours – whether they are inspired or not.

This is a good place to remind you that you must save and back up your work regularly. Computers are notoriously fickle and can ruin your day if your work gets lost or deleted by accident or failure. Keep all your writing saved in at least two – better three, different locations – USB memory sticks, external hard drives, CD-ROMs, your home directory on the university intranet. Make a habit of saving your work manually every 10–15 minutes, and set the program to make auto-recover files every few minutes. We have heard some tragic true stories of work getting 'lost' – perhaps one of the most infuriating and disappointing things that can happen to one's hard-won writing efforts.

What should I do next?

Whatever stage you are at in your project, if you have not done so yet, set up a timetable of work. You can use the example in Figure 7.2 as a model and adjust it to your own particular needs. This was produced using Microsoft® Word's table function, though the Excel® spreadsheet program could also be used. Use the line drawing function on the drawing toolbar for the horizontal time bars. Try to be realistic and take into account your preferred method of working and also your other commitments. It is usually difficult to judge just how long each task will take (usually longer than you think). However, as time will always be a limiting factor you will often have to cut the work to fit the time – a reasonable justification for limiting the scope of your work. The main thing is to get the proportions between the various stages of the work to be reasonable.

Start writing something. If you are still at the beginning, outline the area of your study, bringing in any information or quotations from things you have read. Try to define a focus for your project in the form of questions or aims. If you are further on, you could make a start on your background chapter, using the notes you have made from your reading in order to set the scene for your individual work. You could also write out a structure for your dissertation in the form of a list of headings and subheadings.

If you are unclear of what you want to do, or of how to progress, define the problem as you see it, and try out one or more of the ideas-generating techniques above. You may be faced with a combination of problems that make you feel helpless and lost. Try to break them down into different aspects and tackle each one in turn. Once you have found solutions, start by putting them down in writing and listing what actions you want to take. Even if you do not start working on them straight away, at least you have a record to fall back on.

Further reading

This book is good on motivation, and is referred to in this chapter. Read this to get the full story.

Davies, P. (2001) *Get Up and Grow: How to Motivate Yourself and Everybody Else Too*. London: Hodder and Stoughton.

The following books focus on developing critical thinking skills, with Cottrell's text being a very useful starting point.

Brown, K. and Rutter, L. (2008) *Critical Thinking for Social Work (Post-Qualifying Social Work Practice)*, 2nd edn. Exeter: Learning Matters Ltd.
Cottrell, S. (2005) *Critical Thinking Skills: Developing Effective Analysis and Argument*. Basingstoke: Palgrave Macmillan.
Jones-Devitt, S. and Smith, L. (2007) *Critical Thinking in Health and Social Care*. London: Sage Publications.

There are many books on creative thinking. De Bono became a creative thinking guru in the 1970s and 1980s with a string of books and public appearances. Here are some of his most popular – and easy to read – books.

De Bono, E. (1995) *Serious Creativity: Using the Power of Lateral Thinking to Create New Ideas*. London: Harper Collins.
De Bono, E. (1996) *Teach Yourself to Think*. Harmondsworth: Penguin.
De Bono, E. (2000) *Six Thinking Hats*. Bury St Edmunds: Penguin Books.
De Bono, E. (2007) *How to Have Creative Ideas: 62 Exercises to Develop the Mind*. London: Vermillion.

The following books offer lots of advice on writing. We have put them in order of accessibility and academic stage aimed at.

Clanchy, J. (1998) *How to Write Essays: A Practical Guide for Students*, 3rd edn. Melbourne: Longman.
McMillan, K. and Wevers, J. (2007) *How to Write Essays and Assignments*. Dorchester: Pearson Education Limited.
Bowden, J. (2004) *Writing a Report: How to Prepare, Write and Present Effective Reports*, 7th edn. Oxford: How To Books Ltd.

Murray, R. (2002) *How to Write a Thesis*. Buckingham: Open University Press.

Berry, R. (2004) *The Research Project: How to Write It*, 5th edn. London: Routledge.

Woods, P. (2005) *Successful Writing for Qualitative Researchers*, 2nd edn. London: Routledge.

Hall, G.M. (ed.) (2008) *How to Write a Paper*, 4th edn. London: BMJ Publishing.

Chapter 8

Where Do I Get Hold of All the Necessary Background Information?

Chapter contents

- Information overload?
- What sorts of background information do I need?
- Library searches
- The Internet
- Evaluating web sources
- Search techniques for online catalogues, databases and the Net
- What should I do next?
- Further reading

Information overload?

It is well known that this is an information age; we are drowning in the stuff. There can be no excuse that there is a lack of information on your subject. The problem is in knowing where to look for suitable information and to be able to sort it and select what is relevant and of sufficiently good quality. Any trawl through the Internet will demonstrate what a lot of rubbish there is on every subject under the sun. Even a visit to the library or a good bookshop can be a daunting experience: 'Goodness! Do I really have to read all this stuff!' is a typical reaction. No, you do not. But you will have to read some of it, and the skill is in identifying what the essential information is. Luckily, there are easy-to-learn, sophisticated methods of trawling for information. No need to spend hours in dusty archives (unless that is central to your project), no need to buy lots of expensive books, but there is a need to get skilled in search and find techniques.

Where you look will depend on the subject you have chosen. Some sources cover most subjects; others are specialized in a narrow range, and will hence provide more detail. Here are lists of places you can search.

Libraries

- Your university or college library – this should be your first choice. Here, not only will you find a huge amount of information, but you will also be able to find out about all the other information sources listed below. You should also be able to get help, support and training in information searching from your subject librarian or subject liaison specialist. Many university libraries also offer a degree of one-to-one individual enquiry help as well as group training sessions.

- Specialist libraries – subject libraries in university departments, professional libraries in professional institutions, libraries in research establishments (Wellcome Library) or charitable organizations such as the King's Fund and NSPCC.

- Local NHS trust libraries and Research Development Support Units (RDSUs) (now known as the National Institute for Health Research – Research Design Services [NIHR RDS]) – sometimes have special collections of local interest.

Information services

- Government departments such as standards institutes, Department of Health (DH) for publications, Department of Children Schools and Families (DCSF), public records offices, Office of National Statistics.

- Pressure groups and voluntary organizations in areas such as child and family rights, disability awareness, special needs, older people's health and care needs.

- Health Information Resources (formerly National Library for Health (NLH), – a huge range of resources for NHS professionals and health care students (http://www.library.nhs.uk/).

- The Social Care Institute for Excellence (SCIE) – established by the government in 2001 to improve social care services for adults and children in the UK (http://www.scie.org.uk/).

- The NHS National Institute for Health Research (NIHR) for information on research in the NHS (http://www.nihr.ac.uk/).

- Professional organizations and trade union organizations.

(It is also worth bearing in mind that many of these information services such as governmental departments, the NLH and SCIE provide much of their information via the web, so if you identify their websites you do not need to visit them in person.)

The Internet and intranets

- The full gamut of the World Wide Web.

- Subject specialist web gateways which have health and social care specific sections such as BUBL (http://bubl.ac.uk) and Intute (http://www.intute.ac.uk/healthandlifesciences/) may help you to focus your searching.

- Your own organization's intranet. Often providing lecture notes, course material and other online material as well as other specialist information, e.g. research papers, professorial lectures.

People

There are experts in every field of health and social care. Some will be willing to advise you. Try the members of your own university staff at first, many of whom will be involved in research and or practice. Ask a professor in your subject area to suggest who might have the specialist knowledge that you are seeking. Remember the professionals and experts in the library – seek out your subject librarian or subject liaison specialist who will both be an expert in information finding generally and have some background subject knowledge. If you get the opportunity to attend a professional conference or study day, this might be an opportunity to identify the key researchers and practitioners in the field that interests you. Your library will also contain guides to professionals and experts. In some cases, local knowledge will be needed: search out the relevant local experts through local research and practice networks.

What sort of background information do I need?

A whole range of existing information and background evidence will be available on your subject area. You will undoubtedly wish to focus on primary and secondary sources of research evidence. Primary evidence refers to original empirical research, for example, quantitative and qualitative research studies published in peer-reviewed research journals. Secondary sources refer to sources which summarize and review published empirical research including systematic reviews and literature reviews. In health and social care research there is an increasing focus on evidence-based practice, drawing on primary and secondary sources of evidence, as described in Chapter 1.

In health care, it is well recognized that a hierarchy of evidence exists when looking at how effective or useful a particular treatment intervention is (Greenhalgh, 1997; Summerskill, 2001; Muir Gray, 2008). The hierarchy of evidence is illustrated opposite and is based on the strength of study designs, with evidence from systematic reviews of good quality

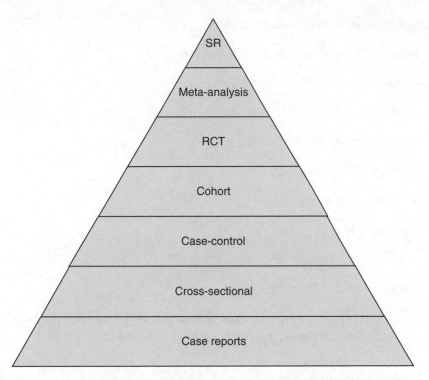

Figure 8.1   Hierarchy of evidence in quantitative research studies
Note: SR = systematic review

Source: Summerskill, W.S.M. (2001) 'Hierarchy of Evidence', in D.P.B McGovern, R.M. Valori, W.S.M. Summerskill and M.Levi Key Topics in Evidence-Based Medicine. Oxford: BIOS Scientific Publishers Ltd.

randomize controlled trials (RCTs) and meta-analysis at the top. This hierarchy is concerned with quantitative studies and is based on the premise that study designs lower down the hierarchy are more liable to bias.

Some hierarchies of evidence do recognize expert opinion while others incorporate qualitative studies. However, it is important to remember that the hierarchy of evidence illustrated previously is concerned with studies examining the effectiveness of clinical interventions, and so would not be appropriate if you have a research question which asks clients how they feel about a particular intervention.

Additional sources of information

In addition to research evidence you will also want to include information in your dissertation from a range of other sources, including:

- books and e-books;
- discussion papers, opinion pieces, news and articles from professional journals;

- government reports and circulars;

- health and social care policy documents;

- national statistics;

- audit data;

- conference papers/proceedings;

- theses and dissertations;

- website information;

- newspapers;

- letters;

- personal opinion from experts.

The next practical step to consider is how to get hold of the information you need to examine your research topic and question.

Library searches

The library will normally be your first access point for information. I am sure that you have used the library many times before, but have you really used all the sophisticated search facilities available? It is not sufficient at this level of study just to visit the shelves to see what is there, even if you have consulted the online catalogue first. There will be a wide range of resources and search facilities provided, together with a series of training sessions (library based and online) and leaflets and downloadable PDFs in the use of these. Find out what is available and attend the training sessions so that you can use the full services of the library with confidence. Being adept at making searches will save you lots of time and frustration, as well as ensuring that you get hold of all the latest information you need.

Try to get the latest publications (unless you have special reasons not to) for two reasons. First, information becomes quickly outdated and new findings are constantly being made; and second, the reference lists at the end of research papers and books which will guide you to further sources will not be too out of date. Here are some of the facilities you should investigate.

Library catalogues

Most libraries now have an electronic catalogue accessed through their computer terminals. You will usually be able to access this online from elsewhere too via the intranet and/or Internet. This means that you can do searches from home or from elsewhere in the university. If the book you want is not on the shelves, reserve it so that you can receive it when it is returned. Do keep track of renewal dates: to forget can turn out to be very expensive.

To widen your search or to locate a book not available in your library, catalogues of other libraries (national and worldwide) can easily be consulted via the web. OPAC (online public access catalogue) is the common system used, and the books can be borrowed through inter-library loans. A fee is usually charged for this kind of loan.

Useful web addresses are:

- The British Library Public Catalogue (BLPC), with details of over 10 million books, journals, reports, conferences and music scores (http://www.bl.uk/).

- Other academic and research libraries in the UK (http://copac.ac.uk/).

- European national libraries (http://www.theeuropeanlibrary.org/portal/index.html).

- The Library of Congress of the USA, with over 17 million books (http://catalog.loc.gov/).

- Looking worldwide, try (http://www.libdex.com/).

- Newspapers, including UK national, many provincial and various international papers, can be found at the British Library Integrated Catalogue: (http://catalogue.bl.uk/) and choose 'Catalogue subset search' then newspapers.

Most importantly, do not forget the journals and newspapers. These are often catalogued and stored separately from the books in the library. As they appear regularly, they tend to be very up to date. They are based on defined subject areas, and vary in content from newspaper type articles to the most erudite research papers. To track down articles and papers in past issues, see the subsections on electronic databases, electronic journals and journals of abstracts and indexes.

If you are at home on holiday, or away on a clinical placement, or if you live some distance away from your university or college, you can probably arrange to use your local university or college library, certainly for reference and possibly for lending (various schemes are in operation: consult your subject librarian).

Electronic databases

These are computer-based lists of publications on CD-ROM, on the university network or on the web. Access to these is, depending on the licensing arrangements, from library terminals, university computers or even your own computer. Databases contain huge amounts of sources, usually searched by using key words. There are many databases to choose from but those that are likely to be of use in health and social care studies are include in Box 8.1.

Box 8.1   Electronic databases relevant to health and social care

Academic Search Complete – a multi-disciplinary database including social work journals and other related areas.

AMED (Allied and complementary medicine) – including occupational therapy, physiotherapy and palliative care.

ASSIA (Applied Social Sciences Indexes and Abstracts) – includes subjects related to social welfare, social policy and social work.

BOPCAS (British Official Publications Current Awareness Service) – contains bibliographic details of government publications with abstracts and some full text links.

BNI (British Nursing Index) – information about nursing, midwifery and community health care, mainly from UK journals.

CAB Abstracts – public health, nutrition, biotechnology, third world development, infectious diseases.

Cancer Library – *US National Cancer Institute, US National Institutes of Health.*

CINAHL (Cumulative Index of Nursing & Allied Health Literature) – includes nursing and health care.

Cochrane Library – systematic reviews of health care evidence.

ERIC – education database, predominantly American material.

HMIC (Health Management Information Consortium) – includes a wide range of non-clinical topics such as hospital policy, administration and management, inequalities in health and user involvement.

MEDLINE/PubMed – medicine and health care.

National Rehabilitation Information Center – disability and rehabilitation databases, produced by the US National Rehabilitation Information Center, Silver Spring, Maryland.

PEDRO – physiotherapy evidence database, produced by the Centre for Evidence Based Physiotherapy at the University of Sydney.

Planex – local public policy and governance including social work. Covers material published since 1980.

ProQuest newspaper library – collection of UK newspapers, including the *Daily Mail, Daily Telegraph, Evening Standard, Financial Times, Guardian, Independent, The Times* and Sunday versions.

PsycINFO – psychology database covering psychological aspects of illness and treatment, psychiatry and child development. It includes abstracts of journal articles, books and dissertations.

Social Care Online – social and community care, includes Department of Health circulars. Produced by the Social Care Institute for Excellence (SCIE).

Social Services Abstracts – journal article abstracts relating to social work, welfare and policy.

- Is it accurate? Does it say what sources the data are based on? Compare the data with other sources. If they diverge greatly, is there some explanation for this?

- What authority is it based on? Find out who authored the pages, and whether they are recognized experts or a reputable organization. Check if other publications are cited or if they provide a bibliography of other articles, reports or books. You may need to track down the 'home page' to get to the details. Also see if there is a postal address and phone number to indicate the 'reality' of the organization. Web addresses that end in 'ac' (meaning academic) are likely to be university or college addresses and therefore point to some intellectual credibility – no guarantee of quality but nevertheless a useful indicator.

- Is it biased? Many pressure groups and commercial organizations use the web to promote their ideas and products, and present information in a one-sided way. Can you detect a vested interest in the subject on the part of the author? Find out more about the authors – e.g. does the information about animal experiments come from an anti-vivisection league, a cosmetics company, or an independent research institute?

- How detailed is the information? Is the information so general that it is of little use, or so detailed and specialized that it is difficult to understand? Investigate whether it is only fragmentary and misses out important issues in the subject, and whether the evidence is backed up by relevant data. There may be useful links to further information, other websites or printed publications.

- Is it out of date? Pages stay on the web until they are removed. Some have obviously been forgotten about and are hopelessly out of date. Try to find a date on the page, or the date when the page was updated (perhaps on the View/Page Info option on your web browser). Note that some updates might not update all the contents. Check any links provided to see if they work.

- Have you cross-checked? Compare the contents with other sources of information such as books, articles, official statistics and other websites. Does the information tally with or contradict these? If the latter, can you see why?

- Have you tried pre-evaluated 'subject gateways'? The information on these sites has been vetted by experts in the relevant subjects, so can be relied upon to be of high quality. Two useful websites which both have sections relating to health and social care are:

    BUBL (http://bubl.ac.uk/)
    Intute (http://www.intute.ac.uk/healthandlifesciences/)

Search techniques for online catalogues, databases and the Net

Here are a few basic hints on how to make effective searches for information. In order to find what you want, it must first be clear what you are looking

Sociological Abstracts – journal article abstracts relating to sociology and political theory.
  Source – the management and practice of primary health care and disability in developing countries.
  Web of Science – includes the Science Citation Index and the Social Sciences Citation Index, providing bibliographic information and journal abstracts.
  ZETOC – The British Library's electronic table of contents, covering the humanities and medicine.

Most databases provide only citations and abstracts and do not usually give the full article. Citations are the basic author and publication details; abstracts are short summaries of the contents of the article. In these cases, you will have to get hold of the book or journal article for the full information. Some databases have full text links and provide the full text of the publication as plain text or even in facsimile, i.e. looking as originally printed. Citation indexes list the publications in which certain books and articles have been used as a reference.

Previous postgraduate dissertations produced in your university should be listed on a database. Copies of undergraduate dissertations might also be, though you might have to consult your own department collection. It is helpful to see what other students have produced before you.

In order to access the many databases identified in Box 8.1, you may need to obtain a password to get access (e.g. Athens authentication); again, consult your librarian or library website. Your library will also provide training sessions in using electronic databases, which will save you much time in the long run.

Electronic journals

Electronic journals (sometimes referred to as e-journals or online journals) contain the full text of published or in-press journal articles, or are solely online publications. Many libraries are increasing their stock of electronic online journals and you will need to become familiar with the e-journals that are particularly relevant to your subject area. You can find out which electronic journals are available by consulting your library catalogue and doing a title search or by reviewing the library's online journal search page.

Journals of abstracts and indexes

These are printed publications that give a summary of articles and papers in a vast range of journals, together with the details required to obtain

Sociological Abstracts – journal article abstracts relating to sociology and political theory.

Source – the management and practice of primary health care and disability in developing countries.

Web of Science – includes the Science Citation Index and the Social Sciences Citation Index, providing bibliographic information and journal abstracts.

ZETOC – The British Library's electronic table of contents, covering the humanities and medicine.

Most databases provide only citations and abstracts and do not usually give the full article. Citations are the basic author and publication details; abstracts are short summaries of the contents of the article. In these cases, you will have to get hold of the book or journal article for the full information. Some databases have full text links and provide the full text of the publication as plain text or even in facsimile, i.e. looking as originally printed. Citation indexes list the publications in which certain books and articles have been used as a reference.

Previous postgraduate dissertations produced in your university should be listed on a database. Copies of undergraduate dissertations might also be, though you might have to consult your own department collection. It is helpful to see what other students have produced before you.

In order to access the many databases identified in Box 8.1, you may need to obtain a password to get access (e.g. Athens authentication); again, consult your librarian or library website. Your library will also provide training sessions in using electronic databases, which will save you much time in the long run.

Electronic journals

Electronic journals (sometimes referred to as e-journals or online journals) contain the full text of published or in-press journal articles, or are solely online publications. Many libraries are increasing their stock of electronic online journals and you will need to become familiar with the e-journals that are particularly relevant to your subject area. You can find out which electronic journals are available by consulting your library catalogue and doing a title search or by reviewing the library's online journal search page.

Journals of abstracts and indexes

These are printed publications that give a summary of articles and papers in a vast range of journals, together with the details required to obtain a full copy of the publications. Although more recent publications are generally recorded on electronic databases, these printed guides cover the older sources – particularly useful for historical studies. Enough information is usually given to enable you to decide if you need to read the full article. They are usually organized in subject areas. Older dissertations and conference proceedings can also be tracked down in this way.

A useful hint when using computer-based searches: instead of printing out your search results on paper, copy them to a USB memory stick or email them directly to your own user account, so that you can easily view and edit them at a later time. The useful references can then be transferred to your bibliography or reference list without having to type them out again (ideally using a bibliographic database program such as EndNote®: see Chapter 17).

Librarians

They are there to help you. Ask at the help desk if you get stuck. There are often subject librarians or subject liaison specialists who have specialist knowledge in health and social care related areas; they will be able to help you explore more elusive sources. Libraries usually run free training sessions on all aspects of searching for information and bibliographic database management, often with specialist advice in the various subject areas. Find out when these take place so that you can make the best use of the services offered.

The Internet

With thousands of pages being added every day, the World Wide Web (WWW) is the biggest single source of information in the world. However, the content is of extremely variable quality. The biggest challenge when using it is to track down good quality material. You can easily waste hours trawling through rubbish in search of the goodies. Careful use of search terms helps to eliminate the trash. Usually, the more precise your search parameters, the more manageable the search results will be. Not all information on the web is free.

There are published Internet guides that can help you to make the best of this resource (try your library for lists devoted to subject areas). Some are specifically aimed at students and list useful search engines, sites and databases. Any Internet guide quickly becomes outdated, so you may have to go and buy one for the current year.

It is worth knowing, however, the different ways that search engines work, so that you can use them to your best advantage and are aware of their limitations. There are four basic types: free text, index based, multisearch engines and intelligent agents.

Free text

These search engines automatically 'trawl' the web and make their own data-base of web pages. These are selections, made at regular intervals, and therefore do not contain all the pages on the web. In response to your search input of one or several words, they produce a list of pages, ranked according to their own parameters, e.g. whether the words appear in the URL, or several times in the text. You will notice that different search engines make completely different selections, so it is worth trying several – Altavista, Google, Hotbot, Infoseek, etc.

Index based

Compilers (yes, actual people) categorize web pages under a series of subject headings and subheadings. To search these you will need to follow a series of links, starting from the general and working down to the particular. This is a help to users unsure of using free text searches, but has the disadvantage of being limited by the particular choices made by the compilers, e.g. an American perspective in Yahoo.com based in the USA.

Intelligent agents

Unlike normal search engines that start a search from scratch every time you use them, these learn from your choices as you accept or reject the results they offer. Every time you rerun them they automatically refine the search on the basis of your past profile. Although these are still being developed, they promise to be a useful labour-saving device.

Multisearch engines

Actually not search engines as such, but web pages that offer several search engines that you can use simultaneously. Just one input will be searched by all the selected engines. However, as they work in different ways, you might get plenty of hits on one, and none on another. The advantage is that they might offer search engines that you have never heard of before. Examples of these are Dogpile, Metacrawler and Mamma.

Evaluating web sources

The WWW is a huge resource and provides a wealth of material which can be used by health and social care professionals. Yet, anyone can add pages to the web, so how can you judge if the information you have found is reliable? Here are seven different tests you can make to judge the quality of websites and their contents.

- Is it accurate? Does it say what sources the data are based on? Compare the data with other sources. If they diverge greatly, is there some explanation for this?

- What authority is it based on? Find out who authored the pages, and whether they are recognized experts or a reputable organization. Check if other publications are cited or if they provide a bibliography of other articles, reports or books. You may need to track down the 'home page' to get to the details. Also see if there is a postal address and phone number to indicate the 'reality' of the organization. Web addresses that end in 'ac' (meaning academic) are likely to be university or college addresses and therefore point to some intellectual credibility – no guarantee of quality but nevertheless a useful indicator.

- Is it biased? Many pressure groups and commercial organizations use the web to promote their ideas and products, and present information in a one-sided way. Can you detect a vested interest in the subject on the part of the author? Find out more about the authors – e.g. does the information about animal experiments come from an anti-vivisection league, a cosmetics company, or an independent research institute?

- How detailed is the information? Is the information so general that it is of little use, or so detailed and specialized that it is difficult to understand? Investigate whether it is only fragmentary and misses out important issues in the subject, and whether the evidence is backed up by relevant data. There may be useful links to further information, other websites or printed publications.

- Is it out of date? Pages stay on the web until they are removed. Some have obviously been forgotten about and are hopelessly out of date. Try to find a date on the page, or the date when the page was updated (perhaps on the View/Page Info option on your web browser). Note that some updates might not update all the contents. Check any links provided to see if they work.

- Have you cross-checked? Compare the contents with other sources of information such as books, articles, official statistics and other websites. Does the information tally with or contradict these? If the latter, can you see why?

- Have you tried pre-evaluated 'subject gateways'? The information on these sites has been vetted by experts in the relevant subjects, so can be relied upon to be of high quality. Two useful websites which both have sections relating to health and social care are:

    BUBL (http://bubl.ac.uk/)
    Intute (http://www.intute.ac.uk/healthandlifesciences/)

Search techniques for online catalogues, databases and the Net

Here are a few basic hints on how to make effective searches for information. In order to find what you want, it must first be clear what you are looking for. Searches rely on single words or a combination of several words. Every subject in health and social care will contain several crucial terms that distinguish it from other subjects, so the trick is to select these. If you are unfamiliar with the subject, look it up in a specialist dictionary or an encyclopaedia to see what terms are used so that you can build up your own list of key words. Remember also the use of different spellings in various parts of the world, e.g. organisation/organization, immunisation/immunization and even different words or phrases for the same meaning i.e. child abuse/child maltreatment.

Databases usually provide the option of a free text search, or a key word, subject or index search. The former looks for your chosen word(s) in all the text contained in the database, while the latter only searches the key words, subject lists or index lists provided by the authors with their books or papers. These lists focus on the subject matter of the publication, so give a more reliable guide to the contents. Many databases include a thesaurus – a list of indexing terms that will help you to use the standard terms. Sometimes the number of articles to which the term is assigned is given.

It is usually possible to narrow your search by indicating place and time, where these are relevant. The publication date is a basic piece of bibliographic data.

Adding a * to words or parts of words automatically widens the search parameters in the form of wildcards. For example, 'nurs*' will find all the words starting with that stem, e.g. 'nurse', 'nurses', 'nursing', etc. Inserting the * symbol into a word takes care of different spelling versions, e.g. 'labo*r' will find 'labour' and 'labor'.

Boolean logic is a fancy word for the technique of using connecting words such as 'and', 'or' and 'not'. These refine the search by defining more closely what you want to include or not. For example:

- School* *and* health: this narrows down your search by only selecting records that contain both terms.

- (Lifts *or* elevators): this widens your search by selecting records that contain either or both terms. Note that brackets are used around terms which mean the same thing, but only in a search which combines both AND and OR statements: e.g.:

  school and health;
  lifts or elevators;
  school and (lifts or elevators);
  (school or college) and (lifts or elevators).

- Nurseries *and* playschools *not* schools: this eliminates the terms that you do not want to consider. However, be careful that you do not eliminate useful records.

It is best if you keep the search terms simple and search several times using different variations and terms. You need to be well organized, clearly focused and systematic in your searching techniques. In addition, what is crucially important is to keep a written record of your search strategy. Record:

- all the databases, online catalogues and websites you search;

- the search terms (key word) you apply and their particular combinations.

For journal articles you also should also record:

- the number of hits (references to potentially useful articles/potentially useful articles) identified in each search;

- the number of hits which on further review are relevant to your question and meet your study inclusion criteria;

- unsuccessful search outcomes.

The latter may occur if you selected the wrong databases, did not use appropriate key words or defined your topic too narrowly (Hewitt, 2000). Conversely finding too many references can also be a problem when searching online databases and this will indicate that you need to narrow the focus of your search, by reducing the number of key words.

Alongside your computerized database searches you will also need to employ some additional types of searching as electronic searches are not comprehensive (Hek and Langton, 2000). For example, hand searching of relevant journals, searching the reference lists of existing papers (sometimes referred to as 'snowballing'), approaching personal contacts, using your personal knowledge and existing resources (Greenhalgh and Peacock, 2005).

What should I do next?

If you have not been to a library training session for some time, now is the time to book yourself in. There are always new sources of information being introduced, especially access to electronic databases, so make sure that you are up to date with all the facilities. You may need a password to access some, so you will not be able to sit at a terminal and work it out yourself. Also look for the latest information bulletins in the library, particularly in your subject.

It is much easier to find information if you know what you are looking for. This might sound obvious, but it does require some careful thought before making searches. Make a list of the all the main concepts and other terms that appear in your title, aims, background, research problem and methods sections of your proposal. This should give you a list of key words on which you can base your searches. Look up the most important ones first.

Once you have found some useful publications, use the reference list at the back to lead you on to other sources. Unfortunately this only goes backwards in time. If you want to look the other way, consult a citation database and look up the title of the book or article you are currently reading. This will list the publications that have cited that one as a reference.

Despite what I said above about knowing exactly what you are looking for, do let chance play some part in your quest. Keep your eyes and ears open for possible leads to information. Discussions on the television or radio, informal conversations, health or social care seminars and chance meetings are all possible sources. In the library, instead of tracking down a particular book, try exploring a section of the shelves containing books with the relevant class number, i.e. the number given according to the subject. For a start, you will immediately see what is actually available, and you may come across authors you are not familiar with.

Do read the next chapter before you return the publications you have borrowed. It is essential that you are systematic in taking notes and making records of the publications, and the next chapter explains how you can do this.

Further reading

We have given a short description of what you may find useful in the following books, starting with searching and reviewing the literature.

Aveyard, H. (2007) *Doing a Literature Review in Health and Social Care: A Practical Guide*. Maidenhead: Open University Press. A very useful and readable text and an excellent guide for beginners.

Fink, A. (2005) *Conducting Research Literature Reviews: From the Internet to Paper*, 2nd edn. London: Sage Publications. This book addresses the key steps of identifying, analysing and interpreting research evidence.

Hart, C. (1998) *Doing a Literature Review*. London: Sage. A guide through the multidimensional sea of academic literature with techniques on how to deal with the information when you have found it.

Hart, C. (2001) *Doing a Literature Search*. London: Sage. A whole book providing a guide on how to search the literature in the social sciences.

Ridley, D. (2008) *The Literature Review: A Step-by-Step Guide for Students*. London: Sage. This text is really targeted at those students undertaking postgraduate studies, but you may find it helpful to dip in to.

And here are some of the multitude of books to help you navigate the Internet. Always try to get the latest edition; they go out of date fast. The first two, as their titles suggest, are specifically aimed at students and we think they are really useful.

Munger, D. and Campbell, S. (2007) *What Every Student Should Know About Researching Online*. London: Pearson Longman.

Winship, I. and McNab, A. (2002) *The Student's Guide to the Internet*. London: Library Association Publishing.

Edwards, M.J.A. (2002) *The Internet for Nurses and Allied Health Professionals*, 3rd edn. New York: Springer.

Sherman, C. (2001) *The Invisible Web: Uncovering Information Sources Search Engines Can't See*. Medford, NJ: CyberAge.

Chapter 9

How Can I Manage All the Notes?

Chapter contents

- Introduction
- Reading techniques
- Identifying useful material
- Organizing your system
- Taking notes
- What should I do next?
- Further reading

Introduction

A good dissertation will be based on wide reading, and contain references to all the important literature in the chosen subject. This means that you will have to spend considerable time trawling through the library, electronic databases and other sources of information, collecting a whole range of relevant information on your subject. All this collected material will have to be recorded somehow and stored for further use in such a way that you can find what you want, when you need it for your writing. This requires considerable organization on your part at the outset, to get your system up and running for when you start. Trying to change your system of recording, storage and retrieval of information halfway through will be an enormous task, well worth avoiding. So you do need to have a sound system to start with, and be very disciplined in following it through. This will ensure that you will not have to waste time searching for that oh-so-important but dimly remembered quotation, on a page you cannot remember in a book you borrowed from the library three months ago, by an author whose name you have forgotten.

The following tips will give you a range of methods to choose from, which you can adapt to your own preferred working methods and the scale of your dissertation. You will find that the skills you develop in this activity will be of invaluable use in many other areas of your work. Remember, this is an information age, so acquiring a sound method of avoiding information overload by good management will be well worth the effort.

Reading techniques

Faced with a line of books on the library shelf that all seem to have some relevance to your subject, it is easy to become overwhelmed by the sheer amount of reading and recording that needs to be done. At this point you need to be aware of methods of 'filleting' a book in order to see quickly how much of it is relevant and what you need to record for later use, and different reading techniques relevant to different stages in the searching process. There is no need to read whole books in order to find the material you require. There are actually several ways of reading that can be used to good effect in the appropriate situations. Freeman and Meed (1993: 31–41) suggest the following levels of reading:

- Scanning – a focused approach, looking for one particular piece of information, as one would look in a dictionary or an encyclopaedia. Here the importance of the index is obvious. The essential thing is that you deliberately ignore everything except the one item for which you are scanning.

- Skimming – a quick review of the contents. With a journal article, you might quickly review the article's abstract. In a book you will probably browse through the contents page, introduction and review in order to get an idea of the content of the book to judge its relevance for your own area of study. A closer look would entail looking at the chapter headings, their introductions and conclusions, and even reading the first and last sentences of paragraphs to get a gist of the main arguments. A review of the diagrams, tables and illustrations also gives valuable clues to the content and approach.

- Reading to understand – involves detailed study of a passage, chapter or article, in order to really absorb all the facts, ideas and arguments. It might be necessary to read it more than once, and to take notes to record and comment on the contents.

- Word-by-word reading – used when following detailed instructions when you need to understand every word. This will be needed when reading assignment and exam questions, and instructions on the use of research methods, such as surveys or experiments.

- Reading for pleasure – used when you read for relaxation and enjoyment, for example, when reading a novel or a magazine.

Another reading technique is called 'speed reading'. This involves a technique of using the eyes to scan pages of text very quickly, getting the brain to absorb the meaning without reading along the lines as you do normally. A ruler is used to guide the eyes' progress down the lines of the pages. This is a skill that undoubtedly needs a lot of practice, and is probably suitable only for the type of reading where you need to find out the outline of a story or argument, rather than particular details. In case you are interested, and have plenty of time to practise, we have added a few references to books on this in the last section of this chapter.

Identifying useful material

First, you really do need to know what you are looking for. The easiest way to limit a search is to select a series of key words that are relevant to your subject. You may not know all of these at the outset, but you will develop a list as you become more familiar with the terminology used and the important concepts and issues involved. These will help you to track down the publications that might be relevant in the library.

Book titles generally contain the most important words used in the text, so this is the obvious place to start. Select the books that mention one or some of your key words in the title, then look at the list of contents at the beginning. Do your key words occur here? Are whole chapters dedicated to them? If so, it is worth investigating more closely. If not, look in the alphabetical index at the back. Are your key words mentioned, and if so, how many pages do they appear on? Look up some of the mentioned pages and read what is written about the word. Do this for several of your key words, and you will be able to decide whether there is enough of interest for you to use the book for further study. If your key words do not appear, or not in the sense or context that interests you, you can reject the book.

This technique can be used on any published information, though the convenient list of contents and index might not be present. Other useful places to look in a book or other publication are the introduction, the reviews on the book cover, and perhaps the conclusions section. Academic journal papers normally have an abstract at the beginning that summarizes the contents very succinctly. They also often identify a list of key words. The use of key words when surfing the Internet is obviously a crucial part of the search process (Chapter 8).

If you find a nugget of information in the text that seems relevant, but you need more, look to see if there is a reference cited in that passage. Then, look up the reference details at the back of the chapter, book or journal article, and there you will have another publication to track down – hopefully with more of the information you need. Getting to the required information on websites requires similar techniques. Look at the contents list for guidance to the contents. More sophisticated sites have a search function where you can insert your key words.

Organizing your system

So now you have a pile of books, or other publications (e.g. journal articles) in front of you, all containing what is probably valuable information.

You cannot be sure if you will use all of this, because you will only discover what is really essential when you get into the writing stage, but you need to record anything that might be useful. This is why it is important to compile your own 'library' of notes that you can draw on at later stages in your dissertation.

Before considering what notes to take and how to take them, let us first look at the formats you could use for recording and storing these notes.

There are two basic formats for notes: paper based; and computer-based.

Paper-based notes

The paper-based format needs no electronic equipment, though a few accessories make life easier. The principle behind this system is to write your notes on sheets of paper or card, and then order the sheets in such a way that you can find the notes when you need them later.

You can use A4 sheets of paper and store them in ring folders, or alternatively you can use index cards (the larger sizes are more useful) and store these in boxes designed for the purpose. The idea is to store your notes under certain headings so that you can find what you have collected on that subject. The headings can be various, depending on your subject and how you will be approaching it. You will have to work out the best method yourself. The kinds of headings commonly used are:

- key words;
- author names;
- publication titles;
- dates;
- subjects – or aspects of the main subject e.g. Main subject – breast feeding and public health, sub-topics – incidence and prevalence rates, health benefits for infants, health benefits for women.

Some academics advise you to make several copies of your notes so that you can file them under several headings. This way you can find the material whether, for example, you are looking for the writings of a particular author, or information about a particular subject or about a particular date. It is best to keep the notes short, that is, concentrated on one topic or aspect of the subject. Start another page or card when the topic or your notes change. This is because you may want to search out all your notes on one topic, so you can pull out all the pages or cards under that topic heading. Several ring binders will be needed for storing your A4 sheets, or filing boxes for storing cards.

The greatest advantage of this format is that you can make and take your notes anywhere without needing any equipment apart from paper or card and a pen. The main disadvantage is that you will need to rewrite the material from your handwritten notes on to the computer when you use them.

Computer-based notes

The computer-based formats rely on various database programs. These are set up to deal with lots of bits of information so that you can easily store and retrieve them. The most common non-specialist database programs come with standard program packages, such as Microsoft® Access®. More specialized programs are aimed at exactly this job of notes and referencing. The current main ones are EndNote®, ProCite® and Reference Manager®. Check if they are available on your university or college network. You can even devise a simple system using your normal word-processing package.

The basic requirements of the system using a computer format are similar to those of a paper-based one. Notes should be short and on a single topic, they should be thoroughly referenced, and they should be stored under allotted headings. The major advantages of a computer-based system are that you have much more powerful search facilities; your notes are easily retrieved, copied, revised and edited; and you do not need to rewrite your reference information (lots of complicated formatting and punctuation), you can just copy it for lists. You can also store all your notes on a USB memory stick or portable external hard drive, these provide a very effective way to back up and transport your work. The main disadvantage is that, in order to avoid copying out, you need to have your own computer (or access to a computer plus your USB memory stick) with you wherever you need to make the notes – not such a problem if you own a laptop. You will also have to spend time learning how to use the program.

Obviously, you can devise a system that uses the best features of each format. Whichever format you want to use, you need to decide exactly how you will do it, and test it out before putting it into general use.

Notes content

There are several bits of information that you must record for each and every one of the notes that you take. These are:

- The author(s) of the text – surname and first names. Perhaps the name on the book is the editor of the book, who has compiled a series of chapters or papers by various authors. In this case you will also need all the name(s) of the author(s) of the relevant text.

- The title of the book – including any subtitle. If it is a journal or a newspaper, you will have to record the full name of the journal or newspaper.

- If it is an article or a paper in an edited book, journal or newspaper with different authors for different chapters or papers, then the title of the relevant chapter or paper is also required.

- If it is a website, the URL (web address) and the date you accessed it.

- The date of the publication (in a book, look on the reverse of the title page for this).

- The place it was published (ditto).

- The name of the publisher (ditto).

- The number(s) of the page(s) containing the information you have made notes from.

- Also useful is a reference to where you found the information, e.g. the library and the book code number, so that you can easily track it down again.

- You might also use material from lectures or conferences. In this case, give full details including speaker, title of talk, conference title, venue and date.

This information, attached to every note, will enable you to fully reference it, and to find the original information again if you need to.

So how will you set about recording the information that you want to collect?

Taking notes

The purposes of note taking are to make:

(1) A record – when you develop your ideas and start writing you will need to have your collected information and ideas to hand. Your notes will be your own 'library' of relevant material. This will include direct quotations as well as transcripts.

(2) A précis – to make the information manageable, it is usually necessary to distil out the valuable essences relevant to your subject of study.

(3) An interpretation – your own view of the value and quality of the information and opinions found in the literature is an important component of the dissertation. Recording these in your notes helps to invoke an analytical approach to reading.

(4) A commentary – notes need not always be directly related to the pieces of text that you are reading. Often it is worth recording your thoughts in relation to your study as they occur. Often, flashes of inspiration or insight occur at unexpected moments, and are quickly forgotten if not written down immediately.

Making notes also helps you to concentrate on what you are reading, and to listen carefully at lectures and conferences.

Notes are really useful when you come to writing the first drafts of your dissertation. You can use them as a prompt to start; after all, you have already begun writing as soon as you have started taking notes. They can be used to help you structure your writing, perhaps by physically laying out the notes in sequence on a table. Reviewing and reordering the sequence is simple and fast. The requirement that notes are single subject, short and well defined is obviously of great value in this context.

There are many recommendations made by lecturers about how to actually do note taking. Here are some dos and don'ts:

- **Do** ensure that you have a supply of your chosen medium for recording notes always to hand, or at least a notebook of some kind. Notes made on the back of an envelope *always* get lost!

- **Do** use your own words. This demands not only that you have understood the text, but that you will understand what it means when you come to read it again. It is best to read the passage in question carefully, then put it aside as you make the notes from memory. This will also avoid any danger of plagiarism.

- **Do** sort your notes into your system as soon as possible, especially if you have made them in a non-standard format that needs transferring to your system (e.g. card system or computer database).

- **Do** make a list of all the publications you have referred to, using a standard format. You can generate this list automatically when using a bibliographic database program such as EndNote®.

- **Do** keep notes to one subject or key word. This will help you greatly when you want to find everything you have noted on one subject or key word.

- **Don't** forget to insert all the reference information on each note, including page number where it can be found.

- **Don't** make notes on the book or publication that you are reading: it spoils your own and anyone else's later reading of the text, and loses the point of extracting information for your own 'library' of notes.

- **Don't** mix up direct quotations, your own notes summarizing the text, and your own commentary on the text (opinions, prompted ideas, comparisons). Make a separate note 'card'/computer record for each. Quotations should be short and make a significant point, or explain an important concept.

What should I do next?

You should, before you start reviewing the literature and taking notes, devise your personal system for recording, storing and retrieving them. The average dissertation might use 100–150 notes based on 40–50 references, so it is definitely worth getting a well-organized system in place. On the basis of what you have read above, explore the options for what format and medium to write your notes, how you will sort them into categories, and how you will store them and retrieve them as you need them.

Here is a set of questions that you should answer. It will provide a checklist to develop and test your system.

(1) Will you use a paper- or card-based system or a computer database system? This is a pretty fundamental decision. It really depends on your familiarity with computers and learning new computer programs whether

you have the confidence (and time) to go electronic. Although you do not necessarily need your own laptop, it does simplify the process and eliminate copying out notes. However, many generations of researchers have managed perfectly well with paper-based systems.

(2) If you decide to use a paper-based system, will you print out standard forms on paper or cards? If you do so, you will be prompted to fill in the important reference details every time you start a new note.

(3) If you decide to use a computer system, which database program will you use? You will have to find out which ones are readily available to you (check on your university or college intranet), and ideally choose one that you can install on your laptop if you have one. The easiest to use will be programs designed for bibliographic purposes, unless you are very familiar with setting up databases from scratch.

(4) How will you store your notes? This is not a problem with computer-based systems, apart from the issue of keeping backups in various formats (e.g. USB memory stick, portable external hard drive or server file). Paper-based formats need more thought. Keep in mind that you may want to search in different ways, e.g. by subject or by author. Consider colour coding and separate folders for paper, or card boxes with dividers for cards (old card boxes are usually easy to acquire cheaply). You might even want to go to the extent of duplicating notes and filing under different headings.

(5) How will you retrieve your notes? This is where the use of key words or subject categories becomes essential. In any system, if you can easily find all the notes you made on the particular aspect of your subject that you want to write about, you are halfway to producing your first draft.

Try out your system with a set of about 10–15 notes. Make real notes that will be useful to you anyway, and make them as diverse as possible, so as to test your storage and retrieval system thoroughly. You could even explain your system to a colleague and ask him/her to try to extract some specific piece of information: unfamiliarity with the notes will create a sterner test.

Further reading

First, some books about note taking and organizing your information. Most books about how to do research will have a section on this, but you may want to compare advice and approaches with those given in this chapter. The first two are examples of these; there are plenty more mentioned at the end of earlier chapters in this book.

Blaxter, L., Hughes, C. and Tight, M. (2002) *How to Research*, 2nd edn. Buckingham: Open University Press. Chapter 4 deals with reading and note taking quite comprehensively.

Rudestam, K.E. and Newton, R. (2007) *Surviving Your Dissertation: A Comprehensive Guide to Content and Process*, 3rd edn. Thousand Oaks, CA: Sage. See Chapter 10 on developing writing skills.
Cottrell, S. (2008) *The Study Skills Handbook*, 3rd edn. Basingstoke: Palgrave Macmillan. This is very good book on study skills that also has useful information on note-taking and writing. See chapters 6, 8 and 9.

Below is information about bibliographic database programs. Check what is available on your college/university network before you make an expensive decision to buy a program yourself.

- EndNote® (http://www.endnote.com).
- ProCite® (http://www.procite.com).
- Reference Manager® (http://www.refman.com).

If you are interested in speed reading, here are some books. But beware, these skills take time and practice to perfect. Have you really got the time now?

Buzan, T. (2007) *The Buzan Study Skills Handbook: The Shortcut to Success in Your Studies with Mind Mapping, Speed Reading and Winning Memory Techniques*. Harlow: BBC Active.
The Princeton Language Institute and Marks-Beale A. (2001) *10 Days to Faster Reading*. New York: Warner Books.

Chapter 10

How Do I Make an Effective Argument?

Chapter contents

Introduction

Your dissertation is probably your first lengthy piece of independent writing. The big question when faced with such a task is how to structure the work so that it forms an integral whole. The structure will provide a guide to the reader, as well as a framework for you to fill as you write. In academic writing, the aim is not to tell a story as one might in a novel, but to set up an argument to support a particular view, analysis or conclusion. In fact, argument will pervade all that you write: you will be trying to persuade the reader that what you have done is worthwhile and based on some kind of intellectual process.

Whatever the subject of the inquiry, there has to be a focus; a central issue that is being considered. You should be able to define this quite clearly when you prepare your proposal, by explanation and persuasion. The body of the dissertation will then revolve around this focal point, perhaps considering it from different perspectives, or examining causes or finding explanations for the situation. At the end you will have to come to some conclusions, and this is where argument is required. You will need to base these conclusions on evidence, and you should produce some reasoned argument about how this evidence leads to your conclusions.

You will also have to argue why you have gone about your investigations in the way you have. Lots of choices will be open to you as to how to carry out your investigations, e.g. which issues to treat as important, which data to collect and which to ignore or reject, whom to consult and how to analyse the data. It is up to you to convince the reader that you have good reasons for doing what you have done, and to demonstrate that it needed to be done in order to produce suitable evidence on which to base your conclusions.

No wonder that argument is an important topic to understand. So, as argument will feature as a basic ingredient of your dissertation, what exactly does an argument consist of and are there different types of argument?

The use of language

Let us just start with a quick review of some of the most important aspects of language. Why? Because language is the medium for argument. An argument without language becomes a fight.

We often fail to appreciate the complexity and subtlety of the many uses of language. Here, as in many other situations, there is a danger in our tendency to oversimplify. Copi and Cohen (2005: 69–71) divided the use of language into three very general categories, which have been found useful by many writers on logic and language.

To communicate information, to inform

Normally this is done by devising propositions and then maintaining or refuting them, or presenting an argument about them. This is not to say that the information is true or that the arguments are valid; misinformation is also included in this category. The function of informative discourse is to describe the world and to reason about it.

To express

Poetry, evocative prose, even sales talk and political haranguing, exploit expressive possibilities to the full. Alliteration, analogies, rhythms, rhymes and other devices are often used.

To direct

For the purposes of causing (or preventing) overt action. The most obvious examples of directive discourse are commands and requests. When a theatre nurse is told to pass the surgeon a scalpel, there is no informative or emotional content in the command. The form of language is directed at getting results.

In your dissertation you will primarily use the informative function of language. In order to inform, it is necessary to assert a statement in such a manner as to get the reader to believe in it. So, what are statements and how are they used?

Statements

According to Reynolds (2006: 67–76), statements can be classified into two groups: those that state that a concept exists, and those that describe a relationship between two concepts.

Existence statements

These state that a concept exists, and provide a typology or a description. Here are some statements that make existence claims:

> That object is a cat.
>
> That hospital is grey and white.
>
> That (event) is a rainstorm.

Each of these statements follows the same basic pattern: it provides a concept, identifies it by a term, and applies it to a thing or an event. The above are examples of existence statements in their simplest form. They can, however, be more complicated without losing their basic form. For example:

> If
>
> there are four nurses in a team;
>
> each nurse has a different role in the team; and
>
> each nurse co-operates and works in the team to care for patients in a local area;
>
> then this group is a district nursing team.

Existence statements can be 'right' or 'wrong' depending on the circumstances. Take for example the rather abstract statement 'It is 5 o'clock in the afternoon here'. This can be seen to be correct anywhere once a day. If, however, we state in a more concrete fashion that 'It is 5 o'clock in the afternoon on 15 November in London', this can only be correct once and in one place. It can thus be seen that the level of abstraction of a statement has a powerful influence on its potential for correctness, i.e. the more abstract a statement, the more capacity it has for being right, and conversely the more concrete a statement, the more capacity it has for being wrong.

Relational statements

These impart information about a relationship between two concepts. By referring to the instance of one concept, they state that another concept exists and is linked to the first. We rely on relational statements to explain, predict and provide us with a sense of understanding of our surroundings.

There are two broad classifications of relational statements. The first describes an association between two concepts, and the second describes a causal relationship between two concepts.

Here is an *associational statement*:

If a person is an athlete, then he will be physically fit.

By slightly changing the wording of this sentence you can transform it into a *causal statement*:

Becoming an athlete will make a person be more physically fit.

That is, becoming an athlete will cause that person to be more physically fit.

There are three possible types of *correlation* between two concepts:

- Positive – e.g. occupational therapy students gaining high grades in written assignments gain high grades in clinical practice (and vice versa), i.e. high value in one concept associated with high value in second concept, or low value associated with low value.
- Negative – e.g. greater affluence is associated with lower levels of malnourishment, i.e. high value in one concept associated with low value in second concept.
- None – e.g. men and women have equal rights in a democracy, i.e. no information about associated high or low values in either concept.

The degree of association is often measurable and is usually expressed as 1.0 for maximum positive correlation, 0.0 for no correlation, and –1.0 for maximum negative correlation.

Causal statements describe what is sometimes called a 'cause and effect' relationship. The concept or variable that is the cause is referred to as the 'independent variable' (because it varies independently), and the variable that is affected is referred to as the 'dependent variable' (because it is dependent on the independent variable). For example, in 'running fast makes you out of breath', 'running fast' is the independent variable and 'out of breath' is the dependent variable.

Causal statements can be deterministic, meaning that under certain conditions an event will inevitably follow, e.g. 'if you drop an apple, it will fall'. However, it is not always possible to be so certain of an outcome, so a probabilistic statement might be more suitable, e.g. 'if parents are intelligent, their children are likely to be intelligent too'.

Abstraction

Statements of any kind can be made on three levels of abstraction:

- Theoretical statements – abstract statements based on theoretical concepts, e.g. 'bodily comfort depends on environmental conditions'.

- Operational statements – less abstract in that they are based on the definitions of theoretical concepts, which are capable of measurement, e.g. 'the rate of heartbeat relates to the surrounding still air temperature and the level of activity'.

- Concrete statements – based on specific findings, i.e. the measurements themselves, e.g. 'the heart beats at 102 beats per minute at a surrounding air temperature of 32 degrees centigrade at an energy consumption level of 42 kilocalories per hour'.

Argument

Statements on their own provide information on discrete units. When they are strung together to form a larger structure, they are often referred to as a discourse. Just as with language generally, discourse can be used for information, expression or direction. Again, for your dissertation you will primarily be using the informative type of discourse, sometimes called assertive discourse. This type of discourse consists of, or contains, assertive statements. These are the discourses that invite us to approach them from a logical point of view.

In some assertive discourses, statements are not merely presented for our information (or misinformation, as the case may be); they are connected in a specific logical way. Some of the statements are offered as reasons for others. This kind of discourse is termed an argument. It is a discourse that not only makes assertions but also asserts that some of those assertions are reasons for others.

In the case of ordinary speech the term 'argument' is often used when referring to a dispute, or a situation in which people who hold different views on some controversial subject try to bring the other person around to their way of thinking. But as a technical term in logic, argument is a special kind of discourse, in which a claim is made that one or more particular statements should be accepted as true, or probably true, on the grounds that certain other statements are true. Put another way: by the process of reasoning, using the operation of logic, a conclusion is inferred from the statements given. An argument can be seen as the verbal record of this reasoning.

The minimal ingredients of an argument are:

- At least one statement that is reasoned for (this is the conclusion of the argument). This can be detected by words such as: therefore, hence, thus, so, implies that.
- At least one statement that is alleged to support the conclusion (this is the premise of the argument). This can be detected by words like this: for, since, because, for the reason that, in view of the fact that.
- Some signal or suggestion that an argument is under way.

It is sometimes difficult to determine whether a discourse is an argument: there are cases, especially in a complex piece of text, when it is impossible to be sure whether the minimal ingredients of an argument are indeed present.

Different types of argument

In essence, your whole dissertation should be in the form of an argument. Why is this? Because whatever you are writing about, it must be your concern to persuade the reader that you are writing sense, that your conclusions follow from your evidence, and that you are making some valid points about your chosen subject. A dissertation that comes to no conclusions is not worthy of the name; it would be better called a summary or an account.

In the light of what has been discussed previously, the nature of your argument will be very much influenced by your philosophical standpoint. It may be based on a purely scientific approach, dealing with facts and looking for verifiable causes and effects, or alternatively it may be based on gaining some kind of understanding of complex social issues where nothing can be stated for certain. You may combine the two approaches where it is relevant. Whatever you do, though, your dissertation should convince the reader that there are good reasons why you come to your conclusions.

So, what are the characteristics of an argument? The most important requirement is the use of logic. This allows us to move from making statements to reaching conclusions. Here are two examples of very basic arguments:

All cows are animals.
Daisy is a cow.
Therefore Daisy is an animal.

Fred is rich and drives a large car.
John is rich and drives a large car.
Mike is rich and drives a large car.
Therefore rich people probably drive large cars.

Compare these two short arguments, and you will doubtless notice that the conclusions differ. The first conclusion is a categorical statement, while the second only asserts a probability. In fact these arguments start from exactly opposite directions.

Deductive thinking

The first is an example of deductive thinking. It starts by making a general statement and then deducing a particular instance from this. The second is an example of an inductive argument. It makes statements about particular cases and then draws a general conclusion from these.

If the statements (premises) of a deductive argument are true, and if the argument correctly follows the rules of logic (i.e. is valid), then the conclusion must be true. In this way it is like a mathematical calculation, either true or false depending on the correctness of the input and the method. There is nothing you can add to the premises to make the conclusion more true (e.g. that all cows have four legs, they all drink water, etc.).

Inductive thinking

Inductive arguments are more flexible in the sense that, even with correct logic, the conclusion cannot be said to be definitely true or false, only more or less probable. The more the supporting evidence you can bring to bear, the greater the probability of the conclusion being correct. For example, if you could name thousands of rich people, all of whom drove large cars, your conclusion would be strengthened. Even if one or two of them only had small cars, the conclusion would not be incorrect.

Just to make things a bit more complicated, inductive arguments do not necessarily only use individual cases to make a general conclusion.

They can also be turned round to make a conclusion about a particular case from a general statement, for example:

> Most clever students get good exam grades.
> Julie is a clever student.
> Therefore Julie will probably get a good grade in her finals.

What really marks this out from a deductive argument is that additional statements (premises) can have serious effects on the probability of the conclusion. If Julie also got good grades in her last exams, she attends all the lectures, works hard etc., then the conclusion will be reinforced. If however she is bone idle, never reads a book or goes to lectures, and gets paralysed by nerves during examinations, then you might reach just the opposite conclusion.

Do I need to use logic in my argument?

The simple answer is yes! Whatever argument you follow, even if it is based on qualitative data of the most subjective kind, you need to make a case to support your conclusions. In order to do this, your argument needs to be based on a logical sequence of evidence and conclusions. What does this involve? Well, there are basic rules of logic that can be simply learned, though applying them in a complex argument is a bit more difficult. The aim is to be able to detect a correct logical structure in an argument to determine whether the argument is valid or invalid. So what are the characteristics of logic that govern the structure of argument?

You must remember that logic is concerned not with the truth or falsity of premises (statements) or conclusions, but rather with the correctness of arguments. Therefore we do not say that arguments are true, incorrect or untrue, but we say that they contain valid deductions, correct inductions, or at the other extreme, assorted fallacies. The strict rules below really apply only to deductive arguments as these are limited to reaching firm conclusions solely based on the stated premises: no 'probably', 'might', 'likely to' as is seen in the conclusions of inductive arguments.

Validity of deductive arguments

The validity of deductive arguments is determined only by their logical form, not by the content of the statements which they contain. When the premise or premises of such an argument are related to the conclusion in such a way that the conclusion must be true if the premises are true, then the argument is said to be 'valid'. Any argument where this is not the case is called invalid.

Consider the following examples:

All diamonds are hard.
Some diamonds are gems.
Therefore some gems are hard.

All birds have wings.
All cats are birds.
Therefore all cats have wings.

All fat cats can fly.
Some pigs are fat.
Therefore some pigs can fly.

Some animals eat grass.
Animals that eat grass are herbivores.
Therefore (all) animals are herbivores.

Although some of the premises in the first and second arguments are obviously false, if they were true, the conclusions would have to be true. These arguments are based on valid logical structures. The structure of the third argument is not valid, even if the premises were true, because it is necessary to be a cat rather then fat in order to fly! In the fourth argument the premises are true but the conclusion is not – invalid logic.

It might be easy in simple sentences like the above to distinguish between valid and invalid arguments, as the premises are short and unambiguous and the construction of the arguments is simple. But arguments are not often stated quite so succinctly in books or research papers, or even in undergraduate dissertations, so it is usually necessary to read the text very carefully to distil the argument down to a series of simple statements.

Fallacies in argument

Logic is the protection against trickery and sloppy thinking. Logic deals with arguments that are based on reason. Mistakes are possible and even frequent in applying forms of logical argument. These mistakes are termed fallacies. However, not all mistakes in argument are genuine mistakes; there are innumerable examples of the calculated use of quasi-reasoning used in order to convince or convert the unwary.

The recognition of fallacies is not new, many of them having been noted as early as Aristotle. You can probably devise an argument yourself which is entirely logical, whose validity is clearly demonstrated by the conclusion being derived from the premises, and which carefully follows all the rules of syllogism, but which is based on premises that are phoney, tricks and delusions. There are brilliant deceptions for getting people to accept all sorts of false premises as true, and these tricks of argument are so common that even when people realize that they are being hood-winked they tend to let it pass.

The daily use of argument in health and social care practice and academic life is a highly complicated human activity and you cannot successfully study it in a sort of vacuum. There is no simple connection between the presentation of an argument on one side, and the acceptance of it on the other. Emotional and referential signals often add a significant subtext. For example, even the most abstract and exotic television commercial usually contains some kind of argument, some assertion of reasons and drawing of conclusions, e.g. 'must buy this because it's so romantic'. Even when you read books on logic you find that the arguments are seldom spelled out fully, except in the examples.

The word 'fallacy' is often used in two ways. Sometimes it is used to describe any kind of attitude that is fraudulent or deceitful, and at other times it is used, in a more narrow sense, to indicate a defective manner of reasoning or a wily or cunning form of persuasion. In the following analysis of fallacies, it is the second meaning that is taken, i.e. when an argument purports to abide by the rules of sound argument but in fact fails to do so. There are two main categories of fallacy: formal and informal.

Formal fallacies have some error in the structure of the logic. Although they often resemble valid forms of argument, the logical route only takes us from A to B by way of disjointed or missing paths. In brief, the fallacy occurs because the chain of reasoning itself is defective.

Informal fallacies, on the other hand, often use valid reasoning in terms that are not of sufficient quality to merit such treatment. They can be linguistic, and allow ambiguities of language to admit error, and leave out something needed to sustain the argument, or permit irrelevant factors to weigh on the conclusion, or allow unwarranted presumptions to alter the conclusions that are reached.

There is not room here to discuss all the different types of fallacy in detail, but we have selected some of those with the greatest relevance to academic research work. Most types of fallacy have been given titles or technical names and are well known to logicians. It is not necessary that you remember the names, though it will impress people if you point out the shortcomings in their arguments by quoting the type of fallacy by its name. The following examples demonstrate a few of these:

(1) 'If I run too much I will be tired. Since I have not run at all, I am not tired.'

Formal fallacy – denying the antecedent. The writer does not recognize that the same result can be produced by different causes.

(2) 'The duchess has a fine ship, but she has barnacles on her bottom.'

Informal fallacy – linguistic. This is a case of careless grammatical construction that causes an ambiguity of meaning.

(3) 'The ship of government, like any other ship, works best when there is a strong captain in charge of it. That is why government by dictatorship is more effective.'

Informal fallacy – relevance presumption. Analogies are often a useful way of describing unfamiliar concepts: in the above, equating government to a ship. The mistake is to assume further similarities that may not exist.

(4) 'Talk of the Loch Ness monster is nonsense. We know that it does not exist because every single attempt to find it has failed utterly.'

Informal fallacy – relevance intrusion. Just because we lack knowledge about something, it is a fallacy to infer that the opposite is the case.

(5) 'All health care professionals are really sensitive people. It happens that some really sensitive people are not properly appreciated. So some health care professionals are not properly appreciated.'

Formal fallacy – undistributed middle. The middle term 'really sensitive people' in this example does not refer to all sensitive people – so health care professionals might not be included.

(6) 'If the Americans wanted good trade relations, they would encourage the production of specialist goods in other countries. Since they do support this type of production, we know that they want good trade relations.'

Formal fallacy – affirming the consequent. In an 'if … then' construction, the 'if' part is the antecedent, and the 'then' part is the consequent. It is all right to affirm the antecedent, but not vice versa. Affirming the consequent is fallacious because an event can be produced by different causes.

(7) 'I don't think we should employ Mr Smith. I am told that he is a poor golf player. Careless people are bad at golf, so I don't think it is a good omen.'

Informal fallacy – omission. When statements are made about a class, they may be about all or some (or none) of the members. This fallacy occurs when ambiguity of expression permits a misunderstanding of the quantity that is spoken of (i.e. in this example, is it all or some careless people who are bad at golf?).

The above examples will give you an idea of some logical pitfalls. In more sophisticated arguments the logic can become very complex, with parts of an argument depending on others, e.g. if not this, then that. Obviously, it is important to recognize fallacies when you read or listen to people's arguments. It is just as important to avoid fallacies in your own writing. At this level, you will have to rely on careful reading and analytical thinking and quite a lot of common sense. The above examples are only a small selection of types of fallacy.

Building up your argument: the essential thread

So, what has all this theoretical stuff got to do with your dissertation work? As has been mentioned several times before, the whole point of doing a dissertation is to identify a particular problem or question, to collect information and to present some answers or solutions. It is up to you to convince the reader that you have collected information relevant to the question or problem and that you have based your answers and conclusions on the correct analysis of this information. You will need to use some logical argument in order to do this convincing.

Taylor (1989: 67) offers a useful list of the sorts of argument you might make in your dissertation. You might:

- agree with, accede to, defend or confirm a particular point of view;

- propose a new point of view;

- concede that an existing point of view has certain merits, but that it needs to be qualified in certain important respects;

- reformulate an existing point of view such that the new version makes a better explanation;

- dismiss a point of view or other person's work on account of its inadequacy, irrelevance or incoherence;

- reject, rebut or refute another's argument on various reasoned grounds;

- reconcile two positions that may seem at variance by appeal to some 'higher' or 'deeper' principle;

- retract or recant one's own position in the face of arguments or evidence.

Imagine yourself to be a lawyer making a case in court. You set out to solve the problem (who committed the crime and how) by analysing the situation, collecting the evidence, then making a case for your conclusions about 'whodunnit' and how. The jury will have to decide whether the argument is convincing and the evidence is sufficiently strong. In the case of a dissertation, you will be setting the problem and laying out your case, and the examiner will be your jury.

Just as a lawyer will be careful to make it clear just how he/she has reached his/her conclusions, so must you make it obvious how you came to yours. Always refer to the evidence when you make statements, whether it be by citing some kind of authority or by referring to your data and analysis. Careful cross-referencing is essential here. Always give page numbers of where the evidence is to be found (whether in a reference or in your dissertation), and refer to diagrams, tables and graphs by number when relevant.

Practical steps

It is a good idea initially to set up a skeleton of your argument by making a diagram that starts with the problem or question at the top, then follows logical steps to the conclusions. There may be branches along the way that take in particular aspects of the subject, i.e. subquestions that need to be covered. But all the threads should come together at the end to provide the main answer or solution to the main problem or question. In this way, you will be able to track the route of your argument and spot gaps, fallacies, meanderings or dead-ends. The examiner should be able to draw a similar diagram from reading your completed dissertation.

Obviously, before you have completed the work, you will not be able to finalize the argument. But it is important to have a clear 'route map' so that you can check your progress and fill in gaps. Expect to change some components of your argument as you get further advanced in your work. When you have completed the first draft, consciously check, by scanning through your main sections, that you have clearly stated the question or problem, that you have explained how you will tackle it, that the data collected are relevant, the analysis produces good reasons for your conclusions, and your conclusions actually address the problem or question stated at the outset. It is surprising how often students get somehow lost in the process and come to conclusions that do little to address the initial problem. If you do this preparation and checking, you won't be one of them.

Gathering your results

Ideally, you will have the research questions at the forefront of your mind throughout your time working on your dissertation. However, this is not always possible as you grapple with the learning of new techniques and methods and the problems of organizing your data collection and analysis. But you must come back to them regularly in order to ensure that you are keeping to the intentions of the project, and will end up with relevant material in order to be able to suggest answers to the questions.

Coming to conclusions is a cumulative process. It is unlikely that the problem you have chosen is simple, with questions raised that can be answered with a simple yes or no. Even if they can, you will be required to describe why it is one or the other, and make an argument to support your case. Normally, you will find that the questions have several subquestions, and even these can be broken down into components requiring separate investigation. Throughout the analysis part of your work you will be able to make conclusions about these fragments of the main issues. The skill is to gather these up at the end in the concluding chapter to fit them together into a 'mosaic' that will present the complete picture of the conclusion to the entire dissertation.

Just as you should be able to summarize the main problem that your dissertation addresses in one or two sentences, so you should be able to state the conclusion equally briefly. This belies the complexities that lie in between. You can picture your dissertation as having a continuous thread of argument running through it. The beginning and end of the argument are fat and tightly woven. But in between, the separate strands fan out, become twisted and frayed as different aspects are investigated, but manage to web together before reaching the end.

The secret to success lies in the sound construction of your argument.

Figure 10.1

What should I do next?

Why not try to construct a diagram as suggested above? One way to do it is to write all the elements of the argument on bits of paper, and then arrange them on a tabletop until you are satisfied that they follow through logically. You will see where there are missing links, where additional evidence is needed, and what is the shortest route to the conclusions. You can easily reject or add bits of paper. You will also be able to track any parallel arguments that you may need to make when you take several aspects of the problem into account. Do they all add up at the end to form a plausible main conclusion?

When you are satisfied with the framework, you can produce a diagram to record your 'route map'. You could also do this exercise on a computer, using a program that is designed to create diagrams of this kind. The next thing to do is to translate how this map will guide the structure of the written work. Does it fall neatly into chapters? Ensure that the steps in the argument remain clear. It is also a good idea to explain the structure of your argument in the introductory chapter. This not only forms a useful guide to the reader, but will impress the examiner with your lucid thinking and organization.

Further reading

You can quickly get into deep water on the subject of thinking and argument. We would recommend Brink-Budgen or Cottrell to start with, and perhaps follow up the references in these if you want to find out more on specific issues.

Brink-Budgen, R. (2000) *Critical Thinking for Students: Learn the Skills of Critical Assessment and Effective Argument*, 3rd edn. Oxford: How To Books.

Cottrell, S. (2005) *Critical Thinking Skills: Developing Effective Analysis and Argument*. Basingstoke: Palgrave Macmillan. See in particular Chapters 3, 4, 6 and 7.

Fisher, A. (2004) *The Logic of Real Arguments*, 2nd edn. Cambridge: Cambridge University Press.

Kuhn, D. (1991) *The Skills of Argument*. Cambridge: Cambridge University Press.

Chapter 11

What Sorts of Data Will I Find?

Chapter contents

- The nature of data
- Primary and secondary data
- Quantitative and qualitative data, and levels of measurement
- Where do I find the necessary data?
- Sampling
- What should I do next?
- Further reading

The nature of data

'Data' means information, or according to the *Oxford English Dictionary* (2002: 603), 'things known or assumed as facts, and made the basis of reasoning or calculation'. Strictly speaking, 'data' is the plural of 'datum', and so is always treated as plural. When you do any sort of enquiry or research, you will collect data of different kinds. In fact, data can be seen as the essential raw material of any kind of research. They are the means by which we can understand events and conditions in the world around us. This chapter discusses the nature of data, their different characteristics, where data can be found and data sampling techniques.

Data, when seen as facts, acquire an air of solidity and permanence, representing the truth. This is, unfortunately, misleading. Data are not only elusive, but also ephemeral. They may be a true representation of a situation in one place, at a particular time, under specific circumstances, as seen by a particular observer. The next day, all might be different. For example, a daily survey of people's voting intentions in a forthcoming general election will produce different results each time, even if exactly the same people are asked – because some change their minds according to what they have heard or seen in the interim period. If the same number of people is asked in a similar sample, a different result can also be expected. Anyway, how can you tell whether they are even telling the truth about their intentions? Data can therefore only provide a fleeting and partial glimpse of events, opinions, beliefs or conditions.

Not only are data ephemeral, but they are also corruptible. Inappropriate claims are often made on the basis of data that are not sufficient or close enough to the event. Hearsay is stated to be fact, second-hand reports are regarded as being totally reliable, and biased views are seized on as evidence. The further away you get from the event, the more likely it is that inconsistencies and inaccuracies creep in. Memory fades, details are lost, recording methods do not allow a full picture to be given, and distortions of interpretations occur. Harold Pinter, the English playwright, described the situation like this:

> Apart from any other consideration, we are faced with the immense difficulty, if not impossibility, of verifying the past. I don't mean merely years ago, but yesterday, this morning. What took place, what was the nature of what took place, what happened? If one can speak of the difficulty of knowing what in fact took place yesterday, one can I think treat the present in the same way. What's happening now? We won't know until tomorrow or in six months' time, and we won't know then, we'll have forgotten, or our imagination will have attributed quite false characteristics to today. A moment is sucked away and distorted, often even at the time of its birth. We will all interpret a common experience quite differently, though we prefer to subscribe to the view that there's a shared common ground all right, but that it's more like a quicksand. Because 'reality' is quite a strong firm word we tend to think, or to hope, that the state to which it refers is equally firm, settled and unequivocal. It doesn't seem to be, and in my opinion, it's not worse or better for that. (1998: 21)

It is therefore a rash researcher who insists on the infallibility of his or her data, and of the findings derived from them. A measure of humility in one's belief in the accuracy of knowledge, and also practical considerations which surround the research process, dictate that the outcomes of research tend to be couched in 'soft' statements, such as 'it seems that', 'it is likely that' and 'one is led to believe that'. This does not mean, however, that progress towards useful 'truths' cannot be achieved.

It is important to be able to distinguish between different kinds of data, because their nature has important implications for their reliability and for the sort of analysis to which they can be subjected. Data that have been observed, experienced or recorded close to the event are the nearest one can get to the truth, and are called *primary data*. Written sources that interpret or record primary data are called *secondary sources*. For example, you can only have an approximate and less complete knowledge of a political demonstration if you read the newspaper report the following day than if you were at the demonstration and had seen it yourself. Not only is the information less abundant, but it is coloured by the commentator's interpretation of the facts.

A pair of other distinctions can be made between types of data. Much information about health care and society is recorded in the form of numbers, e.g. temperatures, respiratory rates, population densities, cost indices. The nature of numbers allows them to be manipulated by the techniques of statistical analysis. This type of data is called *quantitative data*. In contrast, there is a lot of useful information that cannot be reduced to numbers. People's opinions, feelings, ideas and traditions need to be described in words. Words cannot be reduced to averages, maximum and minimum values or percentages. They record not quantities, but qualities. Hence they are called *qualitative data*. Given their distinct characteristics, it is evident that when it comes to analysing these two forms of data, quite different techniques are required.

Let us examine the nature of these two pairs of characteristics of data.

Primary and secondary data

Primary data

Primary data are present all around us. Our senses deal with them all our waking lives – sounds, visual stimuli, tastes, tactile stimuli. Instruments and records also help us to keep track of factors that we cannot judge so accurately through our senses: thermometers record the exact temperature, clocks tell us the exact time and our bank statements tell us how much money we have. Primary data are as near to the truth as we can get about things and events. Seeing a football match with your own eyes will certainly get you nearer to what happened than reading a newspaper report about it later. Even so, the truth is still somewhat elusive – 'Was the referee really right to award that penalty? It didn't look like a handball to me!'

There are many ways of collecting and recording primary data (see Chapter 14 for more detail). Some are more reliable than others. It can be argued that as soon as data are recorded, they become secondary data owing to the fact that someone or something had to observe and interpret the situation or event and set it down in the form of a record; i.e. the data have become second-hand. But this is not the case. The primary data are not the actual situation or event, but a record of it, from as close to it as possible – that is, the first and most immediate recording. 'A researcher assumes a personal responsibility for the reliability and authenticity of his or her information and must be prepared to answer for it' (Preece, 1994: 80). Without this kind of recorded data it would be difficult to make sense of anything but the simplest phenomenon and be difficult to communicate the facts to others.

So, what sorts of primary data are there? There are four basic types:

* Observation – records, usually of events, situations or things, of what you have experienced with your own senses, your eyes, ears etc., perhaps with the help of an instrument, e.g. camera, digital recorder, microscope.

- Participation – data gained by experiences can perhaps be seen as an intensified form of observations, e.g. the experience of learning to drive a car tells you different things about cars and traffic than just watching.

- Measurement – records of amounts or numbers, e.g. population statistics, instrumental measurements of height, weight, blood pressure, temperature.

- Questioning – data gained by asking and probing. For example, information about people's beliefs or motivations.

These can be collected, singly or together, to provide information about virtually any facet of our life and surroundings. So, why do we not rely on primary data for all our research? After all, they get as close as possible to the truth. There are several reasons, the main being time, cost and access. Collecting primary data is a time consuming business. As more data usually means more reliability, the efforts of just one person will be of limited value. Organizing a huge survey undertaken by large teams would overcome this limitation, but at what cost? Also, it is not always possible to get direct access to the subject of research: for example, many historical events have left no direct evidence. Also, if you are undertaking a critical literature review you will be reviewing primary research studies (empirical research) and using someone else's primary data, to make sense of the research literature on a particular topic, a process known as secondary analysis.

Secondary data

Secondary data are data that have been interpreted and recorded, they often summarize or quote content from primary sources (Burns and Grove, 2004). We could drown under the flood of secondary data that assails us every day. News broadcasts, magazines, newspapers, documentaries, advertising and the Internet all bombard us with information wrapped, packed and spun into digestible soundbites or pithy articles. We are so used to this that we have learned to swim, to float above it all and only really pay attention to the bits that interest us. This technique, learned through sheer necessity and quite automatically put into practice every day, is a useful skill that can be applied to speed up your data collection for your dissertation.

Chapter 8 discusses the sources of secondary information. Here we will look at the different types of secondary data that you might want to uncover. Depending on the subject of your dissertation, particular types of data will probably be more important to you than others. The descriptions given later in the chapter will help you to decide where to focus your search efforts.

Books, journal papers, magazine articles, newspapers and clinical guidelines present information in published written form. The quality of the data depends on the source and the methods of presentation.

For detailed and authoritative information on almost any subject, go to refereed journals, or systematic reviews produced through the Cochrane Collaboration: all the papers will have been vetted by leading experts in the subject. Other serious journals, such as some professional journals, will also have authoritative articles by leading figures, despite the tendency of some to emphasize only one side of the issue. There are magazines for every taste, some entirely flippant, others with useful and reliable information. The same goes for books – millions of them. They range from the most erudite and deeply researched volumes, e.g. specialist encyclopaedia and academic tomes, to ranting polemics and commercial pap.

It is therefore always important to make an assessment of the quality of the information or opinions provided. You actually do this all the time even without noticing it. We have all learned not to be so gullible as to believe everything that we read. A more conscious approach entails reviewing the evidence that has been presented in the arguments. When no evidence is provided, on what authority does the writer base his/her statements? It is best to find out who are the leading exponents of the subject you are concentrating on. Apart from getting marks for recognizing these and referring to them, you will be able to rely on the quality of their writings. At this stage of your studies, you are not expected to challenge the experts – leave this for when you do a PhD. (See Chapter 12 for more detail on critical appraisal.)

Television broadcasts, films, radio programmes, podcasts, recordings of all sorts provide information in an audiovisual non-written form. The assertion that the camera cannot lie is now totally discredited, so the same precautions need to be taken in assessing the quality of the data presented. There is a tendency, especially in programmes aimed at a wide public audience, to oversimplify issues. Also, the powerful nature of these media can easily seduce one into a less critical mood. Emotions can be aroused that cloud one's better judgement. Repeated viewings help to counter this.

The Internet and CD-ROMs combine written and audiovisual techniques to impart information. Remember the issues raised in Chapter 8 about assessing the accuracy of any data presented on the World Wide Web.

You cannot always be present at an event, but other people might have experienced it. Their accounts may be the nearest you can get to an event. Getting information from several witnesses will help to pin down the actual facts of the event.

It is good practice, and especially necessary with secondary data, to compare the data from different sources. This will help to identify bias, inaccuracies and pure imagination. It will also show up different interpretations that have been made about the event or phenomenon. Far from being an annoyance, this could provide a rich subject of debate in your dissertation. Academic writing thrives on controversy. You will thus have the opportunity to weigh up the evidence, to set up your argument, and to come to your own conclusions on the matter.

Quantitative and qualitative data, and levels of measurement

The other main dual categories applied to data refer not to their source, but to their nature. Can the data be reduced to numbers or can they be presented only in words? It is important to make a distinction between these two types of data because it affects the way that they are collected, recorded and analysed. Numbers can provide a very useful way of compressing large amounts of data, but if used inappropriately they lead to spurious results. So how can these two categories be distinguished?

Quantitative data

Quantitative data have features that can be measured, more or less exactly. Measurement implies some form of magnitude, usually expressed in numbers. As soon as you can deal with numbers, then you can apply mathematical procedures to analyse the data. These might be extremely simple, such as counts or percentages, or more sophisticated, such as statistical tests or mathematical models.

Some forms of quantitative data are obviously based on numbers: population counts, economic data, scientific measurements, to mention just a few. There are, however, other types of data that initially seem remote from quantitative measures but can be converted to numbers. For example, people's opinions about home births might be difficult to quantify. But if, in a questionnaire, you give a set choice of answers to the questions on this subject, then you can count the various responses. The data can then be treated as quantitative.

Typical examples of quantitative data are census figures (population, income, living density), epidemiological data (prevalence rates, incidence rates, standardized mortality rates), economic data (share prices, gross national product, tax regimes), performance data (sport statistics, medical measurements, engineering calculations) and all measurements in scientific endeavour.

There are different ways of measuring data, depending on the nature of the data. These are commonly referred to as *levels of measurement* – nominal, ordinal, interval and ratio.

Nominal   If you have a diverse collection of different animals, you could sort them into groups of the same type, e.g. lion, tiger, elephant, giraffe. This most basic level of measurement is called nominal (i.e. referring to names). You might think that there is not much mathematical analysis you can apply to a list of names – counting the number of names and the number of cases in each category is about it. However, you can represent this information on a bar graph to compare the different sizes of the groups. You can also compare percentages of each group to the total, or one to another, and find the mode (the value that occurs most frequently in the groups). If you have two types of nominal measurement of a group, e.g. types of front teeth (sharp and pointy or flat and blunt) and eating habits (carnivore, herbivore, mixed), you can use the *chi-squared* statistical test to show up the differences between the expected and the observed values (more about straightforward statistical tests in Chapter 15).

Common uses of the nominal level of measurement in health and social care research are male/female, socio-economic groups, religious affiliations, ethnicity, occupations, birth place, smoker/non-smoker, geographical location, health care organization, i.e. Acute Trust, Foundation NHS Trust or Primary Care Trust.

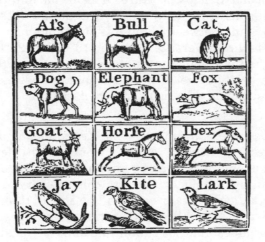

Figure 11.1 Nominal

Ordinal If the animals were well behaved, you could perhaps stand them in a row in order of height. Now you have measured them in an ordinal fashion, i.e. put them into an order – big to small – by comparing bigger and smaller rather than actually measuring their size. They probably will not be in equal steps of size; there may be a few very big or very small animals, and a lot somewhere near the middle. Now you can analyse data measured at this level by finding the mode and the median (in this case the middle size). You can also determine the percentage or percentile rank, and again, if you have two types of measurement (e.g. size and fierceness), you can use the chi-squared test. You can also show relationships by means of rank correlation.

Examples of the ordinal level of measurement in health and social care are levels of education (none, primary, secondary, college or university), skills (unskilled, semi-skilled, skilled), and many multiple-choice answers to patient satisfaction questionnaires (like very much, like, neutral, dislike, dislike very much).

Interval If you ask some people how much they like the different animals in your collection, scoring them in a range from 1–10 (the higher the more liked), then you will be getting them to measure on an interval scale. Unlike the uneven steps in animal sizes, the equal steps in this measurement scale give an accurate gauge of the distance between levels of liking, e.g. you can work out an average score for each animal and get an accurate comparison of their popularity. However, as there is no meaningful nought, you cannot say that a score of 4 indicates half the popularity of a score of 8. This would be like saying that a room with a temperature of 10°C is half as hot as one measured at 20°C.

Actually, temperature is a good example of an interval scale: in neither Fahrenheit nor Celsius measures does 0° mean a total absence of warmth. You can however truthfully say that the difference between scores of 4 and 8 and between 2 and 6 is the same, just as you can say that the temperature difference between 10°C and 20°C and between 15°C and 25°C is the same. You can use additional quite sophisticated statistical tests on this level of measurement (e.g. standard deviation, t-test, F-test and the product moment correlation).

Ratio If you counted how many lions, tigers, elephants, giraffes you had in your collection, then you would be using the ratio level of measurement. Here the nought will mean no animals. Any kind of measurement that has a meaningful nought falls into this category, e.g. measures of height and weight, age in years – you will be able to think of many more yourself. The distinctive quality of the ratio level of measurement is that you can express values in terms of multiple and fractional parts, e.g. half as big, three times as expensive. This is the most versatile level of measurement, open to a wide range of statistical tests.

Qualitative data

Qualitative data cannot be accurately measured and counted, and are generally expressed in words rather than numbers. The study of human beings and their societies and cultures requires many observations to be made that are to do with identifying, understanding and interpreting ideas, customs, beliefs and other essentially human activities and attributes. These cannot be pinned down and measured in any exact way. These kinds of data are therefore descriptive in character, and rarely go beyond the nominal and ordinal levels of measurement. This does not mean that they are any less valuable than quantitative data; in fact their richness and subtlety lead to great insights into human behaviour and society

Words, and the relationships between them, are far less precise than numbers. This makes qualitative research more dependent on careful definition of the meaning of words, the development of concepts and the plotting of interrelationships between variables. Concepts such as poverty, comfort, social capital, while elusive to measure, are nonetheless real and detectable.

Typical examples of qualitative data are literary texts, minutes of meetings, observation field notes, interview transcripts, video recordings of observations, documentary films, historical records, photographs, memos and recollections. Some of these are records taken very close to the events or phenomena, while others may be remote and highly edited interpretations. As with any data, judgements must be made about their credibility. Qualitative data, because they cannot be dispassionately measured in a standard way, are more susceptible to varied interpretations and valuation. In some cases even, it is more interesting to see what has been omitted from a report than what has been included. You can best check the reliability and completeness of qualitative data about an event by obtaining a variety of sources of data relating to the same event; this is called triangulation.

The distinction between qualitative and quantitative data is one of a continuum between extremes. You do not have to choose to collect only one or the other. In fact, there are many types of data that can be seen from both perspectives. For example, a questionnaire exploring people's attitudes about parenting may provide a rich source of qualitative data about their aspirations and beliefs, but might also provide useful quantitative data about levels and types of support available to parents. What is important is that you are aware of the types of data that you are dealing with during collection or analysis, and that you use the appropriate levels of measurement.

Where do I find the necessary data?

Data are the raw materials of research. You need to mine your subject in order to dig out the ore in the form of data, which you can then interpret and refine into the gold of conclusions. So where can you as a prospector for data find the relevant sources in your subject?

Although we are surrounded by data, in fact bombarded with them every day from television, posters, radio, newspapers, magazines and books, it is not so straightforward to collect the correct data for our research purposes. You need to carefully consider whether you are going to be collecting mainly primary or secondary data to address the research question you have posed.

You are probably wasting your time if you amass data that you are unable to analyse, either because you have too much, or because you have insufficient or inappropriate analytical skills or methods to undertake the analysis. We say probably, because research is not a linear process, so it is not easy to predict exactly how many data will be 'enough'. What will help you to judge the type of and amount of data required is to decide on the methods that you will use to analyse them (see Chapters 15 and 16 for this). In turn, the decision on the appropriateness of analytical methods must be made in relation to the nature of the research problem and the specific aims of the research project. This should be evident in your overall argument that links the research question/problem with the necessary data to be collected and the type of analysis that needs to be carried out in order to reach valid conclusions.

Collecting secondary data

Whatever the topic of your research, collecting secondary data will be a must. You will inevitably need to ascertain the background to your research problem/question, and also get an idea of the current theories, relevant policies and latest ideas. You have probably already been doing this to some extent when preparing the groundwork for your dissertation. All subjects require secondary data for the background to the study. Others rely greatly on them for the whole project, for example when undertaking a critical literature review, or doing a historical study (i.e. of any past events, ideas or objects, even the very recent past) or a secondary analysis of a large scale database (i.e. Millenium Cohort Study data, the General Household Survey, the 10-yearly National Census data, the British Crime Survey), or a review of statistical data from the Office of National Statistics (ONS). Wherever there exists a large body of recorded information, there are data for study.

Secondary data come in the form of literary sources, such as histories, commentaries, diaries, letters and records, which are contemporary, impersonal recordings of events, situations and states (e.g. patient, hospital and local government records), and may be descriptive or statistical. Any of them can be quantitative or qualitative in nature.

One of the main problems faced by the researcher seeking historical and/or recorded data is that of locating and accessing them. Another is often that of authenticating these sources, another is the question of interpretation. For example, a detailed historical analysis of an event will be worthless if the historical data have not been correctly interpreted, for example, if you did not detect that the evidence was highly biased. Locating secondary data can take a considerable amount of time for example, rummaging through dusty archives in a specialist library or downloading the latest government statistical data from the Internet. Gaining permission to use existing health and social care data can also be time consuming and may require ethics committee review.

Below are some of the principal sources of secondary data that might be relevant to undergraduate student research in health and social care:-

Libraries and archives   These are generally equipped with sophisticated catalogue systems which facilitate the tracking down of particular pieces of data or enable a trawl to be made to identify anything which may be relevant (see Chapter 8). International computer networks can make remote searching possible. See your own library specialists for the latest techniques. Valuable historical material is also contained in charitable institutions such as the Wellcome Library for archives and collections relating to the history of medicine. The UK Data Archive stores the largest collection of digital data sets relating to the social sciences and humanities.

Government departments   These often hold much statistical information, both current and historic. Indeed the National Library for Health (NLH), Social Care Institute for Excellence (SCIE) and government departments provide much of their information via the web, so you do not need to visit them in person. See for example the UK Statistics Authority and the ONS (http://www.statistics.gov.uk/); the Information Centre for Health and Social Care (http://www.ic.nhs.uk/statistics-and-data-collections); and for information and publications on health care, public health, workforce, social care statistics (http://www.dh.gov.uk/en/publicationsandstatistics/index.htm).

The Internet   This is a rapidly expanding source of information of all types.

Professional bodies   Many have libraries or information resource centres that hold collections of current and historical statistical information or provide access links to such resources/databases.

Existing data sets   Where data previously collected for another study is re-analysed to examine different research hypotheses or questions.

The wealth of statistical data contained in archives, especially those of a more recent date, provides a powerful resource for research into many health and social care subjects. You will often find, however, that the data recorded are not always in the exact form that you require (for example, when making international comparisons on child maltreatment, the data might be compiled in different ways or using alternative definitions in the different countries under consideration). In order to extract the exact data you require, you will have to extrapolate from the existing data.

Collecting primary data

Collecting primary information is much more subject specific, so you will have to judge what is appropriate here. Consider whether you need to get information from people, in single or large numbers, or whether you will need to observe and/or measure things or phenomena. You may need to do several of these: for example, for a nursing degree you may be examining both people and their treatments, or in social work you may be looking at organizational systems and their effects on staff.

Primary data collection entails going out and collecting information by observing, recording and measuring the activities and ideas of real people, or perhaps observing health care interventions, or experiencing events in social care. This process of collecting primary data is often called survey research. You should only be interested in collecting data that are required in order to investigate your research problem and help answer your research question. Even so, the amount of relevant information you *could* collect is likely to be enormous, so you must find a way to limit the amount of data you collect to achieve your aims. The main technique for reducing the scope of your data collection is to study a sample, i.e. a small section of the subjects of your study. There are several things you must consider in selecting a sample, so before thinking about the different methods of data collection, let us first deal with the issue of sampling.

Sampling

When you organize any kind of limited survey to collect information, or when you choose some particular cases to study in detail, or select papers to appraise in a literature review the question that inevitably arises is: how representative will the collected information be of the whole population? In other words, will the relatively few people you ask, or situations you study, or research papers you review be typical of all the others?

When we talk about 'population' in research, it does not necessarily mean a number of people. Population is a collective term used to describe the total quantity of cases of the type that are the subject of your study. So a population can consist of cases that are objects, people, organizations or even events, e.g. school buildings, occupational therapists, local authorities.

Where the objects of study are big and complex, for example hospitals or Local Safeguarding Children Boards, it might only be possible to study one or very few cases. Here, a case study approach is applicable, which enables a detailed investigation into the selected case or cases. You will have to judge which cases you choose on the basis of how typical they are of their type (population).

If you wish to survey the opinions of all the primary care staff working in a small GP practice, there might be no difficulty in getting information from each member of staff, so the results of the survey will represent the opinions of the whole practice. However, if you wish to assess the opinions of the members of a large health care trade union, apart from organizing a national ballot you will have to devise some way of selecting a sample of the members you are able to question, and who are a fair representation of all the members of the union. Sampling must be done whenever you can gather information from only a fraction of the population of a group or a phenomenon that you want to study. Ideally, you should try to select a sample that is free from bias. You will see that the type of sample you select will greatly affect the reliability of your subsequent generalizations.

There are basically two types of sampling procedure – random and non-random. Random sampling techniques give the most reliable representation of the whole population, while non-random techniques, relying on the judgement of the researcher or on accident, cannot generally be used to make accurate generalizations about the whole population.

Random sampling

In random sampling, each member of the target population has an equal probability of being selected. Random sampling at its simplest is like a competition draw. Represent all the cases in your population on slips of paper, put them into a hat, and draw out the slips in a random fashion. As with all samples, the larger the sample, the better. However, the issues are not always as simple as this. Here are a few basic guidelines.

First, a question should be asked about the nature of the population: is it homogeneous or are there distinctly different classes of cases within it? Different sampling techniques are appropriate for each. The next question to ask is which process of randomization will be used? The following gives a guide to which technique is suited to the different population characteristics.

Simple random sampling   This is used when the population is uniform or has similar characteristics in all cases e.g. a production of chocolate bars from which random samples are selected to test their quality.

Simple stratified sampling   This should be used when cases in the population fall into distinctly different categories (strata), e.g. a hospital whose employees are divided on different 'Agenda for Change' pay bands. An equally sized randomized sample is obtained from each stratum separately to ensure that each is equally represented. The samples are then combined to form the complete sample from the whole population.

Proportional stratified sampling   Used when the cases in a population fall into distinctly different categories (strata) of a known proportion of that population, e.g. a university in which 40% of students study arts and 60% study sciences. A randomized sample is obtained from each stratum separately, sized according to the proportion of each stratum to the whole population, and then combined as previously to form the complete sample from the population.

Cluster sampling or area sampling   Here, cases in the population form clusters by sharing one or some characteristics but are otherwise as heterogeneous as possible. It is a strategy commonly employed when the population is spread over a wide geographical area and the researcher wishes to include groups of participants' from a number of different locations, e.g. a study investigating nurses attitudes to PREP requirements across England, could select a cluster sample of nurses in each of the 10 Strategic Health Authority Regions.

Systematic sampling   This is used when the population is very large and of no known characteristics, e.g. the population of a town. Systematic sampling procedures involve the selection of units in a series (for example, on a list) according to a system. Perhaps the simplest is to choose every nth case on a list, for example, every 50th person in a telephone directory or list of council tax payers. It is important to pick the first case randomly, i.e. do not necessarily start counting from the first name on the list. The type of list is also significant – not everyone in the town owns a telephone or is a council tax payer.

Non-random sampling

Non-random sampling can be useful for certain studies, but it provides only a weak basis for generalization.

Accidental sampling or convenience sampling   This involves using what is immediately available, e.g. studying the ward you happen to be on during a clinical placement, examining the work practices in your occupational therapy department. There are no ways of checking to see if this kind of sample is in any way representative of others of its kind, so the results of the study can be applied only to that sample.

Quota sampling   Used regularly by reporters interviewing on the streets, quota sampling is an attempt to balance the sample interviewed by selecting responses from equal numbers of different respondents, e.g. equal numbers from different political parties. This is an unregulated form of sampling, as there is no knowledge whether the respondents are typical of their parties. For example, Labour Party respondents might just have come from an extreme left-wing rally.

Theoretical sampling   A useful method of getting information from a sample of the population that you think knows most about a subject. A study on homelessness could concentrate on questioning people living in the street. This approach is common in qualitative research where statistical inference is not required.

Another four methods can be briefly mentioned. *Purposive sampling* is where the researcher selects what he/she thinks is a 'typical' sample. With *volunteer sampling* people volunteer to take part through self-selection; it is therefore a sample of convenience. *Systematic matching sampling* is when two groups of very different size are compared by selecting a number from the larger group to match the number and characteristics of

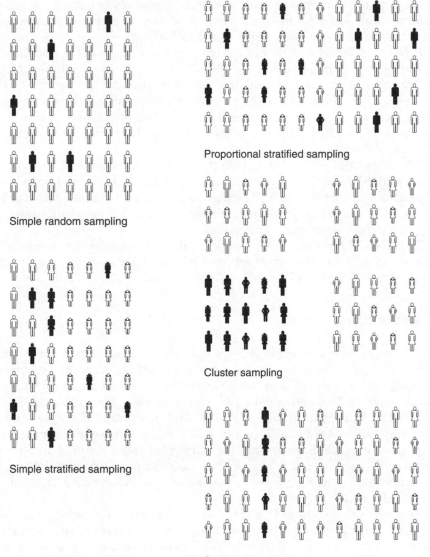

Figure 11.2   Random sampling diagrams

the smaller one. Finally, the *snowball* technique is when you contact a small number of members of the target population and get them to introduce you to others, e.g. parents of children with a peanut allergy.

Sample size

Once you have selected a suitable sampling method, the remaining problem is to determine the sample size. There is no easy answer to this problem.

If the population is very homogeneous, and the study is not very detailed, than a small sample will give a fairly representative view of the whole. In other cases, you should consider the following.

If you want great accuracy in the true representation of the population, then the sample must be large. It should also be in direct relationship to the number of questions asked and the amount of detail required in the analysis of the data. Normally, conclusions reached from the study of a large sample are more convincing than those from a small one. However, you have to take into account the practicalities of your resources in terms of time, cost and effort.

The amount of variability within the population (technically known as the standard deviation) is another important factor in deciding on a suitable sample size. Obviously, in order that every sector of a diverse population is adequately represented, a larger sample will be required than if the population were more homogeneous.

If statistical tests are to be used to analyse the data, there are usually minimum sample sizes specified from which any significant results can be obtained. Chapter 15 deals briefly with statistical methods.

Case studies

Sometimes you may want to study a system, an organization, an event, a family unit, or even a person or type of personality. It can be convenient to pick one or a small number of examples of these to study them in detail, and make assessments and comparisons. These are called case studies. This is usually based on the argument that the case studies investigated are a sample of some or many such systems or organizations, and so what you can find out in the particular cases could be applicable to all of them. You need to make the same kind of sampling choice as described above in order to reassure yourself, and the reader, that this in fact holds good.

Alternatively, if there is a large variation between such systems or organizations it may not be possible to find 'average' or representative cases. What you can do here is to take several very different ones, e.g. those showing extreme characteristics, those at each end of the spectrum and perhaps one that is somewhere in the middle. Take for example exercise regimes for increasing fitness. You could compare the results of one that is based purely on weight training, one based purely on aerobic exercises and one that combines both approaches. Other examples could be an examination of different treatment regimes for managing obesity, density of housing accommodation, top-bottom and bottom-top management structures or different types of parenting programmes. You can probably think of some more relevant to your topic area.

If you are going to do some kind of a survey or case study research, you might think that all this about sampling is a bit elaborate for the scale of your dissertation. But in fact, you will gain extra marks if you can show that you have considered the issue of sampling, even if your survey is small or your case study is an obvious choice. Demonstrate your knowledge by briefly discussing the relevant options and argue the case for your conclusions. Describe how you have carried out the sampling.

What should I do next?

You will soon have to begin collecting information about your topic of research. When doing your background reading, you have probably already seen what information has been collected and analysed by other people. This could give a good indication of what kind of data you will be searching for. Consider the types of data that you might, or are planning to collect, and first ask yourself these questions:

- Has the information you want already been recorded somewhere by someone else?

- Or do you have to go out to collect the information yourself directly from people or by observing phenomena? If so you will need to think about ethical approval issues (See Chapter 13) and sampling.

- Are the data you will collect easily quantifiable and measurable?

- Or are they difficult to describe and pin down exactly?

These might be surprisingly difficult questions to answer, as it is not always obvious what data will be required and from where they can be obtained. You might well have to spend some time thinking about this. It is a good idea to make some lists of data you will need to collect, and then try to sort them into categories: primary and secondary; quantitative and qualitative. These pairs are not connected, so do the same exercise with each pair.

If, for example, you are interested in the types and quality of nursing care in old people's homes, the data might be already available in statistics collected by the government or other organizations (secondary data). Or you might undertake a critical review of the literature when you will be reviewing someone else's primary research data on nursing care in old people's homes (if so see the next chapter, Chapter 12, on critical appraisal). Conversely, you may want to pinpoint particular homes to see how these compare (primary data). How you measure the type and quality of nursing care is not easy to do in a general way. What does 'type of nursing care' mean? Can you break it down into several categories (nominal measurement) or into degrees of care (ordinal measurement)? Both of these will be quantitative data in the sense that you are putting some kind of measurement to them, though you will have to make a qualitative assessment in order to fit them into these orders. How do you measure quality? Can you do it by counting the number of nurses and the hours they are in attendance (quantitative data) or will you assess the attitudes of the nurses to the patients by observing their behaviour (qualitative data)?

Very often, unmeasurable, abstract concepts such as effectiveness, efficiency and so forth have to be broken down into components in order to apply them in a meaningful way to your investigation. Some of these components will be measurable and dealt with quantitatively; others will be qualitative and rely on descriptions and comparisons. So if you are using general abstract terms like this in your dissertation title, and in the questions you are posing, ask what they mean in the context you are using them. Try to see how they can be broken down into less abstract components that can be studied and measured more easily.

You are likely to end up with a variety of data types you need to collect. This is altogether normal, and actually an advantage, as you can then demonstrate to the examiner of your dissertation how well you can deal with the collection and analysis of a range of different kinds of data.

Further reading

What is considered to be data, and what to do with them, is a big subject in research and gets dealt with exhaustively in most books about academic writing, which can be overwhelming at this stage of your studies. Below are some useful other ways of looking at this aspect, without getting too deeply into technicalities. If you have other books about research to hand, look up the index to see what they have to say about data.

Blaxter, L., Hughes, C. and Tight, M. (2006) *How to Research*, 3rd edn. Maidenhead: Open University Press. The first part of Chapter 6 provides another angle on data and its form.

Denscombe, M. (2007) *The Good Research Guide: For Small Scale Social Research Projects*, 3rd edn. Buckingham: Open University Press.

Leedy, P. and Ormrod J.E. (2005) *Practical Research: Planning and Design*, 8th edn. Upper Saddle River, New Jersey: Pearson, Merrill Prentice Hall. Part II, Chapter 5 provides a rather nice philosophical approach to the nature and role of data in research.

Robson, C. (2002) *Real World Research: A Resource for Social Scientists and Practitioners Researchers*, 2nd edn. Oxford: Blackwell.

These books have useful chapters on sampling:

Brett Davies, M. (2007) *Doing a Successful Research Project: Using Qualitative or Quantitative Methods*. Houndsmill, Basingstoke: Palgrave McMillan. See Chapter 4.

Fox, N., Hunn, A. and Mathers, N. (2000) 'Chapter 2: Sampling', in N. Mathers, M. Williams and B. Hancock (eds), *Statistical Analysis in Primary Care*. Oxford: Radcliffe Medical Press. This chapter focuses on sampling and sample size in quantitative research.

And a couple of books which are just about sampling:

Fink, A. (1995) *How to Sample in Surveys*. Volume 6 of The Survey Kit. London: Sage.
Scheaffer, R.L. (2005) *Elementary Survey Sampling*, 6th edn. Belmont, CA: Duxbury.

Chapter 12

How Do I Critically Appraise Research Evidence?

Chapter contents

- What is critical appraisal?
- Why do we do it? Why is it important?
- The steps of critical appraisal
- Summarizing the evidence
- What should I do next?
- Further reading

What is critical appraisal?

Critical appraisal of the research literature is an important step in determining the quality of research evidence and is a central component of evidence-based health and social care practice. Critical appraisal can be defined simply as 'a systematic way of considering the truthfulness of a piece of research, the results and how relevant and applicable they are' (Bury and Jerosch-Herold, 1998: 138). The process involves an objective critique and evaluation of the strengths and weaknesses of a research paper, to determine its design quality and merits, and its relevance for health or social care practice. With new research evidence constantly emerging, practitioners need to have the skills to be able to read and critically consider the quality of that evidence and whether it is relevant to their work. Research evidence comes in many different forms ranging from large scale randomized controlled trials (RCTs) to very small qualitative case studies. In the current climate of evidence-based practice, all practitioners, including students, are increasingly being required to understand where evidence exists, to have the skills to appraise the quality of that evidence and to assess where information is weak, contradictory or even absent.

Why do we do it? Why is it important?

Evidence-based practice involves appraising and evaluating the quality of research evidence to assess its potential to underpin decision making and practice in health and social care. As Earl-Slater has pointed out 'the rationale for critical appraisal stems from the fact that we need to know what is going on and we need to know if and how we can do it better' (2001: 60). Earl-Slater (2001: 60) argues that the critical appraisal process is also important for a number of other reasons including:

- Large quantities of evidence have to be made into smaller digestible bite sized pieces.

- It enables a distinction to be made between the quantity of research information and its quality.

- A critical appraisal can integrate data from a number of different sources.

- It is usually quicker and cheaper to conduct than a new research study.

- It can help specify generalizability of the research evidence.

- It can help to identify gaps and inconsistencies in the evidence base.

Critical appraisal also enables flaws and potential biases in the research process to be identified. Most importantly, by thoroughly reading a research article and applying a process of structured critical appraisal, this should ensure that a thorough assessment of all aspects of a research paper is undertaken. Critical appraisal requires lots of in-depth reading and as you are learning the techniques, can initially be quite time consuming. It is a skill that has to be learnt and practised (Bury and Jerosch-Herold, 1998). However, as practitioners increase in confidence this should help to prevent them skipping over certain sections of a research paper which may lead to a misinterpretation of the results or findings (Bury and Jerosch-Herold, 1998). It can also aid understanding of the research process. Critical appraisal should be balanced in its approach and should never be used as a critical attack on another's work (Polit and Tatano Beck, 2004).

If you are undertaking a literature review project for your dissertation, you will need to demonstrate sound skills in critically appraising your research literature. This will involve three key elements:

(1) Deciding whether a study's design is appropriate to answer the research question.

(2) Looking at how the research has been conducted and deciding whether it was done properly.

(3) Analysing the study findings and examining the conclusions based on that evidence (Avis, 1994; NHS Executive, 1996).

You will also need to evaluate and consider the relevance of the study findings to your own dissertation question and study objectives.

The steps of critical appraisal

The first step in the critical appraisal process should begin with a thorough reading of each original research article. Get to know your research papers, perhaps make notes on the main research approaches used, the study's main findings and conclusions. You will need to read each paper on several occasions to become familiar with the content and to be able to discuss key issues with your supervisor. Having familiarized yourself with the content of the research papers, you will then need to undertake an in-depth critique of each paper. You must make a decision for yourself whether or not the research article is high quality and whether you are convinced about they study's results.

As Hewitt (2000: 48) has outlined, the critical appraisal process will involve you asking a series of questions, such as:

- Is the purpose of the research clear and the research question well defined?

- How was the study conducted?

- Are the methods clearly articulated and appropriate?

- Is the sample and sampling procedure clearly described?

- How were data analysed?

- Are results presented clearly and in an understandable format?

- Is the interpretation of the study results consistent with the results presented?

- Are the conclusions drawn justified or are there other explanations that could account for the findings?

- What are your overall impressions of the research?

- Where is the research published and the type of publication?

There are several very useful tools and checklists available that can help you in the process of critical appraisal of empirical research. These research appraisal tools tend to consist of more detailed sets of questions than those outlined above, in the form of checklists. Some critical appraisal tools are generic, while others focus specifically on appraising quantitative research, systematic reviews, qualitative research evidence or a range of other research designs. You will find that most research textbooks contain detailed checklists for critical appraisal of research articles (e.g. Polit and Beck, 2005) and that there are also a number of specialist books on the topic (e.g. Muir Gray, 2001; Straus et al., 2005; Greenhalgh, 2006). Critical appraisal tools are also available on the Internet and The Critical Appraisal Skills Programme (CASP) based in Oxford (http://www.phru. nhs.uk/Pages/PHD/resources.htm) has produced a range of such tools for appraising studies with different research designs. Each CASP tool consists of a set of about 10 questions and additional prompts to take you through the appraisal process in a systematic fashion.

If you are undertaking a critical literature review for your dissertation thesis, you will need to select a critical appraisal tool and justify your selection of that particular framework. In a clearly labelled Appendix you should include an example of the appraisal framework(s) and questions that you use in your dissertation, you should also include one fully worked example i.e. one of your research papers fully appraised using the critical appraisal framework.

Summarizing the evidence

Once you have appraised each research article you will need to consider how you will present the summaries of your critiques of the research evidence. Each summary should briefly cover your critical appraisal of each research paper and your assessment of the quality of each paper. At this stage you will need to consider presenting the results of your critique in a summary table. It is usual for a summary table to include the following information for each research paper:

- author(s) and year of study;

- study design;

- sample size;

- methods of data collection;

- main findings;

- conclusions;

- the study's strengths and limitations.

Once you have produced a table summarizing the results of your critical appraisal of each of the studies, you will be in a position to make comparisons across the set of papers. See Aveyard (2007) for a good discussion of a simple approach to comparing and contrasting the results of your research papers, using a process of coding and thematic development. See also Chapter 16.

What should I do next?

If you are undertaking a critical literature review for your dissertation thesis, you will need to critically appraise each of the research articles that you have selected (your sample) and that are relevant to your research question. You have to make a judgement about the quality and relevance of each research paper to your study question. Therefore:

- Don't forget that the critical appraisal process should begin with a thorough reading of each original research article. So initially keep reading your research papers so that you get to know the material thoroughly.

- Once you are very familiar with the content of the research papers, you will need to select a critical appraisal tool to undertake a more in-depth critique of each research paper.

- Your examiner will expect you to justify why you have selected the particular appraisal tool/framework you choose to use. You will need to provide a rationale for this in your dissertation methods chapter and an explanation of how you conduct your appraisals.

- Do start thinking about how you will summarize the data from the critical appraisal of the research papers early on. Start reading about how you will go on to identify and illustrate the key themes that emerge from your analysis across your sample of research papers.

Further reading

The following books provide some really useful detail about critically appraising research literature in health and social care:

Aveyard, H. (2007) Doing a Literature Review in Health and Social Care. A Practical Guide. Maidenhead: Open University Press.

Chambers, R., Boath, E. and Rigers, D. (2007) Clinical Effectiveness and Clinical Governance Made Easy, 4th edn. Oxford: Radcliffe Publishing Limited.

Crombie I.K. (2007) A Pocket Guide to Critical Appraisal, 2nd edn. Oxford: Wiley-Blackwell.

Greenhalgh, T. (2006) How to Read A Paper: The Basics of Evidence-Based Medicine, 3rd edn. Malden, MA: Blackwell Publishing.

Helewa, A. and Walker, J.M. (2000) Critical Evaluation of Research in Physical Rehabilitation. Philadelphia, PA: W.B. Saunders Company.

Muir Gray J.A. (2001) Evidence-based Healthcare: How to Make Health Policy and Management Decisions, 2nd edn. Edinburgh: Churchill Livingstone.

You may also find it useful to access the critical appraisal sections and tools on the following websites:

http://www.shef.ac.uk/scharr/ir/netting/
http://www.phru.nhs.uk/Pages/PHD/resources.htm

Chapter 13

What About Research Ethics and Research Governance?

Chapter contents

Introduction

Ethics is about moral principles and rules of conduct. What have these got to do with writing a dissertation? Quite a lot actually; they focus on your behaviour towards other people and their work. You are not producing your dissertation in a vacuum. You will naturally be basing your information and ideas on work done by other people, and you may well be interacting with other people during your study. It is important to avoid unfairly usurping other people's work and knowledge. In addition to this, research participants have a right to privacy, and their autonomy, safety and well-being must be protected at all times. If you are planning to collect primary data you will need to obtain ethics review for your research study. Research that is undertaken within the UK NHS will also need to be reviewed to ensure it complies with national arrangements for research management and governance.

Acknowledging other people's work

An important part of a dissertation is to find out what has already been written by other people on the chosen subject. You will be expected to collect and report facts and ideas from a wide range of sources, so there is no need to feel that *everything* you write has to be 'original'. Even the greatest thinkers have 'stood on the shoulders of giants' in order to make their discoveries. There is real truth in the view that other people's work can be an inspiration and guide to ones' own. The point is that the sources of work on which you base your writing must be acknowledged. In order to maintain an honest approach, there must be a clear distinction between your ideas and those of other people.

Your university or college will have strict regulations covering the issues of plagiarism and syndication, and you should make yourself familiar with these. These extracts taken from the Oxford Brookes University Student Conduct Regulations (2007) provide a typical example:

> Students must ensure that they do not plagiarise (i.e. take and use another person's thoughts, writings, inventions as their own) any part of any work submitted for assessment in fulfillment of course requirements. Quotations from whatever source must be clearly identified and attributed at the point where they occur in the text of the work by use of one of the standard conventions for referencing. Any student whose work submitted for assessment is plagiarised, in whole or in part, may be subject to disciplinary action in accordance with the University's Disciplinary Procedure.
>
> Except where written instructions specify that work for assessment may be produced jointly and submitted as the work of more than one student, students must not collude with others to produce a piece of work jointly, copy or share another student's work or lend their work to another student in the reasonable knowledge that some or all of it will be copied. Such collusion is cheating and any student who participates in collusion may be subject to disciplinary action in accordance with the University's Disciplinary Procedure.

You may think that you could easily get away with copying chunks of text from the Internet; after all, there are millions of pages to choose from. However, the source can easily be tracked down by typing a string of four or five words from the text into a search engine such as Google. There are also software programmes available to universities (i.e. Turnitin®) that allow checks to be run on coursework to prevent plagiarism. The penalties for transgressing university and college regulations, even inadvertently, are heavy; so how can problems be avoided?

The solution lies in a good system of referencing and acknowledgement. Credit will be given for evidence of wide reading of relevant texts, so there is no need to be shy about quoting your sources. There are two ways of incorporating the work of others into your text: the first is by *direct quotation*, and the second by *paraphrase*. These can be referenced in several widely recognized systems, for example, the Harvard system. Generally, all systems identify the sources in an abbreviated form within the text to pinpoint the relevant sections, and cross-reference these to a full description in a list at the end of the chapter or dissertation, or in some cases in a footnote at the bottom of the page. You should decide on one system and then use it consistently. Advice might be given in your course description as to which system your university prefers. For a full account of the practical aspects of how to do your referencing, refer to Chapter 17.

How much referenced material should you use? This depends on the nature of your dissertation. Obviously, if you are undertaking a literature review comparing the published works of several people, it will be appropriate to have numerous references. In other cases, say a report on a laboratory experiment, fewer references may be sufficient to set out the background to the study. You should be able to get further advice on this issue from your dissertation supervisor.

Where does the boundary lie between paraphrasing (which requires referencing) and your own writing based on the ideas of others (which does not)? This is a matter of judgement. Substitution of a few words, reordering sentences, or cutting out a sentence here and there, are not enough to make it your own work. A sound method of avoiding accusations of plagiarism is to carefully read the source material, and then put it away out of sight. Rely on your memory and own words to describe and interpret the ideas.

Here is a brief example in two parts to demonstrate skills in paraphrasing, using a quotation from Leedy's (1997) book *Practical Research*. First the quotation – a word-for-word copy of a section of his text. Note the citation at the end.

> Any research endeavour that employs human subjects may raise questions of propriety, create misunderstandings, or ask subjects to go beyond demands consistent with pure research objectivity. A statement signed by the subject, indicating a willingness to co-operate in the research and acknowledging that the purpose and procedure of the research project have been explained, may well be a safeguard for both researcher and subject. Such a statement should contain a clause indicating that if, at any time during the research procedure, the individual should not wish to continue to be associated with the research effort, he or she shall have the right to withdraw. (Leedy, 1997: 116–17)

In the first example below, we have made a summary in our own words of the main points, which are attributed to the author. We kept the text in front of us so that I could make an accurate account. The length was reduced to a couple of sentences, and again there is the citation.

> Leedy (1997: 116–17) states that research using human subjects may raise issues of propriety, misunderstandings and objectivity. To mitigate problems, a signed statement should be obtained from the subject indicating agreement to participate in the project, and containing the

option for him or her to opt out of the research exercise should he or she so wish ...

In the following example we put the text aside and wrote a commentary in our own words on the content, i.e. our interpretation of the issues raised. The source does not need to be cited in this case.

> Use of a signed agreement between researcher and participants will help to reduce any misunderstandings and misgivings on the part of participants in research projects. An opt-out clause should be included to enable participants to terminate their agreement to participate during the course of the project.

If your dissertation were to be published, there are strict limitations as to how much direct quotation or illustrative material you are allowed to use without asking permission from the original author or copyright holder. This does vary. For example, all government statistics, as well as illustrations and figures, need permission for reproduction. However, for unpublished student academic work such as yours, these limits do not apply. Even more reason, then, to acknowledge your sources, in gratitude that you do not need to go through the process of gaining permissions.

Seeking Research Ethics Committee review

If you are intending to collect primary data as part of your research dissertation you must seek ethics review and approval of your research. As a student researcher you will undoubtedly need to seek initial permission from your university or academic school's research ethics committee. Check if your university school or department has a research ethics officer who can provide further information for you on the university ethics review processes. The main reason for research ethics review is to ensure that the dignity, rights, safety and well-being of research participants are not compromised in any way by their participation in a study.

In the UK, all research involving NHS staff, patients, premises and clinical records must be approved by the National Research Ethics Service (NRES). Audit and service evaluation are excluded from this requirement. All applications are made via the central allocation service (CAS) or directly to a local NHS Research Ethics Committee (REC). A multi-site study will need to be identified as such on the application form and then will reviewed by the main REC. Site specific assessments (SSA) are required from each of the research sites involved. The major issues that an ethics committee will be concerned with are outlined in Table 13.1. For further guidance see the NRES website at http://www.nres.npsa.nhs.uk/. A new online ethics form has been designed so that a research and development (R&D) form for research governance purposes is generated at the same time as the online ethics application form. For more detailed information on the Integrated Research Application System (IRAS) see https://www.myresearchproject.org.uk/, where detailed guidance is available. Most local authorities and many charitable organizations will also have an ethics committee or the equivalent of an ethics review procedure. It is worth reflecting on the point that research on sensitive topics will be difficult in terms of gaining permissions; but that research of a more evaluative nature that may benefit the organization may be more likely to meet with success.

Negotiating access to the field

If you are planning to undertake empirical research, a service evaluation or an audit study within a health, social care, voluntary or university setting, you will need to seek approval from the senior manager at the organization.

Table 13.1   Ethical review – issues considered

---

* Scientific design and conduct of the study
  - Appropriateness of research study design
  - Statistical methodology, sample size and randomization
  - Criteria for ending the study or prematurely withdrawing research study participants
  - Arrangements for monitoring and auditing the research
  - Adequacy of the research site
  - Research reports and publishing

* Recruitment of research participants
  - The population characteristics of the study sample (i.e. gender, culture, age, ethnicity, economic status) and a justification for this
  - Research reports and publishing
  - Initial contact with participants and their recruitment
  - Inclusion and exclusion criteria for research participants
  - The process of providing information for potential research study participants

* Care and protection of research participants
  - The safety of any research intervention
  - The researcher's qualifications and experience
  - Any plans to withdraw or withhold standard care or therapies and justification
  - The care to be provided to research study participants both during and after the research study and for those who withdraw during a study
  - Arrangements for informing the participant's GP
  - Financial rewards and compensation for study participants and researchers and their organizations

---

Table 13.1　(Continued)

- Protection of research participants' confidentiality
  - Access to personal data, medical records and biological samples; process of consent for this, how data will be obtained and used
  - Security and confidentiality of personal information.
  - Storage and distribution of data and samples

- Informed consent process
  - Full description of the process of gaining informed consent
  - Adequacy, readability and coherency or written and verbal information
  - A clear justification for involvement of individuals who are unable to give consent.
  - Provision of information to participants which becomes available during the course of a study
  - Process for receiving and dealing with queries and complaints.

- Community considerations
  - Consultation with users/communities during the design of the research study.
  - The impact and relevance of the research on the local community and the concerned communities
  - Contribution of the research to capacity building e.g. enhancing local services or ability to respond to local health needs
  - Availability and affordability to concerned communities of any successful study product following the research
  - The availability of the research study results to study participants and concerned communities.

Source: After Department of Health (2001). Crown copyright material is reproduced with the permission of the Controllor Office of Public Sector Information (OPSI).

This individual's support will be required to gain access to the study site where you want to conduct the study, for example, a local authority setting, hospital ward, or voluntary organization. For example, in a study surveying social workers about children in need issues, you would need to seek permission from the Children's Services Safeguarding Manager. Initial permission to seek access to the research setting should be sought by writing to the senior manager, enclosing a copy of your research proposal. You might then need to follow this up with a meeting in person to provide more detail about the study before formal permission to access the field can be given.

Research governance

In the UK, R&D approval must be sought from each organization for all research and audit conducted in NHS settings to ensure that the study complies with local arrangements for research governance. The Department of Health (2005) has published a Research Governance Framework for Health and Social Care (see http://www.doh.gov.uk/reesrach), which sets out a framework for the governance of research in these settings. It includes information about the standards required for research, the responsibilities and accountabilities of all involved in research and information on monitoring of and audit of research. All NHS Trusts have mechanisms to examine the R&D management and governance aspects of research, to ensure that any proposed study is conducted to the highest scientific and ethical standards and is justified organizationally. Many local authorities are also establishing similar research governance approval procedures.

Respect for other people

Many dissertation topics in health and social care will involve collecting information from people, whether they are experts or members of the general public. This data collection may be in the form of interviews or questionnaires, but could also be types of experiments. Whenever you are dealing with other people, you must be sensitive to issues of autonomy, privacy, fairness, consent, safety, confidentiality of information and impartiality. This is actually quite a complex subject, and it requires real thought about how your plans for getting information or opinions from people can be achieved in a way that meets these ethical obligations. As students and trainee professionals you are also required to adhere to your professional ethical frameworks or professional codes of conduct.

Here are some of the main aspects to consider.

Inform people

A participant information sheet will need to be drafted to explain to potential recruits what your study is about and what is required of them, any risks involved and to what use the findings would be put. It should provide sufficient information to enable people to decide whether or not they want to take part. Munhall (1988: 151) highlights the 'on-going process' of seeking informed consent from potential respondents and emphasizes that consent is not a one off process but needs to be continually negotiated and agreed. Participants have a right to know why you are asking them questions and to what use you will put the information that they give you. Reiterate before interviewing and add an explanatory introduction to questionnaires. If you will be conducting some kind of test or experiment, you should explain what methods you will use.

Potential recruits to your research study must be given sufficient information to allow them to decide whether or not they want to take part.

- **Example** – You are planning to interview school nurses about their role in obesity prevention amongst school aged children. You might hold a preliminary discussion meeting with the school nurses at a team meeting to give details about your proposed research. Explain that you are conducting a study as part of a BSc in Community Health Care Nursing to examine through individual one to one interviews the school nurses' role in obesity care and management. You will then send a formal letter of invitation and a participant information sheet to each school nurse in the PCT outlining the study and the nature of their proposed involvement. This allows the school nurses further time to reflect on their decision about whether or not to be involved in your study before they are provided with the opportunity to opt in.

Ask permission and anticipate refusal to participate

Do not assume that everyone is willing to help you in your research. Once people are informed about the project they should be clearly given the choice to take part or not. All participant information sheets should emphasize that participation in the research study is entirely voluntary. Potential recruits should also be reassured that they can withdraw from a study at any point without having to give a reason and without it affecting the care/services they receive.

- **Example** – You want to test people's skills in balancing on a tightrope, depending on the tension of the rope. You will need to explain exactly what you wish them to do, safety measures to be taken, clothing and footwear required, time and place of the experiment, who will be observing, and other data required (e.g. age, weight, size, etc.) This will enable the potential participants to judge if they want to take part.

Respect privacy through anonymity

Most surveys rely on the collection of data, the sources of which do not need to be personally identified. In fact, people are far more likely to give honest replies to questions if they remain anonymous, that is, if a person's identity cannot be linked to their response. You should check that the way data are collected and stored ensures anonymity – omission of names and addresses. Treat data as numbers wherever possible.

- **Example** – You are distributing a questionnaire to households about vandalism and intimidation on a housing estate, asking questions about the extent and causes of the problems. To ensure anonymity, the questionnaires must not contain anything that may identify the respondent, e.g. even a family profile might do this. Delivery and return of the questionnaires should also be considered to ensure that the information cannot get into the wrong hands.

Protect participant confidentiality

It is essential that all information gathered from participants is kept strictly confidential. People who take part in research have a right to privacy. Confidentiality must be maintained at all stages in the research process and individuals must not be identified in a dissertation or a subsequent publication. You must be very clear about how you will maintain confidentiality and manage personal information. You will need to obtain a person's written agreement/consent to collect information about them and to access their health or social care records. Written consent should also be obtained to use anonymized quotes in a final report/publication. You also need to be familiar with the requirements of the Data Protection Act 1998.

- **Example** – You are interviewing a small number of health care lecturers from your local university about occupational stress in nursing. You will need to explain exactly how you will maintain confidentiality and manage personal information at all times during: recruitment, data collection, data analysis processes and dissemination. You will also need to be clear about how you will store and manage confidential data and personal information.

Obtain informed consent

It is essential to obtain a person's written consent to collect information about them and to access their health or social care records. Written agreement should also be obtained to use anonymized quotes in your dissertation or in a final report/publication. It is also good practice to return an anonymized interview transcript to the individual respondent, asking them to check that the transcript is an accurate record of the interview and to ensure that they are happy to allow quotes to be included in your dissertation.

- **Example** – In the above example, ask before the interviews if you will be allowed to quote the health care lecturers anonymously in your dissertation and if they agree, gain their written consent to do so. Provide respondents with an opportunity to check their transcripts after the interview. If you say you will do this in advance, you will be likely to get a less cautious response during the interview, as there is an opportunity for the interviewee to check for accuracy. When writing up your dissertation, consider using pseudonyms

to maintain confidentiality. You may also need to remove potentially iden-
tifiable details from the lecturer's accounts, but without altering the content or meaning of the interview.

Fairness

In any tests or experiments, thought should be given to ensure that
they are fair, and can be seen to be so. Participants will feel cheated
if they feel that they are not treated equally or are put at some kind of
disadvantage.

- **Example** – A common issue is the exclusion of people in a research study
  on the basis of race due to assumptions about their ability to understand
  English. A further example about fairness is providing realistic information
  about the duration of, say an interview, and keeping to it.

Management of unexpected outcomes

When planning research it is always important to plan ahead and have
contingencies in place to manage unexpected eventualities or outcomes,
such as the observation of poor practice, the disclosure of personal or inti-
mate experiences, or distressed participants. The dignity, rights, safety
and well-being of study participants must always take precedence over
the research aims at all times. All health and social care trainees must
ensure that they adhere fully to the ethical framework and professional
codes of conduct of their professional bodies. It is good practice to ensure
that additional support and or debriefing opportunities are available for
study participants following an interview.

- **Example** – Discussing personal experiences may raise sensitive issues for
  participants, which may cause them to become distressed. If a patient
  became upset during an interview, the interview should be stopped immediately and appropriate support offered/given. The patient should be
  offered the opportunity to continue the interview on another occasion. The
  interview should only be resumed if the patient gives their explicit permission for it to do so. There should also be an opportunity at the end of
  the interview for the participant to debrief (e.g. with a specialist nurse)
  and discuss any questions they may have with the researcher.

Avoid sexism

The way language is used can often lead to sexism, particularly the use
of masculine labels when the text should actually refer to both men

and women. Bias, usually towards the male, is also to be avoided in your research.

- **Example** – The use of words such as 'manpower' rather than 'labour power', 'one-man show' rather than 'one-person show', and the generic 'he' or 'his' when you are referring to a person of either sex. Research bias can occur when you devise a study that assumes the 'boss' is a man, or that all midwives are women.

Be punctual, convenient and brief

Punctuality, brevity and courteousness are essential qualities to help your efforts to gain information. Appointments should be made and kept punctually. Time is a valuable commodity for almost everybody, so it will be appreciated if you regard it as such.

- **Example** – You need to get expert information on the intricacies of managing an acute surgical ward in your local hospital. You turn up three-quarters of an hour late, just at a time when two patients return from theatre and the ward is very busy. You have missed your 'slot' and will cause real inconvenience if you start asking questions now.

Be diplomatic and avoid offence

On the whole, people are willing to help students in their studies. However, do not abuse this willingness by being arrogant and insensitive. You might be dealing with delicate issues, so consider and anticipate the sensitivities and feelings of the participants. Above all, do not make people appear ridiculous or stupid.

- **Example** – Do not regard yourself as the host of a chat show when, say, interviewing a group of elderly people in a residential home about their past lives. They may have very different views on what is proper to talk about, so avoid the pressure tactics and 'clever' questions used to prise out information not willingly given.

Give thanks

It is good practice to thank people who have participated in or helped with your research study. Any help should be acknowledged with thanks, whether verbal or, in the case of questionnaires, interviews or letters asking for information, written.

- **Example** – Adding a short paragraph at the end of the questionnaire thanking the person for answering the questions is simply done. A simple expression of thanks before leaving after an interview is important and should always be followed up with a thank you letter/email.

Academic integrity

This refers back to some of the issues raised in Chapter 5 about philosophy. The main point we want to make here is that of being scrupulously honest about the nature of your findings, even (and especially) if they tend to contradict the main thrust of your argument. Good quality research is not achieved by using the techniques of a spin doctor. Politicians might want to put the right kind of gloss on data collected for them in order to bolster their arguments, but this is not appropriate in academic work. Data should speak for themselves. Your analysis should reveal the message behind the data, and not be used to select only the results that are convenient for you.

As with most things, this kind of honesty can be more complicated than at first glance. Consider the following scenario. A study is being carried out on the use of animals in experiments to develop new products, in this case, an anti-ageing pill that may have useful properties for treating Alzheimer's disease. The data on the level of discomfort that the animals suffer, based on medical measurements and observations, are contradictory and difficult to quantify. The researcher carrying out the study feels that an anti-ageing pill is not really a medicine, so testing on animals is not justified. However, the experimenters argue that if many human lives can be prolonged by pre-empting the effects of Alzheimer's, then the slight suffering of some animals is justified.

How will the researcher present the data in an honest and balanced way?

It would be easy to present one side of the argument and stress the amount of suffering caused to animals in the search for an elixir of youth. That the animals suffer can be derived from the data. By interpreting the data on the animals' discomfort level as demonstrating cruelty, and by ignoring the likely medical benefits of the pill, a strong case could be made for discontinuing the experiments.

But such certainty is not inherent in this situation. Much better, that is, more honest, if the researcher discussed the issues driving the research, and the difficulty of gauging the level of suffering of the animals, and concentrated on assessing the strengths of the opposing arguments, taking into account the uncertainties of the data and of the eventual properties of the product.

If you can achieve a balanced view, it is probably not necessary to specifically state your personal attitude to the issues. However, there are situations where it is impossible to rise above the events and be a detached observer. For example, if you are a committed and active supporter of alternative therapies, and make a study of an aspect of alternative therapy, you should declare your interest. Your arguments may well be valid and based on good evidence, but you are unlikely to seek supporting evidence for the other side.

Another way to ensure that you will avoid being accused of spin or false interpretation of the evidence is to present all the data you have collected as fully and clearly as possible. This may be the results of a questionnaire, measurements of activities or any other records relevant to your study. You can then base your analysis on these data, and it is open to the reader to judge whether your analysis is correct and whether your conclusions are valid. All arguments are open to challenge, but if you present the raw materials on which your arguments are based, then at least the discussion has a firm foundation.

What should I do next?

The issues of ethics in academic work pervade almost all aspects. Some of these issues are based on simple common sense and civilized behaviour, such as one's relationships with colleagues and other people. Others are more formal in character and require real organizational effort in order to fulfil the requirements, such as seeking research governance approval and/or formal ethics review, or systematically employing a sound referencing system and gaining permissions for use of information. You should therefore:

- Consider carefully how you will use the written work and ideas of other people in your dissertation. Will you be discussing and comparing their ideas, or will you be developing ideas of your own based on those of others? You will probably do some of both. Consciously devise a method to differentiate between quotation, summary, paraphrase and commentary so that you will be aware of which mode you are writing in at any time.

- If you are planning/intending to collect primary data as part of your dissertation work you must seek formal ethics committee review of your research. Sometimes, it may be necessary to seek an ethical review opinion from more than one committee.

- Before conducting a research study or audit project in a UK health care setting, R&D management approval must be obtained, as well as ethics approval via the NRES.

- Examine your plans for gathering information from other people. Systematically organize them to take account of all the relevant ethical issues. This will involve matters of procedure as well as content in written and verbal form. You can use the bullet points outlined in Table 13.1 and above as a checklist.

Further reading

Although ethical behaviour should underlie all academic work, it is in the fields of health and social care that the really difficult issues arise. Researching people, health and society raises many ethical questions that are discussed in the books below. The first book has two sections that are short and useful. The other books on this list are far more detailed and really aimed at professional researchers – though the issues remain the same for whoever is doing it.

Geraldi, O. (ed.) (2000) *Danger in the Field: Ethics and Risk in Social Research.* London: Routledge. Read this if you are going into situations that might be hazardous.

Laine, M. de (2000) *Fieldwork, Participation and Practice: Ethics and Dilemmas in Qualitative Research.* London: Sage. The main purposes of this book are to promote an understanding of the harmful possibilities of fieldwork; and to provide ways of dealing with ethical problems and dilemmas. Examples of actual fieldwork are provided that address ethical problems and dilemmas, and show ways of dealing with them.

Mauthner, M. (ed.) (2002) *Ethics in Qualitative Research.* London: Sage. This book explores ethical issues in research from a range of angles, including: access and informed consent, negotiating participation, rapport, the intentions of feminist research, epistemology and data analysis, tensions between being a professional researcher and a 'caring' professional. The book includes practical guidelines to aid ethical decision-making rooted in feminist ethics of care.

Robson, C. (2002) *Real World Research: A Resource for Social Scientists and Practitioner-Researchers, 2nd edn.* Oxford: Blackwell Publishers See pp. 65–76, 501–3.

There are also books about ethics that specialize in certain fields. Here are some examples.

College of Occupational Therapists (2005) *Code of Ethics and Professional Conduct for Occupational Therapists.* London: College of Occupational therapists. This booklet is available by this public link: http://www.cot.co.uk/public/publications2/categoryshow.php?c=1

Graue, M.E. (1998) *Studying Children in Context: Theories, Methods, and Ethics.* London: Sage.

Leathard, A. and McLaren, S. (2007) *Ethics: Contemporary Challenges in Health and Social Care.* Bristol: Policy Press, University of Bristol. Have a look at the chapters relating specifically to research ethics.

Long, T. and Johnson, M. (eds) (2007) *Research Ethics in the Real World: Issues and Solutions for Health and Social Care.* London: Churchill Livingston.

Royal College of Nursing (2007) *Research Ethics RCN Guidance for Nurses*. London: Royal College of Nursing, Research Advisory Group.

The Social Research Association has also produced a useful code of practice for the safety of social researchers which is available at: http://www.the-sra.org.uk/staying_safe.htm

The Chartered Society of Physiotherapy also has guidance on research ethics and ethics committees available at: http://www.csp.org.uk/

Chapter 14

How Do I Collect Primary Data?

Chapter contents

- Introduction
- Research methods
- Questionnaires
- Interviews
- Focus groups
- Standardized scales and tests
- Observation
- Experiments
- What should I do next?
- Further reading

Introduction

Collecting primary data for research purposes needs a plan of action that identifies and uses the most effective and appropriate methods of data collection. This chapter briefly introduces the most common primary data collection techniques used in health and social care dissertations. You should read this chapter with your research problem and question in mind, so that you can select the most promising approaches for further investigation. As data collection must be rigorous to ensure that you have enough of the right data, you will undoubtedly need to do further reading on your chosen methods in books providing more comprehensive guidance. A list is provided at the end of this chapter. Use this chapter as a basic introduction to the variety of methods available to you.

Research methods

One of the main points of doing a dissertation is to gain some experience of applying research methods – valuable marks are allotted for this.

Box 14.1 illustrates some of the primary data collection methods that are commonly used in dissertations in health and social care research. Clearly some research questions in health and social care research benefit from taking a mixed method approach, combining both qualitative and quantitative data collection techniques. Above all, the methods selected should be appropriate to the particular question being asked and must at all costs be applied in a rigorous and sensitive way.

Box 14.1   Primary data collection methods

Questionnaires
Interviews
Focus groups
Standardized scales and tests
Experiments
Observational methods
Measuring tools i.e. physiological measures

Questionnaires

The asking of questions is an obvious method of collecting both quantitative and qualitative information from people. Using a questionnaire enables you to organize the questions and receive replies without actually having to talk to every respondent. As a method of data collection, the questionnaire is a very flexible tool, but you must use it carefully in order to fulfil the requirements of your research. While there are whole books on the art of questioning and questionnaires, it is possible to isolate a number of important factors to consider before deciding to use a questionnaire.

Before examining the form and content of a questionnaire, let us briefly consider why you might choose this form of data collection, and the ways in which you could deliver the questionnaire.

One of the main features of a questionnaire is its impersonality. The questions are fixed, that is, do not change according to how the replies develop. They are the same for each respondent and the person posing the questions is remote. The responses can be completely anonymous, allowing potentially embarrassing questions to be asked with a fair chance of getting a true reply. Another feature is that there are no geographical limitations: the respondents can be anywhere in the world as long as they can be reached by post or via the Internet. Questionnaires can be a relatively economic method, in cost and time, of soliciting data from a large number of people. Time for checking facts and for pondering on the questions can also be taken by the respondents, which tends to lead to more accurate information.

Developing a questionnaire

Here are some simple rules to devising a questionnaire. It is not always easy to carry them out perfectly.

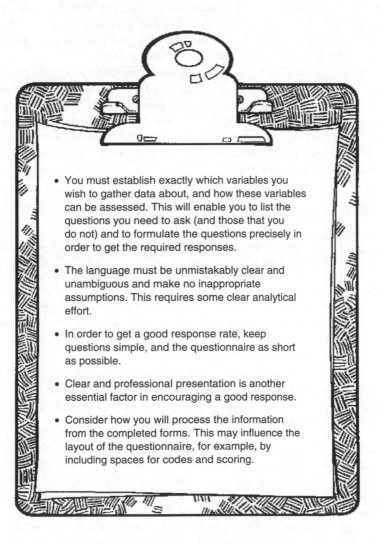

- You must establish exactly which variables you wish to gather data about, and how these variables can be assessed. This will enable you to list the questions you need to ask (and those that you do not) and to formulate the questions precisely in order to get the required responses.

- The language must be unmistakably clear and unambiguous and make no inappropriate assumptions. This requires some clear analytical effort.

- In order to get a good response rate, keep questions simple, and the questionnaire as short as possible.

- Clear and professional presentation is another essential factor in encouraging a good response.

- Consider how you will process the information from the completed forms. This may influence the layout of the questionnaire, for example, by including spaces for codes and scoring.

It is a good idea to pre-test the questionnaire on a small number of people before you use it in the main study. This is called a pilot study. If you can, test it on people of a type similar to that of the intended sample to anticipate any problems of comprehension or other sources of confusion. You will get some good marks for this.

It is good practice, when sending out or issuing the questionnaire, to courteously invite the recipients to complete it, and encourage them by explaining the purpose of the survey in a covering letter or email, how the results could be of benefit to them, and how little time it will take to complete. Include simple instructions on how to complete the responses. Some form of thanks and appreciation of their efforts should be included at the end. If you need to be sure of a response from a particular person, send a preliminary letter, with a reply-paid response card, to ask if he/she is willing to complete the questionnaire before you send it.

For the actual design of the questionnaire, you should consult books that deal with this in detail. This will speed up the process and help you to avoid common pitfalls. If you get it right you have a good foundation for your data collection. See later for useful references.

A useful and simple-to-use program for compiling and analysing questionnaires is called PinPoint 3. This might be available to you on your university network. It provides standard formats for setting up the questions, with response boxes and integrated coding systems that allow analysis later. When you have the responses, you can simply type them onto the chosen questionnaire format and the press of a button will produce graphs that display the results.

Delivering questionnaires

There are three basic methods of delivering questionnaires: *personally*, by *post* and via the *Internet*.

Personal   The advantages of personal delivery are that you can help respondents to overcome difficulties with the questions, and that you can use your own personality and reminders to ensure a high response rate. You can also find out the reasons why some people refuse to answer the questionnaire, and you can check on responses if they seem odd or incomplete. This personal involvement enables you to devise more complicated questionnaires. Obviously, there are problems both in time and in geographical location that limit the scope and extent to which you can use this method of delivery.

Postal   Postal questionnaires do not suffer from the limitations of time and geographical location. However, the most serious problem with postal questionnaires is that the rate of response is difficult to predict or control, particularly if there is no system of follow-up. Postal questionnaires are notorious for their low response rates. The pattern of non-response can have a serious effect on the validity of your sample by introducing bias into the data collected. Consider the cost in choosing postal distribution.

It might be your only method of questioning people spread over a large area or situated in relatively inaccessible regions. The key strategy that can be used to improve response rates, is to office code the questionnaires and use follow ups or reminders. The chief advantages of using postal surveys are that they are a fairly cheap method of gathering data and require a lot less time and energy to administer than Internet-surveys and interviews.

Internet   Internet-administered surveys are becoming increasingly popular, particularly for market research purposes. They can be distributed via:

- a simple Email survey with questions in the main body of the email;
- by emailing an Internet link directly to potential respondents;
- by setting up a website and posting a survey on the site.

Internet survey tools to assist in the development of web-based surveys are widely available online, with some even being free for very simple tools. If you are interested in exploring these further, run a quick online search using 'Internet survey tools' or check out some of the references to Internet research methods at the end of the chapter.

While Internet surveys can be helpful in enabling researchers to reach a large number of respondents spread over a wide geographical area, they are not without limitations. Learning to use online software and setting up a questionnaire can take a considerable amount of time and effort. It can take a lot of time either to email a group of potential respondents or set up a web-posted survey and advertise the link. Response rates can be low. It is generally thought that email surveys are more likely to gain higher response rates than web-posted surveys (Hewson et al., 2003). Response rates may also be improved by keeping the questionnaire content simple and the completion time short. People dislike complicated layouts and spending a long time reading on screen, others worry about confidentiality and whether their personal details can be identified. One of the main problems with web-posted surveys is the 'lack of a sampling frame'; while you may get 150 completed questionnaires, this may account for only a small percentage of visitors to the website and it is impossible to assess how representative your sample is, as there may be an over-representation from frequent or other users (Hewson et al., 2003: 8)

Interviews

While questionnaire surveys are relatively easy to organize, and prevent the personality of the interviewer having effects on the results, they do have certain limitations. They are not suitable for questions that require probing to obtain adequate information, as they should only contain simple, one-stage questions. It is often difficult to get responses from the complete sample; questionnaires tend to be returned by the more literate sections of the population, or people who feel very strongly about the issue under study.

The use of interviews to question samples of people is a very flexible tool with a wide range of applications. Because of their flexibility, interviews are a useful method of obtaining information and opinions from experts during the early stages of your research project. Though suitable for quantitative data collection, they are particularly useful when qualitative data are required. There are two main methods of conducting individual interviews: face-to-face and telephone.

Face-to-face interviews

Face-to-face interviews can be carried out in a variety of situations: in the home, at work, outdoors, on the move (e.g. while travelling). They can be used to question members of the general public, health and social care experts or leaders, specific groups of society, for example, elderly or disabled people, ethnic minorities, both singly and in groups. Interviews can be used for subjects both general or specific in nature, and even, with the correct preparation, for very sensitive topics. They can be one-off or repeated several times over a period to track developments. As the interviewer, you are in a good position to judge the quality of the responses, to notice if a question has not been properly understood and to encourage the respondent to be detailed in his/her answers. Using visual signs, such as nods and smiles, helps to get good responses.

Telephone interviews

Telephone interviews avoid the necessity of travelling to the respondents, and all the time and problems associated with contacting people in person. They are particularly useful for gathering data from respondents based across a wide geographical area. Telephone surveys can be carried out more quickly than face-to-face interviews, especially if the questionnaire is short (20–30 minutes at the most). However, you cannot use visual aids to explain questions, and there are no interpersonal cues such as eye contact, smiling, puzzled looks between you and the interviewee. Voice quality is an important factor in successful phone interviews. You should speak rapidly and loudly, using standard pronunciation and sounding competent and confident. For telephone interviews where possible, it is good practice to pre arrange a suitable time to ring – but do be punctual.

Different types of interview structure

How you structure the interview depends on the type of information you wish to collect. If you want very precise answers to very precise questions, perhaps for statistical analysis, then use a tightly structured interview with closed questions similar to a questionnaire. At the other extreme, if you want to explore a situation and get information that you cannot foresee, then an open and unstructured form of interview is best. A semi-structured interview falls between the two, achieving defined answers to defined questions, while including more open-ended questions for issues to be explored.

The most important point when you set up an interview is to know exactly what you want to achieve by it, how you are going to record the information and what you intend to do with it. Although there is a great difference in technique for conducting interviews 'cold' with the general public and interviewing professional experts by appointment, in both cases the personality and bearing of the interviewer are of great importance. You should be well prepared in the groundwork (i.e. writing letters for appointments, explaining the purpose of the interview), in presenting the interview with confidence, friendliness and good appearance, gathering the appropriate written consents and in the method of recording the responses (digital recording, writing field notes, completing forms, etc.).

Focus groups

A focus group is where a group of people are interviewed together to explore in-depth a particular topic. Focus groups, sometimes called 'group discussions' are led by the interviewer (sometimes referred to as the moderator) who guides the discussion around pre-determined topics. The moderator needs to be a skilled communicator to ensure that there is fair representation among the group members and to ensure that no one person dominates the group discussion and at the same time facilitating less vocal participants to speak (Krueger and Casey, 2008). This method of qualitative data collection is increasingly popular in health and social care research, as it provides an opportunity to obtain the views of several participants at one time. It is generally recommended that groups should be homogenous e.g. similar age group or client group, as too diverse a group may mean that responses are not representative and participants may feel less secure and less able to contribute. The optimum size of a focus group is between seven and 10 participants.

A strength of focus groups is that they can promote lively and stimulating interaction and discussion and may explore aspects of a topic that may not have been raised in an individual interview. Participants often enjoy taking part in focus group discussions and can feel stimulated by the experiences and views of other people. It is a relatively cheap method and time efficient for the researcher. On a practical level focus groups can be quite difficult to organize in terms of getting groups of people together at a time which suits everyone, this is particularly the case with busy health and social care practitioners who may commit to attending a focus group, but may have to pull out on the day when faced with unexpected events in practice (Appleton et al., 2001). Potentially the group's discussion may be dominated by one or two individuals. To counter this it is advisable to facilitate the group to negotiate some 'ground rules' prior to starting the discussion to enable people to identify their expectations. The 'moderator' is responsible for facilitating group dynamics and guiding the discussion in order to ensure representation from all participants (Krueger and Casey, 2008).

Generally it is recommended that focus groups are recorded, and that in addition, written notes are also taken by an observer, who may also comment on group dynamics. Since the information must come directly from the focus group respondents, the moderator must take care to avoid leading questions, excessive guidance and other factors which may cause distortion. Following each focus group, the recorded discussion should be fully transcribed and the working transcripts coded and analysed. There is more about this in Chapter 16.

Standardized scales and tests

A wide range of standardized scales and tests have been devised by social scientists and psychologists to establish people's abilities, attitudes, aptitudes and opinions. A well-known example of one of these is the IQ or intelligence test, other examples relevant to health and social care include Goodman's (1997), the Strengths and Difficulties Questionnaire, The Parenting Stress Index (PSI) (Abidin, 1995) and the Hospital Anxiety and Depression Scale (HADS) (Zigmond and Snaith, 1983; Snaith, 2003). The objective of the tests is usually to measure in some way the characteristics, abilities or behaviour of the respondents according to a standardized scale, so that easy comparisons can be made. One of the main problems is to select or devise a suitable scale for measuring the often rather abstract concepts under investigation, such as attitude (e.g. to school meals, parenting, capital punishment, etc.).

It is safer to use tried and tested standard scales, of which there are several, each taking different approaches according to the results aimed at. One of the most commonly used is the Likert scale which has a summated rating approach. Here is an example of a Likert scale so that you get the idea of what it is like:

Strongly agree 1 2 3 4 5 Strongly disagree.

The 'questions' are expressed as statements (e.g. women should be able to choose where to give birth) and the respondent is asked to ring one of the numbers in the scale 1–5 from strongly agree to strongly disagree. Another way of expressing the same thing is just to use words:

Strongly agree. Agree. Uncertain. Disagree. Strongly disagree.

You can use any dichotomous combination such as like/dislike, satisfied/satisfied, want/not want, probable/improbable. You just have to be careful that there are gradations of the opinion or feelings, unlike accept/reject, which is either one or the other. As an alternative to five, you can have three or seven stages (best to keep to odd numbers so that you get a middle value).

You can see that a score is automatically given by the response, so you can easily count the number of different scores to analyse the results. A useful precaution to prevent oversimplification of responses is to ask many questions about the same topic, all from different angles. This form of triangulation helps to build up a more complete picture of complex issues. You can then also weight the results from the different questions: that is, give more importance to those that are particularly crucial by multiplying them by a chosen factor.

Other scales used in health and social care research include the *semantic differential scale* and the *visual analogue scale*. The semantic differential scale was developed by Osgood et al. (1957) to measure beliefs and attitudes. A seven-point scale usually used with two opposing adjectives, such as hot/cold or strong/weak. The respondent is asked to place a tick at the appropriate place along the scale. An example is given below:

Example of a semantic differential scale

Question: How would you rate the student's performance in practice?

Excellent	1	2	3	4	5	6	7	Very poor

The semantic differential scale is very flexible and quite easy to develop. However care must be taken to ensure that the pair of adjectives selected are measuring the same dimension, or part of the same concept and are mutually exclusive (Oppenheim, 1992).

The visual analogue scale (VAS) is increasingly used in health care clinical settings and particularly in nursing and clinical therapy, to measure patients' subjective experiences for example, pain, fatigue and nausea. The VAS is similar to the semantic differential scale, but rather than having gradations on a scale, it is a straight line (placed either vertically or horizontally) usually 100 cm in length, with extreme limits of responses to the concept being measured at either end. Respondents can place their response anywhere on the line. See the example below:

Example of a visual analogue scale

No pain ————————————————————————Pain is unbearable.

While visual analogue scales are fairly easy to construct and can be useful for measuring changes over a period time, they are widely recognized as being difficult to interpret.

Observation

Observation is a method of recording conditions, events and activities through looking, not asking. In research, the aim is to take a detached view of the phenomena, and be 'invisible', either in fact or in effect (i.e. by being ignored). When observation takes place in the natural setting, it is unstructured, the researcher is often actively engaged in the situation under study and therefore adopts a participant observation role. Observation can also be used for recording the nature or conditions of objects, for example, hospital buildings. This type of observation is often referred to as a survey, and can range from a preliminary visual survey to a detailed survey using a range of instruments for measurement.

Health and social care practitioners are well versed in using observation skills as many aspects of patient/client care require skilled observation and measurement skills, for example, measurement of vital signs and wound assessment. As an activity, as opposed to a method, observation is of course required in many research situations, for example, observing the results of experiments, or the reactions of people to questions in an interview. Observation can be used to record both quantitative and qualitative data.

The researcher can observe behaviour or events taking place as they occur. Observation can record whether people act differently to what they say or intend. They can sometimes demonstrate their understanding of a process better by their actions than by verbally explaining their knowledge. For example, a radiographer may probably demonstrate more clearly his/her understanding of the techniques of operating an X-ray machine by working with it than by verbal explanation. Observation is not limited to the visual sense. Any sense – smell, touch, hearing – can be involved, and these need not be restricted to the range perceptible by the human senses, for example, a microscope can be used to extend the capacity of the eye.

On the one hand, observations of objects can be a quick and efficient method of gaining preliminary knowledge or making a preliminary assessment of their state or condition. On the other hand, observation can be very time consuming and difficult when the activity observed is not constant (i.e. much time can be wasted waiting for things to happen, or so much happens at once that it is impossible to observe it all and record it). Instrumentation can sometimes be devised to overcome the problem of infrequent or spasmodic activity, for example, automatic cameras or video recordings. The use of such recording devices can increase accuracy and can enable recorded observations to be reviewed. In unstructured observation, field notes (jotted notes written inconspicuously during the observation period) provide descriptive observation data and a record of events as they occur (Lofland and Lofland, 1995), while structured observation methods use checklists or rating scales to record behaviours or events using pre-defined categories.

Gathering data through observation

Here are a few basic hints on how to carry out observations:

- Make sure you know what you are looking for. Events and objects are usually complicated and much might seem to be relevant to your study. Identify the variables that you need to study, and concentrate on these.

- Devise a simple and efficient method of recording the information accurately. Rely as much as possible on ticking boxes or circling numbers, particularly if you need to record fast-moving events. Obviously, you can leave yourself more time when observing static objects to notate or draw the data required. Record the observations as they happen. Memories of detailed observations fade quickly.

- Use instrumentation when appropriate or necessary. Instruments that make an automatic record of their measurements are to be preferred in many situations.

- If possible, process the information as the observations progress. This can help to identify critical matters that need study in greater detail, and others that prove to be unnecessary.

- Covert observation is really to be avoided.

Experiments

The world around us is so complicated that it is often difficult to observe a particular phenomenon without being disturbed by all the other events happening around us. Wouldn't it be useful to be able to extract that part of the world out of its surroundings and study it in isolation? You can sometimes do this by setting up an experiment in which only the important factors (variables) that you want to consider are selected for study. This enables you to manipulate the variables in order to see what happens if you make certain changes. The results can then be used to collect data on the observed phenomenon, which in turn can be analysed, often providing information to form the basis of further testing. Experiments are used in many subject areas, but particularly those that are based on things or the interaction between things and people ('things' include systems or techniques as well as objects or substances).

There are many locations where experiments can be carried out, but the laboratory situation is the one that provides the greatest possibilities for control. Checks should be carried out on experiments to test whether the assumptions made are valid. In experiments, a control group is used to provide a 'baseline' against which the effects of the experimental treatment may be evaluated. The control group is one that is identical (as near as possible) to the experimental group, but does not receive experimental treatment (for example, in a medical experiment, the control group will be given placebo pills instead of the medicated pills). As you see in this example, experiments are not only a matter of bubbling bottles in a laboratory. They can involve people as well as things – only it is more difficult to control the people!

Experimental designs

Generally, experiments are designed and carried out in order to examine causes and effects (studying dependent and independent variables), and are used to find explanations for them – e.g. what happens if, and why? The design of the experiments depends on the type of data required, the level of reliability of the data required, and practical matters associated with the problem under investigation.

There is plenty of scope for setting up experiments that so simplify, and even falsify, the phenomenon extracted from the real world that completely wrong conclusions can be arrived at. This is why it is important to briefly explain the different kinds of experiment that can be set up, and the strength of the conclusions that can be drawn from the observations. Campbell and Stanley (1963: 171–246) divided experiments into four general types:

- pre-experimental designs;
- true experimental designs;
- quasi-experimental designs;
- correlational and *ex post facto* designs.

To explain how they work, here is a brief summary of the different designs commonly used in health and social care research under these headings. These are illustrated with an example using the following hypothesis: mental health practitioners who complete a training course on safeguarding children have improved levels of knowledge about categories of abuse.

Pre-experimental designs

One-shot case study (after only)   This is the most primitive type of design where observations are carried out only after the experiment, lacking any control or check.

- **Example** – A group of mental health nurses who completed a training course on safeguarding children had their knowledge levels about categories of abuse tested after the course. Conclusion: we have a measure of the group's knowledge levels after the course, but we cannot conclude a great deal from this, because we do not know what the mental health nurses' knowledge levels were in the first place.

One-group pre-test/post-test (before–after)   Here the subject (group) is examined before the experiment takes place and afterwards, but there is no control group.

- **Example** – Mental health nurses' knowledge levels of categories of abuse are measured before the intervention (the training course) and afterwards. Conclusion: while there may be a significant increase in knowledge levels following the course, this may be due to the assessment process itself, as the mental health nurses might have gained knowledge from the test process. There might also be other explanations for the improvements noted.

The trouble with these designs is the lack of control of the variables, which can seriously affect the study outcomes, for example, a case of child abuse in clinical practice or a change of job.

True experimental designs

Pre-test/post-test control group (before–after)   This is the commonest true experimental design.

- **Example** – Two groups of mental health practitioners are selected in the same random procedure, and knowledge levels about categories of abuse tested. They are then allocated to either an intervention group who receive the independent variable (a safeguarding training programme) or a control group (who receive no training). The groups' knowledge levels about categories of child abuse are tested again and the results (the dependent variables) are compared. Best results are gained if both samples achieve identical results in the pre-test.

Solomon four-group (before–after)   This is a refinement of the previous design, using four samples, which additionally tests the effects of the pre-test.

- **Example** – Four groups of mental health practitioners are selected in the same random procedure. This design divides the randomly selected set of subjects into four groups: two groups receive the intervention and two do not. Two groups undergo a pre-test and two do not. Two groups are pre-tested on their knowledge levels about categories of abuse, one group receives the intervention the safeguarding training course. Of the two groups not pre-tested, one receives the safeguarding training programme and the other does not. All four groups are tested at the end of the study period on their knowledge levels about categories of child abuse and the results compared. This is a more complex study design, but it will be detectable if the pre-testing of two of the groups affected their subsequent performance by comparing them with those mental health practitioners who were not pre-tested. This design is more robust than other experimental designs but the analysis of the results is more complex; it also requires a sample size twice that of other experimental designs.

Post-test only, control group (after only)   This is used when a pre-test is not possible, such as in a one-off situation like admission to a coronary care unit (CCU) or during a one-off course.

- **Example** – Two groups of mental health nurses are selected in the same random procedure. One is allocated to either an intervention group who receive the independent variable (a safeguarding training programme) or a control group (who receive no training). Both are tested for their knowledge levels about categories of child abuse and the results compared. The validity of this test critically depends on the randomness of the sample.

Quasi-experimental designs

These types of experiments are undertaken when it is not possible to fulfil all the elements of a true experiment, that is, they lack either randomization or a control group.

Non-randomized control group, pre-test/post-test   When random selection cannot be achieved, the control group and the experimental group should be matched as nearly as possible.

- **Example** – Two similar groups of mental health practitioners have their knowledge levels about categories of child abuse tested. They are then allocated to either an intervention group who receive the independent variable (a safeguarding training programme) or a control group (who receive no training). The groups' knowledge levels about categories of child abuse are tested again and the results (the dependent variables) are compared.

Time-series experiment   Repeated identical experiments are made. Then one variable is changed to produce a new outcome, and the new experiment is repeated, to check if the variable consistently creates the changed outcome.

- **Example** – A group of mental health practitioners are repeatedly tested about their knowledge around categories of child abuse. The group then attend a safeguarding training programme, and the groups' knowledge levels are repeatedly tested after the course. The danger with this design is that, over time, other unknown factors might affect the results.

Control group, time series   The same process as above, but with a parallel control group which does not undergo the variable change.

- **Example** – As above but with a parallel group that does not attend a safeguarding training programme and is used to compare outcomes.

Correlational and *ex post facto* designs

It is worth pointing out that many textbooks, unlike Campbell and Stanley (1963), regard these as non-experimental designs.

Correlational Can be used to describe or predict associations between variables. This is prone to misuse. After a correlation between two factors is statistically proved, a claim is made that one factor has caused the other. Life is rarely so simple. Correlation does not imply causation – more robust designs are needed to determine this. There may be many other factors that have not been recognized in the research, one, or some of which could be the cause, or could have contributed to the cause.

Ex post facto This is not really an experimental approach in that the investigation begins after the event has occurred, so no control over the event is possible. These designs can be retrospective (a group's history can be traced backwards in time) or prospective (follow a group forward in time). The search for the cause of the event, for example, a plane crash or the outbreak of an unknown disease, relies on the search for and analysis of relevant data. The most likely cause has to be discovered from among all possible causes, so there are many opportunities to search in the wrong area. This is a common form of scientific investigation, and needs the skills of a detective in addition to those of a scientist.

Internal and external validity

In order for the experiment to be of any use, it must be possible to generalize the results beyond the confines of the experiment itself. For this to be the case, the experiment should really reflect the situation in the real world – that is, it should be valid. The level of sophistication of the design and the extent of control determine the *internal validity* of the experimental design, and the extent of the legitimate generalizability of the results gives a rating for the *external validity* of the design.

Cohen et al. (2007: 135–7) have listed the factors which cause a threat to internal and external validity, and which are worth summarizing briefly here. First, those affecting internal validity:

- History – unnoticed interfering events between pre-test and post-test observations may affect the results.

- Maturation – when studied over time, the subjects of the experiment may change in ways not included in the experimental variables, for example, samples deteriorate with age.

- Statistical regression – the tendency for extreme results in the tests to get closer to the mean in repeat tests.

- Testing – pre-tests can inadvertently alter the original properties of the subject of the experiment.

- Instrumentation – faulty or inappropriate measuring instruments and short-comings in the performance of human observers lead to inaccurate data.

- Selection – bias may occur in the samples owing to faulty or inadequate sampling methods.

- Experimental mortality – dropout of experimental subjects (not necessarily through death) during the course of a long-running experiment tends to result in bias in what remains of the sample.

And second, those affecting external validity:

- Vague identification of independent variables – subsequent researchers will find it impossible to replicate the experiment.

- Faulty sampling – if the sample is only representative of what (or who) is available in the population rather than of the whole population, the results cannot be generalized to that whole population.

- Hawthorne effect – people tend to react differently if they know that they are the subject of an experiment.

- Inadequate operationalization of dependent variables – faulty generalization of results beyond the scope of the experiment.

- Sensitization to experimental conditions – subjects can learn ways of manipulating the results during an experiment.

- Extraneous factors – these can cause unnoticed effects on the outcome of the experiment, reducing the generalizability of the results.

If doing an experiment is appropriate, then you will have to decide what kind of experimental design is possible in the circumstances. This will depend on the availability of type and number of materials or subjects, timing, test facilities, practical opportunities and so forth. When you have judged what is possible, then consider how reliable the resulting data will be. Even if they are not 100% reliable, you may be able to argue that they are the best possible in the circumstances and that they will still be useful despite being subject to certain caveats. Also try to predict how the results of the experiments will help you to find answers to your research problem and question.

What should I do next?

Having waded through this rather long chapter, you will have got a good idea of what your options are for getting hold of the necessary data required for your dissertation research. What you really need to decide now is just what data you will have to gather, and then choose suitable data collection methods. You will probably find that your project is not so simple as to require only one data collection method. In all cases, secondary data will be required, if only to provide some background information on which to base the research. Occasionally you might need to use two or three different methods for data collection, one for each aspect of your investigations, or to triangulate the information on just one subject.

For example, if you were studying the effect of particular television programmes on children's play habits, you might want to make observations and set up questionnaires to get the children's and their parents' view; consult statistics about publicity and toy and video sales to get data about the promotion of the programmes; and read previous research on the subject to find methodological approaches to studying this subject; and so on.

A good way to approach primary data collection is to ask yourself the following questions:

- Who/what/where are the different people/things/phenomena that need to be investigated?

- In each case, what sort of data are needed?

- In each case, what is the best method for obtaining those data?

You should make a list of the answers to the above questions, and then see how you could organize the data collection in a manageable way. You will quickly see whether it is practicable to do everything on the list. Consider not only the amount of data you need to collect (e.g. how many questions you need to ask of how many people) but also the issues of where you have to go, and when and how you can get access to the information. Don't attempt too much – you will stress yourself out. Rather, narrow the scope of the research to ensure that it can be reasonably completed on time. For example, in the television programme project above, you could restrict your investigations to the children's perspective, and avoid the commercial and production aspects.

The results of your deliberations can now be fed into your project plan, with time allocated for each data collection task.

Further reading

There are hundreds of books about data collection methods. In addition, there are the examples in previous dissertations, which you can consult for more information about the nature of data collected and use of methods. Also have a look at a few of the books below which examine in more detail different aspects of data collection. For more choice, look up key words such as interviews, questionnaires, survey research etc. in your library catalogue.

Here are some books on research in general. We have pointed out the sections on data, data collection, sampling and so forth which are useful because of their brevity:

Seale, C. (ed.) (2004) *Researching Society and Culture,* 2nd edn. London: Sage. See Chapter 13 on 'Doing Social Surveys'.

Holliday, A. (2007) *Doing and Writing Qualitative Research*, 2nd edn. London: Sage. Consult Chapters 4 and 5 for what counts as data and writing about data.

Fowler, F.J. (2008) *Survey Research Methods,* 4th edn. London: Sage. This book goes into great detail about all aspects of the subject of doing surveys. Good on sampling, response rates, methods of data collection – particularly questionnaires and interviews. Use it selectively to find out more about the particular methods you want to use. This book will also be useful later for analysis, and has a section on ethics too.

Robson, C. (2002) *Real World Research: A Resource for Social Scientists and Practitioner-Researchers,* 2nd edn. Oxford: Blackwell. Part III gives valuable information and advice on the tactics of data collection using a wide range of methods. See Chapter 10, pp. 292–308, for an explanation of standard scales.

Aldridge, A. (2001) *Surveying the Social World: Principles and Practice in Survey Research*. Buckingham: Open University Press. Another comprehensive book: find what you need by using the contents list and index.

Fink, A. (2003) *The Survey Kit,* 2nd edn. London: Sage. Ten volumes covering all aspects of survey research. This must be the ultimate.

Some books specifically on questionnaires:

Dillman, D.A. (2007) *Mail and Internet Surveys: The Tailored Design Method*, 2nd edn. Hoboken, NJ: Wiley and Sons Inc.

Frazer, L. (2000) *Questionnaire Design and Administration: A Practical Guide*. Chichester: Wiley.

Gillham, W.E. and William E.C. (2008) *Developing a Questionnaire,* 2nd edn. London: Continuum.

Oppenheim A.N. (1992) *Questionnaire Design, Interviewing and Attitude Measurement*, 2nd edn. London: Pinter Publishers. A classic and very useful text on questionnaire design.

Peterson, R.A. (2000) *Constructing Effective Questionnaires*. London: Sage Publications.

And a few books on interviewing:

Gubrium, J.F. and Holstein, J.F. (2002) *Handbook of Interview Research: Context and Method*. London: Sage Publications.

Keats, D.M. (2000) *Interviewing: A Practical Guide for Students and Professionals*. Buckingham: Open University Press.

Kvale, S. (2009) *InterViews: Learning the Craft of Qualitative Research Interviewing: An Introduction to Qualitative Research Interviewing*, 2nd edn. London: Sage Publications.

Wengraf, T. (2001) *Qualitative Research Interviewing: Biographic, Narrative and Semi-Structured*. London: Sage Publications.

And a couple on case studies:

Stake, R.E. (1995) *The Art of Case Study Research*. London: Sage Publications.

Yin, R.K. (2009) *Case Study Research: Design and Methods*, 4th edn. Thousand Oaks, CA: Sage Publications.

Some books dedicated to experimental methods:

Field, A. and Hole, G. (2003) *How to Design and Report Experiments*. London: Sage Publications.

McKenna, R.J. (1995) *The Undergraduate Researcher's Handbook: Creative Experimentation*. Needham Heights, MA: Allyn & Bacon.

Dean, Angela (1999) *Design and Analysis of Experiments*. New York: Springer.

Montgomery, Douglas C. (2008) *Design and Analysis of Experiments*, 7th edn. New York: John Wiley and Sons.

Finally some useful books on virtual methods:

Hewson, C., Yule, P., Laurent, D. and Vogel, C. (2003) *Internet Research Methods*. London: Sage Publications.

Hine, C. (ed.) (2005) *Virtual Methods: Issues in Social Research on the Internet*. Oxford: Berg.

Mann, C. and Stewart, F. (2000) *Internet Communication and Qualitative Research: A Handbook for Researching Online*. London. Sage Publications.

This is a useful website for examining online methods:

http://www.geog.le.ac.uk/ORM/

Chapter 15

How Do I Analyse Quantitative Data?

Chapter contents

- Raw data
- Refer to the research question
- Analysis according to types of data
- Quantitative analysis
- Parametric and non-parametric statistics
- Statistical tests: parametric
- Statistical tests: non-parametric
- Discussion of results
- What should I do next?
- Further reading

Raw data

The results of your survey, experiments, archival studies, or whatever methods you used to collect data about your chosen subject, are of little use to anyone if they are merely presented as raw data. It should not be the duty of the reader to try to make sense of them, and to relate them to your research questions or problems. It is up to you to use the information that you have collected to make a case for arriving at some conclusions. How exactly you do this depends on what kind of questions you raised at the beginning of the dissertation, and the directions you have taken in order to answer them.

The data you have collected might be recorded in different ways that are not easy to read or to summarize. Perhaps they are contained in numerous questionnaire responses, in handwritten laboratory reports, recorded speech, as a series of photographs or observations in a diary. It can be difficult for even you, who have done the collecting, to make sense of it all, let alone someone who has not been involved in the project.

The question now is how to grapple with the various forms of data so that you can present them in a clear and concise fashion, and how you can analyse the presented data to support an argument that leads to convincing conclusions. In order to do this you must be clear about what you are trying to achieve and the type of data you have collected, whether it be quantitative or qualitative.

Refer to the research question

This is a very good time to return to your research proposal, and to any revisions you might have made in the interim, to refocus on exactly what you intended to do so many weeks/months ago. What are the burning issues that you wanted to tackle? What were the stated aims of your research? What specific problem or question was raised? What sort of answers were you aiming at?

Now you can briefly review that information you have collected and assess whether you really have kept to the issues raised in the proposal. Are the data likely to produce the answers you were seeking? If you have not strayed from the intended route, then it is likely that you will be able to go on to analyse the data successfully as intended. But what if you feel that as time went by you got diverted from your original intentions, that unexpected events occurred that led you to consider different, perhaps more important issues, or that your interests were drawn to aspects about which you were not aware before? Now is the time to consider the best way ahead in the light of changed circumstances.

Your original proposal was not written in stone. You based it on the knowledge and understanding you had at the time. The process of collecting data about your subject has put you in a much stronger position to know more about the important issues in your chosen field. In order to produce a good dissertation, you must now reconsider the main aims of the research and revise them on the basis of your new direction. We presume that the changes will not be huge, more a realignment than a new beginning. But what is important is that you redefine questions or problems so that you will be able to produce some answers or solutions based on the data that you have collected. It is best to actually formulate these questions or problems in writing; you will need to discuss them anyway at the beginning of your dissertation. If you have already written the first chapters, review these in the light of your most recent thoughts.

Analysis according to types of data

There are several reasons why you may want to analyse data. Some of these are the same as the reasons why you wanted to do the study in the first place. Analytical methods enable you to:

- measure;

- make comparisons;

- examine relationships;

- make forecasts;

- test hypotheses;

- construct concepts and theories;

- explore;

- control;

- explain.

This book is much too short to be able to describe all the analytical methods possible. However, this chapter will review some of the main methods, and refer you to more specialized publications where you can get detailed instructions on how to carry out the analysis.

The common way to categorize data for both collection and analysis is to distinguish between quantitative and qualitative data (see Chapter 11). You must have done this already when you did your data collection. However, life is rarely as tidy as theory. You possibly have some of both types of data – not a bad thing as they can provide different perspectives on a subject. In fact, some of the analytical methods can be used both quantitatively and qualitatively. These are mentioned where appropriate. As the subject of analysis of primary data is rather large and of essential importance to your dissertation, it is spread over two chapters. This chapter continues with a discussion of quantitative analysis, and Chapter 16 describes the techniques of qualitative analysis. For those of you undertaking a critical review of the literature for your dissertation, see Chapter 12 for a discussion on critical appraisal methods.

Quantitative analysis

Quantitative analysis deals with numbers and uses mathematical operations to investigate the properties of data. The levels of measurement used in the collection of the data, that is, nominal, ordinal, interval and ratio (see Chapter 11), are an important factor in choosing the type of analysis that is applicable, as is the number of cases involved. Statistics is the name given to this type of analysis, and is defined in this sense as: 'the field of study that involves the collection and analysis of numerical facts or data of any kind' (Oxford Encyclopaedic Dictionary, 2002: 3010).

Most surveys result in quantitative data, such as the numbers of people who believed this or that, how many pre-school children have had which immunisations or levels of family income. However, not all quantitative data originate from surveys. For example, content analysis is a specific method of examining records of all kinds (e.g. radio and television programmes or films, documents or publications). A checklist is made to count how frequently certain ideas, words, phrases, images or scenes appear in order to be able to draw some conclusions from the frequency of their appearance (e.g. the perceptions of palliative care in the media).

One of the primary purposes of doing research is to describe the data and to discover relationships among events in order to describe, explain, predict and possibly control their occurrence. Statistical methods are a valuable tool to enable you to present and describe the data and, if necessary, to discover and quantify relationships. And you do not even have to be a mathematician to use these techniques, as user-friendly computer packages (such as Excel® and Statistical Package for the Social Sciences [SPSS®]) will do all the presentation and calculations for you. However, you must be able to understand the relevance and function of the various displays and tests in relation to your own sets of data and the kind of analysis required.

The most straightforward process is to describe the data in the form of tables, graphs and diagrams. For this, a spreadsheet program, such as Excel®, is quite sufficient. This will order and display the data in a compact form so that you can make comparisons, detect trends and measure amounts and combinations of amounts. If you do not know how to use a spreadsheet for this, attend a course of instruction or find a handbook to guide you.

If you need to do more sophisticated analysis, then there are a wide range of statistical techniques that you can employ using SPSS. Many tests bear exotic names like the Kruskal–Wallis test, Kendall's coefficient of concordance, chi-square and Kolmogorov–Smirnov tests. However, do not be put off by these, as you will only be required to use the most common ones and there are simple rules as to when and how they should be applied. Even so, it is always advisable to consult somebody with specialist statistical knowledge in order to check that you will be doing the right thing before you start. Also, attend a course, usually made available to you by your college or university, in the use of SPSS® or any other analysis program that is available to you. Also it is worth checking with your dissertation supervisor if there is a statistics learning pack for your dissertation module.

Another factor to be taken into account when selecting suitable statistical tests is the number of cases about which you have data. Generally, statistical tests are more reliable the greater the number of cases. Usually, more than about 20 cases are required to make any sense of the analysis, though some tests are designed to work with fewer. Always consult the instructions on this issue for the particular tests you want to use. It may affect your choice.

There is not space (or need) in this book to explain in detail the range of tests and their uses. There are many books that specialize in just this. It will, however, help your understanding if we give a general description of statistics and the various branches of the discipline.

Parametric and non-parametric statistics

The two major classes of statistics are parametric and non-parametric statistics. You need to understand the meaning of a parameter in order to appreciate the difference between these two types. A parameter of a population (i.e. the things or people you are surveying) is a constant feature that it shares with other populations. The most common one is the 'bell' or 'Gaussian' curve of a normal frequency distribution.

This parameter reveals that most populations display a large number of more or less 'average' cases with extreme cases tailing off at each end. For example, most people are of about average height, with those who are extremely tall or small being in a distinct minority. The distribution of people's heights shown on a graph would take the form of the normal or Gaussian curve.

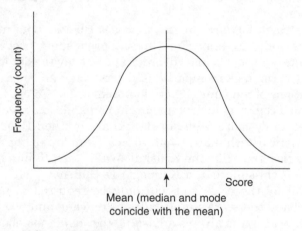

Figure 15.1   A Gaussian curve

Although the shape of this curve varies from case to case (e.g. flatter or steeper, lopsided to the left or right), this feature is so common amongst populations that statisticians take it as a constant – a basic parameter. Calculations of parametric statistics are based on this feature.

Not all data are parametric, that is, populations sometimes do not behave in the form of a Gaussian curve. Data measured by nominal and ordinal methods will not be organized in a curve form. Nominal data tend to be in the dichotomous form of either/or (e.g. male or female), while ordinal data can be displayed in the form of a set of steps (e.g. the first, second and third positions on a winners' podium). For those cases where this parameter is absent, non-parametric statistics may be applicable.

Non-parametric statistical tests have been devised to recognize the particular characteristics of non-curve data and to take into account these singular characteristics by specialized methods. In general, these types of test are less sensitive and powerful than parametric tests; they need larger samples in order to generate the same level of significance.

Statistical tests: parametric

The two classes of parametric statistical tests are descriptive and inferential.

Descriptive statistics

Descriptive statistics are primarily concerned with describing and organizing the data sample, for example, in tables, bar charts, histograms, pie charts, graphs, box plot and scatter diagrams. They are used all the time in health and social care practice to summarise data on for example patient or client groups, their age, gender and socio-economic background or the numbers and types of referrals to social care services. Descriptive statistics provide a method of quantifying the characteristics of the data, where their centre is, how broadly they spread and how one aspect of the data relates to another aspect of the same data. The 'centre of gravity' of the data, their point of central tendency, can be determined by finding the 'mode' or the 'median' and any one of several 'means'. These measures have their own characteristics and applications and should be chosen with regard to the data being analysed.

The measure of the dispersion (or spread) of the data, how flat or steep the Gaussian curve appears, is an indication of how many of the data closely resemble the mean. The flatter the curve, the greater is the amount of data that deviate from the mean, that is, the fewer that are close to the average. The horizontal length of the curve also gives an indication of the spread of values and the extent of the extremes represented in the data, while the occurrence of a non-symmetrical curve indicates a skewness in the data values.

Apart from examining the qualities of a single set of data, the main purpose of statistical analysis is to identify and quantify relationships between variables. This is the type of research called *correlation* research. But remember, the mere discovery and measurement of correlations is not sufficient on its own to provide research answers. It is the interpretation of these discoveries that provides the valuable knowledge that will give answers to your research question.

The technical term for the measure of correlation is the coefficient of correlation. There are many types of these, the Pearson *r* being the most common. It is possible to measure the correlation between more than two variables if you use the appropriate tests. However, be wary about assuming that, because a strong statistical correlation between variables can be demonstrated, there is necessarily a causal bond between the variables. It may be purely chance or the influence of other factors that, say, leads to areas of high-density development in cities having high crime rates. You must carefully question the assumptions on which such a causal assertion is made, and review the facts to examine if such a causality is verifiable in other ways.

Inferential statistics

Inferential statistical tests go beyond describing the characteristics of data and the examination of correlations between variables. Inferential statistics are 'concerned with the drawing of conclusions about a target population based on the analysis of data obtained from a random sample drawn from that population' (Banerjee, 2005: 2). As the name implies, they are used to produce predictions through inference, based on the data analysed. This entails making predictions about the qualities of a total population on the basis of the qualities of a sample. So the total population could be large or small, for example, all physiotherapists in the country or all the patients registered with one GP practice and a sample will be selected to draw conclusions about the total population. Inferential statistics can therefore be helpful to health and social care professionals wanting to make predictions about what could happen in future similar cases (Cluett, 2000). As with all predictions made from samples, the representative quality of the sample is crucial to accuracy, that is, the sample must be as typical as possible of the whole.

Statistical tests: non-parametric

Statistical tests built around discovering the means, standard deviations and so forth of the typical characteristics of a Gaussian curve are clearly inappropriate for analysing non-parametric data. Hence, non-parametric data cannot be statistically tested in the above ways.

There are tests that can be used to compare the qualities of two or more groups or samples, to analyse the rankings made by different judges, or to compare the data from observed and theoretical sources. Detailed information about which tests to use for particular data sets can be obtained from specialized texts on statistics and your own expert statistical adviser. Here is perhaps a good place to warn you that computer statistical packages (e.g. SPSS®) will not distinguish between different types of parametric and non-parametric data.

In order to avoid producing reams of impressive looking, but meaningless analytical output, it is up to you to ensure that the tests are appropriate for the type of data you have.

Discussion of results

Both spreadsheet and statistical programs will produce very attractive results in the form of charts, graphs and tables that you can integrate into your dissertation to back up your argument. The important issue is that you have carried out the appropriate analysis related to what you want to demonstrate or test. Explain what data you have collected, perhaps supplying a sample to show their form (e.g. a questionnaire return), give the reasons for doing the particular tests for each section of the investigation, and then present the results of the tests.

Graphs, tables and other forms of presentation always need to be explained. Do not assume that the reader will know how to read them and that they are self-explanatory in relation to your argument. Spell out in words the main features of the results and explain how these relate to the parts of the subproblems or subquestions that you are addressing. Now draw conclusions. What implications do the results have? Are they conclusive or is there room for doubt? Mention the limitations that might affect the strength of the result, for example, limited number of responses, possible bias or time constraints. Each conclusion will only form a small part of the overall argument, so you need to fit everything together like constructing a jigsaw puzzle. The full picture should clearly emerge at the end. It is best to devote one section or chapter to each of the subproblems or subquestions. Leave it to the final chapter to draw all the threads together in order to answer the main issue of the dissertation.

Computer programs provide you with enormous choice when it comes to presenting graphs and charts. It is best to experiment to see which kind of presentation is the clearest. Consider whether you will be printing in monochrome or colour, as different coloured graph lines will lose their distinctiveness when reduced to shades of grey. It is also a good idea to set up a style that you maintain throughout the dissertation.

What should I do next?

If you are not experienced in doing quantitative analysis and see the need to do it to analyse your findings, now is the time to learn. You will definitely need to go on a short course in using the relevant computer programs, such as spreadsheets and statistics. SPSS® is the most commonly used statistical package, and has become very user friendly, so you should experience few practical problems. Find out from your computer centre or library when the course takes place, and book yourself in.

One of your first jobs will be to enter all the data onto a spreadsheet, for example, all the answers to all the questions from the questionnaires. Before you embark on any actual analysis, first take time to examine the nature of your data and what kind of analysis you want to subject them to. Will you be measuring them, making comparisons or examining relationships? Are the data parametric or non-parametric? If you are doing some statistical tests, you will have to ensure that you select the right ones. This will require some reading about statistical tests and possibly getting some advice from staff. Do not become too ambitious: keep it simple and within your level of understanding. It is quite easy to get carried away with doing grandiloquent sounding tests as they are carried out just as fast as any other; but could you really explain what they are about?

Leave yourself plenty of time to discuss the results in writing and to work on the conclusions. This is, of course, the whole point of gathering all the data in the first place and making the effort to test them. One of the commonest faults in undergraduate dissertations is that the impressive displays of graphs, tables and charts are left for the reader to interpret. So relate the conclusions directly back to the questions asked or problems posed at the beginning of the dissertation, and check that your overall argument is still sound. Then you will have achieved the purpose of all your research work.

Further reading

The following book chapters give a brief introduction and overview of quantitative analysis and introductory statistics:

Denscombe, M. (2003) *The Good Research Guide for Small-Scale Research Projects*. Buckingham: Open University Press. See Chapter 13 on quantitative data analysis.
Robson, C. (1993) *Real World Research: A Resource for Social Scientists and Practitioner-Researchers*. Oxford: Blackwell. See Chapter 13.

For a more detailed, though straightforward, introduction to statistics, have a look at:

Preece, R. (1994) *Starting Research: An Introduction to Academic Research and Dissertation Writing*. London: Pinter. See Chapter 7.
Diamond, I. and Jeffries, J. (2000) *Beginning Statistics: An Introduction for Social Scientists*. London: Sage Publications. This book emphasizes description, examples, graphs and displays rather than statistical formula. A good guide to understanding the basic ideas of statistics.

For a comprehensive review of the subject see below. You could also have a browse through what is available on your library shelves to see if there are some simple guides there.

Byrne, D. (2002) *Interpreting Quantitative Data*. London: Sage Publications.
Kerr, A.W, Hall, H.K. and Kozub, S.A. (2002) *Doing Statistics with SPSS*. London: Sage Publications.

Wright, D.B. (2002) *First Steps in Statistics*. London: Sage Publications.

Useful guides to SPSS® include:

Colman, A.M. and Pulford, B.D.(2008) *A Crash Course in SPSS for Windows: Updated for Versions 14, 15, and 16,* 4th edn. Chichester: Wiley-Blackwell.

Greasley, P. (2008) *Quantitative Data Analysis with SPSS: An Introduction for Health and Social Studies*. Maidenhead: McGraw-Hill Education.

Chapter 16

How Do I Analyse Qualitative Data?

Chapter contents

- Qualitative research
- Qualitative data collection and analysis
- Preliminary analysis during data collection
- Typologies and taxonomies
- Pattern coding, memoing and interim summary
- Main analysis during and after data collection
- What should I do next?
- Further reading

Qualitative research

Doing research is not always a tidy process where every step is completed before moving on to the next. In fact, especially if you are doing it for the first time, you often need to go back and reconsider previous decisions or adjust and elaborate on work as you gain more knowledge and acquire more skills. But there are also types of research in which there is an essential reciprocal process of data collection and data analysis.

Qualitative research is the main one of these. This does not involve counting and dealing with numbers but is based more on information expressed in words – descriptions, accounts, opinions and feelings. This approach is common whenever people are the focus of the study, particularly small groups or individuals, but can also concentrate on more general beliefs or customs. Frequently it is not possible to determine precisely what data should be collected at the beginning of a study, as the situation or process is not sufficiently understood. Periodic analysis of collected data provides direction to further data collection. Adjustments to what is further looked at, what questions are asked and what actions are carried out are based on what has already been seen, answered and done. This emphasis on reiteration and interpretation is the hallmark of qualitative research.

Qualitative data collection and analysis

The essential difference between quantitative analysis and qualitative analysis is that with the former, you need to have completed your data collection before you can start analysis, while with the latter, analysis is carried out concurrently with data collection. With qualitative studies, there is a constant interplay between collection and analysis that produces a gradual growth of understanding. You collect information, review it, collect more data based on what you have discovered, then analyse again what you have found. This is quite a demanding and difficult process, and is prone to uncertainties and doubts. At the level of an undergraduate dissertation, you will have to be careful not to be too ambitious, as the restricted time you have does not allow for lengthy delving and pondering. Keep the study focused and limited in scope so that you can complete the process. The important criteria for the examiner will be whether you have correctly used the methods and whether your conclusions are based on evidence found in the data collected.

Bromley (1986: 26) provides a list of 10 steps in the process of qualitative research, summarized as follows:

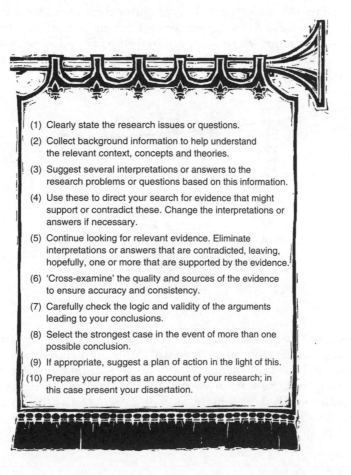

(1) Clearly state the research issues or questions.

(2) Collect background information to help understand the relevant context, concepts and theories.

(3) Suggest several interpretations or answers to the research problems or questions based on this information.

(4) Use these to direct your search for evidence that might support or contradict these. Change the interpretations or answers if necessary.

(5) Continue looking for relevant evidence. Eliminate interpretations or answers that are contradicted, leaving, hopefully, one or more that are supported by the evidence.

(6) 'Cross-examine' the quality and sources of the evidence to ensure accuracy and consistency.

(7) Carefully check the logic and validity of the arguments leading to your conclusions.

(8) Select the strongest case in the event of more than one possible conclusion.

(9) If appropriate, suggest a plan of action in the light of this.

(10) Prepare your report as an account of your research; in this case present your dissertation.

According to Robson, 'the central requirement in qualitative analysis is clear thinking on the part of the analyst' (2002: 459), where the analyst is put to the test as much as the data. Although it has been the aim of many researchers to make qualitative analysis as systematic and as 'scientific' as possible, there is still an element of 'art' in dealing with qualitative data. However, in order to convince others of your conclusions, there must be a good argument to support them. A good argument requires high-quality evidence and sound logic. In fact, you will be acting rather like a lawyer presenting a case, using a quasi-judicial approach such as used in an enquiry into a disaster or scandal.

Qualitative data, represented in words, pictures and even sounds, cannot be analysed by mathematical means such as statistics. So how is it possible to organize all these data and be able to come to some conclusions about what they reveal? Unlike the well-established statistical methods of analysing quantitative data, approaches to qualitative data analysis are still being developed and debated. The certainties of mathematical formulae and determinable levels of probability are not applicable to the 'soft' nature of qualitative data, which are inextricably bound up with human feelings, attitudes and judgements. Also, unlike the large amounts of data that are often collected for quantitative analysis, which can readily be managed with the available standard statistical procedures conveniently incorporated in computer packages, there are no such standard procedures for codifying and analysing qualitative data.

However, there are some essential activities that are necessary in all qualitative data analysis. Miles and Huberman (1994: 10–12) suggest that there are three concurrent flows of action:

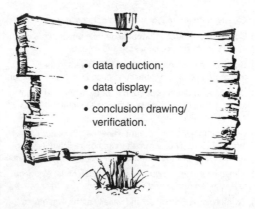

- data reduction;
- data display;
- conclusion drawing/ verification.

Data reduction 'refers to the process of selecting, focusing, simplifying, abstracting and transforming the data' (Miles and Huberman, 1994: 11), as the researcher elicits meanings and insights from field notes and transcripts. Data reduction involves data coding, writing summaries, establishing patterns and themes in the data. It is an inductive, highly interactive and iterative process, which requires the analyst to be extremely well organized and diligent. The activity of *data display* is important. The awkward mass of information that you will normally collect to provide the basis for qualitative analysis cannot be easily understood when presented as extended text, even when coded, clustered and summarized. Information in text is dispersed, sequential rather than concurrent, bulky and difficult to structure. Our minds are not good at processing large amounts of information, preferring to simplify complex information into patterns and easily understood configurations. Consequently, if you use suitable methods to display the data in the form of matrices, graphs, charts and networks, you not only reduce and order the data, but also can analyse it. *Conclusions* are verified as the analysis proceeds and confirmability (validity) of the data is tested.

Preliminary analysis during data collection

When you conduct qualitative research it is important that you keep a critical attitude to the type and amount of data being collected, and the assumptions and thoughts that brought you to this stage. It is always easier to structure the information while the details are fresh in the mind, to identify gaps, to allow new ideas and hypotheses to develop, and to challenge your assumptions and biases. Raw field notes, often scribbled and full of abbreviations, and tapes of interviews or events need to be transcribed and processed in order to make them useful. Much information will be lost if this task is left for long.

The process of data reduction and analysis should be a sequential and continuous procedure, simple in the beginning stages of the data collection, and becoming more complex as the project progresses. To begin with, one-page summaries can be made of the results of contacts, for example, phone conversations, visits. A standardized set of headings will prompt the ordering of the information: contact details, main issues, summary of information acquired, interesting issues raised, new questions resulting from these. Similar one-page forms can be used to summarize the contents of documents.

Typologies and taxonomies

As the data accumulate, a valuable step is to organize the shapeless mass of data by building typologies and taxonomies. These are technical words for the nominal level of measurement (remember Chapter 11), that is, ordering by type or properties, thereby forming subgroups within the general category.

Even the simplest classification can help to organize seemingly shapeless information and to identify differences in, say, behaviour or types of people. For example, children's behaviour in the playground could be divided into 'joiners' and 'loners', or nursing staff in the ward could be classified as charge nurses, staff nurses, student nurses and auxiliary nurses. This can help you to organize amorphous material and to identify patterns in the data. Then, noting the differences in terms of behaviour patterns between these categories can help you to generate the kinds of analysis that will form the basis for the development of explanations and conclusions.

This exercise in classification is the start of the development of a coding system, which is an important aspect of forming typologies. Codes are labels or tags used to allocate units of meaning to the collected data. Coding helps you to organize your piles of data (in the form of notes, observations, transcripts and documents) and to provide a first step in conceptualization, and helps to prevent 'data overload' resulting from mountains of unprocessed data in the form of ambiguous words.

Codes can be used to label different aspects of the subjects of study. Lofland, (1971: 14–16), for example, devised six classes on which you could devise a coding scheme for 'social phenomena':

- acts;
- activities;
- meanings;
- participation;
- relationships;
- settings.

The process of coding is analytical, and requires you to review, select, interpret and summarize the information without distorting it. Normally, you should compile a set of codes before doing the fieldwork, based on your background study, and then refine it during the data collection.

There are two essentially different types of coding, one that you can use for the retrieval of text sequences, the other devised for theory generation. The former refers to the process of cutting out and pasting sections of text from transcripts or notes under various headings. The latter is a more open coding system used as an index for your interpretive ideas – reflective notes or memos, rather than merely bits of text.

Several computer programs used for analysing qualitative data (such as Ethnograph and NVivo) also have facilities for filing and retrieving coded information. They allow codes to be attached to the numbered lines of notes or transcripts of interviews, and for the source of the information/opinion to be noted. This enables a rapid retrieval of selected information from the mass of material collected. However, it does take quite some time to master the techniques involved, so take advice before contemplating the use of these programs. It is also important to bear in mind that while these computer programs can help with data management, handling and retrieval, they do not do the analysis for you!

Pattern coding, memoing and interim summary

The next stage of analysis requires you to begin to look for patterns and themes, and explanations of why and how these occur. This requires a method of pulling together the coded information into more compact and meaningful groupings. Pattern coding can do this by reducing the data into smaller analytical units such as themes, causes/explanations, relationships among people and emerging concepts, to allow you to develop a more integrated understanding of the situation studied and to test the initial explanations or answers to the research issues or questions. This will generally help to focus later fieldwork and lay the foundations for cross-case analysis in multicase studies by identifying common themes and processes.

Miles and Huberman (1994: 70–1) describe three successive ways that pattern codes may be used:

- The newly developed codes are provisionally added to the existing list of codes and checked out in the next set of field notes to see whether they fit.

- Next, the most promising codes are written up in a memo (described below) to clarify and explain the concept so that it can be related to other data and cases.

- Finally, the new pattern codes are tested out in the next round of data collection.

Actually, you will find that generating pattern codes is surprisingly easy, as it is the way by which we habitually process information. However, it is important not to cling uncritically onto initially developed patterns, but to test and develop, and if necessary, reject them as your understanding of the data develops, and as new waves of data are produced.

Compiling memos is a good way to explore links between data and to record and develop intuitions and ideas. You can do this at any time – but it is best done when the idea is fresh! Remember that memos are written for yourself, so the length and style are not important, but it is necessary to label a memo so that it can be easily sorted and retrieved. You should continue the activity of memoing throughout the research project. You will find that the ideas become more stable with time until 'saturation' point, that is, the point where you are satisfied with your understanding and explanation of the data is achieved.

It is a very good idea, at probably about one-third way through the data collection, to take stock and seek to reassure yourself and your dissertation supervisor by checking:

- the quantity and quality of what you have found out so far;

- your confidence in the reliability of the data;

- the presence and nature of any gaps or puzzles that have been revealed;

- what still needs to be collected in relation to your time available.

This exercise should result in the production of an interim summary, a provisional report a few pages long. This report will be the first time that everything you know your data will be summarized, and presents the first opportunity to review emergent explanatory variables.

Remember however that the nature of the summary is provisional. Though it is perhaps sketchy and incomplete, it should be seen as a useful tool for you to reflect on the work done, for discussion with your dissertation supervisor, and for indicating any changes that might be needed in the coding and in the subsequent data collection work. In order to check on the amount of data collected about each research question, you will find it useful to compile a data accounting sheet. This is a table that sets out the research questions and the amount of data collected from the different informants, settings and situations. With this you will easily be able to identify any shortcomings.

Main analysis during and after data collection

Traditional text-based reports tend to be lengthy and cumbersome when presenting, analysing, interpreting and communicating the findings of a qualitative research project. Not only do they have to present the evidence and arguments sequentially, with selected quotations frequently used to illustrate meaning, reports also tend to be bulky and difficult to grasp quickly because information is dispersed over many pages.

This presents a problem for you, the writer, as well as for the final reader, who rarely has time to browse backwards and forwards through masses of text to gain full information. Graphical methods of data display and analysis can largely overcome these problems and are useful for exploring and describing as well as explaining the main emergent themes. They can be used equally effectively for one case and cross-case analysis.

Graphical displays fall into two categories: matrices or tables and networks.

Matrices or tables

The two-dimensional arrangement of rows and columns can summarize a substantial amount of information. You can easily produce these informally in a freehand fashion to explore aspects of the data, to any size. You can also use computer programs in the form of databases and spreadsheets to help produce summary tables (see Table 16.1 for an example of a summary table.). You can use matrices to record variables such as time, levels of measurement, roles, clusters, outcomes and effects. If you want to get really sophisticated, latest developments allow you to formulate three-dimensional matrices.

Networks

A network is made up of blocks (nodes) connected by links. You can produce these maps and charts in a wide variety of formats, each with the capability of displaying different types of data:

- Flowcharts are useful for studying processes or procedures. Not only helpful for explanation, their development is a good device for creating understanding.

- Organization charts display relationships between variables and their nature, for example, formal and informal hierarchies (see Figure 16.1 for an example of data analysis sub-categories).

- Causal networks are used to examine and display the causal relationships between important independent and dependent variables, causes and effects.

These methods of displaying and analysing qualitative data are particularly useful when you compare the results of several case studies, as they permit a certain standardization of presentation, allowing comparisons to be made more easily across the cases.

You can display the information in the form of text, codes, abbreviated notes, symbols, quotations or any other form that helps to communicate succinctly. The detail and sophistication of the display can vary depending

Table 16.1 Summary Table detailing ward staffing numbers (day time)

Hospital 'X'	Senior sister/ charge nurse	Junior sister/ charge nurse	Senior staff nurse	Staff nurse	Health care assistant	Student nurse
			Nursing staff numbers			
Ward A	1	2	1	3	2	5
Ward B	2	2	1	3	3	3
Ward C	1	2	0	3	2	3
Ward D	1	1	1	4	1	2
Ward E	1	1	1	3	3	4
Ward F	1	1	1	4	2	4
Ward G	1	0	2	4	3	2
Ward H	1	1	1	4	2	4

Figure 16.1 Example of an organizational chart (principle categories in a data analysis index system including major subcategories of the assessment category)

on its function and on the amount of information available. Displays are useful at any stage in the research process.

Ordering information in displays

The different types of display can be described by the way that information is ordered in them.

Time ordered displays These record a sequence of events in relation to their chronology. A simple example of this is a project programme giving names, times and locations for tasks of different kinds. The scale and precision of timing can be suited to the subject. Events can be of various types, for example, tasks, critical events, experiences, stages in a programme, activities and decisions.

Some examples of types of time ordered displays are:

- Events lists or networks – showing a sequence of events, perhaps highlighting the critical ones, and perhaps including times and dates.

- Activity records – showing the sequential steps required to accomplish a task.

- Decision models – commonly used to analyse a course of action employing a matrix with yes/no routes from each decision taken.

Conceptually ordered displays These concentrate on variables in the form of abstract concepts related to a theory and the relationships between these. Examples of such variables are motives, attitudes, expertise, barriers or coping strategies. They can be shown as matrices or networks to illustrate taxonomies, content analysis, cognitive structures, relationships of cause and effect, or influence.

Here is a selection of different types:

- Conceptually or thematically clustered matrix – helps to summarize the mass of data about numerous research questions by combining groups of questions that are connected, either from a theoretical point of view, or as a result of groupings that can be detected in the data.

- Taxonomy tree diagram – useful to break down concepts into their constituent parts or elements.

- Cognitive map – a descriptive diagrammatic plotting of a person's way of thinking about an issue, useful to understand somebody's way of thinking or to compare that of several people.

- Effects matrix – plots the observed effects of an action or intervention, a necessary precursor to explaining or predicting effects.

- Decision tree modelling – helps to make clear a sequence of decisions, by setting up a network of sequential yes/no response routes.

- Causal models – used in theory building to provide a testable set of propositions about a complete network of variables with causal and other relationships between them, based on a multicase situation. A preliminary stage in the development of a causal model is to develop causal chains, linear cause–effect lines.

Role ordered displays   These show people's roles and their relationships in formal and informal organizations or groups. A role defines a person's standing and position by assessing their behaviour and expectations within the group or organization. These may be conventionally recognized positions, for example, nurse, mother, social worker; or more abstract and situation dependent, for example, motivator or objector. People in different roles tend to see situations from different perspectives: a strike in a hospital will be viewed very differently by the management and the workforce. A role ordered matrix will help to systematically display these differences or can be used to investigate whether people in the same roles are unified in their views.

Partially ordered displays   These are useful in analysing 'messy' situations without trying to impose too much internal order on them. For example, a context chart can be designed to show, in the form of a network, the influences and pressures that bear on an individual from surrounding organizations and persons when making a decision to act. This will help to understand why a particular action was taken.

Case ordered displays   These show the data of cases arranged in some kind of order according to an important variable in the study. This allows you to compare cases and note their different features according to where they appear in the order.

If you are comparing several case studies, you can combine the above displays to make 'meta' displays that amalgamate and contrast the data from each case. For example, a case ordered meta-matrix does this by simply arranging case matrices next to each other in the chosen order to enable you to simply compare the data across the meta-matrix. The meta-matrix can initially be quite large if there are a number of cases. A function of the analysis will be to summarize the data in a smaller matrix, giving a summary of the significant issues discovered. Following this a contrast table can also be devised to display and compare how one or two variables perform in cases as ordered in the meta-matrix.

Illustrating key themes in diagrams

Another way of illustrating the relationship between key themes in a qualitative study is through the use of diagrams or illustrations. These can help to illustrate in a diagrammatic form the key patterns occurring in the data, their relationship and the resulting interpretive analysis. (See Figure 16.2).

What should I do next?

After reading the above information about qualitative data collection and analysis, how do you think the different techniques could be used in your dissertation? If you are focusing your work on people in health and social care settings, especially at the level of the individual or small groups, or on people's customs or beliefs, you will not be able to do your research by analysing numbers, you will have to deal with lots of information in the form of written material. As you will probably have gathered, the process can be quite complicated and difficult to do for the first time. It is a great help if you can use a previous qualitative research study as a model, perhaps to test out its methods and findings in a different context. For example, if you are interested in examining the factors that influence work motivation in an accident and emergency department, perhaps a research project has already been done on a similar topic but in a different hospital setting. This would provide useful guidance on the main variables to examine, and the practical techniques of data collection, display and analysis.

We suggest that you do the following things to get you on your way. Note how you will be building up an argument for doing your research the way you propose.

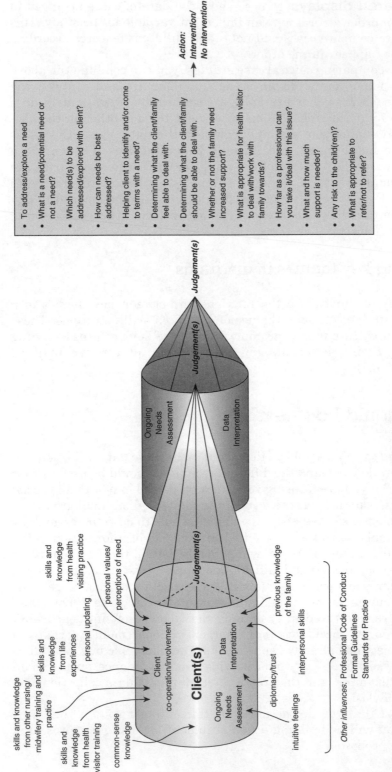

Figure 16.2 Process of health visitor judgement formation

Source: Appleton J.V. and Cowley S. (2003) 'Valuing professional judgement in health visiting practice', *Community Practitioner*, 76 (6): 215–20. Reproduced with the permission of Unite/CPHVA and Ten Alps Publishing.

- Think carefully about your dissertation topic and ask yourself: what is the nature of what you are going to investigate? Are the variables readily recognizable and easily measurable, and are there more than 20 or 30 cases in your study? If so, a quantitative approach is more suitable. Are the variables open to interpretation, difficult to measure, and are there only a few cases to examine? If yes, then you have to use qualitative research methods to examine these. Note that there may be aspects of your dissertation topic that fall into each of these categories. No problem: you will just have to use whichever type of method is appropriate for each of the aspects.

- If you think that a qualitative approach is appropriate for all or some of your research, examine what are the main factors at play. How are they described, for example, belief, loyalty or tradition?

- From your background reading, look for writings that specifically describe and explain investigations dealing with these factors, particularly those that were in your area of study. Examine these to see if there are methods used that you could adapt for your own work to get the answers you seek.

- Set up a plan of work to describe the sequence of data gathering and analysis, the types of activities you will undertake at each step, together with timing. This will help to ensure that you will not bite off more than you can chew. Obviously, there will be some uncertainties: point these out. If there are too many, the project could get horribly out of hand, so alter the setting, eliminate problem areas, find other more familiar ways, or even adjust the research questions to make the work more practicable and achievable.

If you can, it is really worth talking to your supervisor about your plan to discuss the practical and skill issues. Obviously, the clearer you can draw it up, the more use it will be. The main questions to ask are:

1   Is the plan practically possible with your time, skills and access to your study respondents?

2   Will it produce the answers to the questions posed by your project?

3   Will the project fulfil the requirements of the dissertation assignment?

If the answers are 'yes' to the above questions, then things are looking good. If you managed to get some feedback from your supervisor, make sure that you understood what he/she advised, and reflect how this advice might alter your work. Check again against the questions after you have made any alterations.

Further reading

As you would expect with this big and complex subject, there are a myriad books dedicated to explaining all aspects. In the list below, we have tried to explain a bit about each individual book and how it may be of use to you. We have ordered them in what we think is going from simplest to most sophisticated.

Denscombe, M. (2003) *The Good Research Guide for Small-Scale Research Projects*. Buckingham: Open University Press. See Chapter 14 on qualitative data analysis, for a brief introduction and overview of qualitative analysis.

Robson, C. (2002) *Real World Research: A Resource for Social Scientists and Practitioner-Researchers,* 2nd edn. Oxford: Blackwell. A resource book, and should be used as such. Good for getting more detailed information on most aspects of data collection and analysis. Read the recommendations at the beginning (p. xx) of how to use the book.

Flick, U. (2006) *An Introduction to Qualitative Research,* 3rd edn. London: Sage Publications. This book contains lots of really practical advice on the documentation, coding, interpretation and analysis of qualitative data in Parts 4–7. Be selective in picking out what is relevant to you, as a lot of it will not be.

Seale, C. (ed.) (2004) *Researching Society and Culture,* 2nd edn. London: Sage Publications. This edited book has chapters by various authors, each on one aspect of research. There are a number of chapters in Part II which consider qualitative analysis, you need to choose whatever is appropriate for your study.

For a really comprehensive though incredibly dense and rather technical guide to qualitative data analysis, refer to:

Miles, M.B. and Huberman, A.M. (1994) *Qualitative Data Analysis: An Expanded Sourcebook*. London: Sage Publications. This has a lot of examples of displays that help to explain how they work, but is technically sophisticated so you might find it difficult to understand the terminology in the examples.

And a few more books if you don't find what you want in the above. Your library catalogue will list many more.

Coffey, A. and Atkinson, P. (1996) *Making Sense of Qualitative Data: Complementary Research Strategies*. London: Sage Publications.

Silverman, D. (2001) *Interpreting Qualitative Data: Methods for Analysing Talk, Text and Interaction*, 2nd edn. London: Sage Publications.

Holliday, A. (2007) *Doing and Writing Qualitative Research*, 2nd edn. London: Sage Publications. A general guide to writing qualitative research aimed at students of sociology, applied linguistics, management and education.

Schwandt, T. (1997) *The Sage Dictionary of Qualitative Inquiry*, 3rd edn. Thousand Oaks, CA: Sage Publications. To help you understand all the technical jargon.

Chapter 17

What About Referencing?

Chapter contents

- Why should I bother with references?
- Keeping track
- Right ways of doing it
- How many references do I need?
- What should I do next?
- Further reading

Why should I bother with references?

Writing a dissertation is not an exercise in creative writing. You will not be relying on your imagination as a source of your text. Almost everything you write will need to be based on the work or evidence of others and on your own research work. At this level you will not be required to produce an original contribution to knowledge. You might generate some new data if you do empirical work or an audit study, and you will certainly have to express opinions and judgements that are genuinely your own. Your input will primarily be the building up of an argument or discussion from existing material, collected and organized by yourself. To do this you will need to read quite widely in order to study the background to your subject and to investigate what work has already been done in your chosen field. You will also need to consult textbooks about research methodology, and possibly track down relevant statistics and other data.

In order to record the sources of this information, and also to substantiate facts and claims that you make in your text, you must include citations within the text of your dissertation and make a list of references. The use of a sound referencing system is essential. It is also good academic practice, and if properly applied is bound to impress your examiner.

Not only does it demonstrate your high ethical standards, but it also gives a very good record of the number and type of books, journal articles and other publications to which you have referred during your study. Expect the examiner to know who the important writers are in the subject you have chosen, so you need to ensure that you have consulted the appropriate books and journal articles.

From an ethical point of view, correct referencing ensures that you do not pass off as your own any ideas, writings, diagrams or information created by someone else. In academic writing there is absolutely no shame associated with referring to, using or manipulating other people's work. In fact, much time is spent by academics doing just this. As long as you are 'up-front' and acknowledge your sources, you cannot be criticized. If you are reviewing existing ideas and knowledge on a subject, your text could legitimately be riddled with acknowledged excerpts and quotations. If, however, you are sloppy and forgetful, even unintentional borrowings are regarded as theft of intellectual property, commonly referred to as plagiarism. As you will see from your university or college regulations, penalties for plagiarism are stiff, and rightly so. It is not at all difficult to conform to the accepted standards of referencing, it just needs a bit of care and forethought.

Not only is referencing used to acknowledge the contribution of others to your text, it is also very useful as a guide to the reader to check on the quality of the sources and perhaps to acquire more detailed information. The best test of a referencing system is to try to find the original information, opinion, or idea referred to from the reference information given. For example, if you quote that 23 per cent of school leavers cannot read and write sufficiently to fill in a job application form, can the actual published statistic be tracked down from your reference?

Keeping track

There are several established systems for achieving this task. What you need for all of them is a full record of the source of your information. This is why we stressed very strongly in Chapter 9 that you should always attach details of the author, publication, page number, date of publication and publisher to each note that you have taken from your reading sessions. Without this information you will be at a loss to provide a full reference; many wasted hours can be spent trying to track down the source of a really useful quotation or a relevant theory or opinion, perhaps months after you have read them.

It is the best idea to incorporate all the referencing details while preparing your drafts. This is easily done using bibliographic referencing software such as EndNote®. This will prevent references from becoming 'detached' from the relevant text and will save much time later on in the production of the finished script. The citation is the acknowledgement within the text to indicate the source of the opinion or information. This is expanded to the full details in the reference found in the reference list at the end of the dissertation. Do not confuse this with a bibliography, which is a list of books you have referred to or which expand on the subject, but which may not have been actually cited in your text. Correct referencing can quite easily be done if you use one of the systems we suggest below.

Right ways of doing it

It is likely that your university school or department will recommend a particular system of referencing to which you should adhere. There are actually many alternative systems on offer that differ in detail, and publishers usually stipulate which one should be used if you publish your work with them. Here are two alternative systems that you can use. These two commonly used systems – the Vancouver (numeric) system and the Harvard (author–date) system – are explained in some detail to show the principles of referencing.

Vancouver (numeric) system

This referencing system is used internationally and is often adopted in medical and other health care journals. It is ideally used for shorter pieces of text, or for separate chapters, articles or papers. It is suitable for use in a research proposal. The citation is simply a number in superscript at the appropriate spot in the text (i.e. after the statement or piece of information to which it refers). You can include several numbers or a range of numbers to refer to several publications. Note, the punctuation is always before the superscript number. For example, the following abridged extract is taken from a short article [Appleton J.V. (2006) Safeguarding Children] published in *Community Practitioner*:

> The revised guidance for England, *Working Together to Safeguard Children – A guide to Inter-agency working to safeguard and promote the welfare of children*[1] was launched in April 2006 and replaces the 1999 edition ... The new guidance reflects major developments in legislation, policy and practice which followed Lord Laming's Inquiry into the death of Victoria Climbié[2] and the Chief Inspectors' Reports on Safeguarding Children.[3,4] The Government's response to these reports informed the Green Paper *Every Child Matters*[5] and the Children Act (2004),[6] with plans to integrate services around the needs of children ... Safeguarding and promoting the welfare of children is defined as: 'protecting children from maltreatment; preventing impairment of children's health or development; and ensuring that they are growing up in circumstances consistent with the provision of safe and effective care; and undertaking that role so as to enable those children to have optimum life chances and to enter adulthood successfully'.[1(p5)]

The reference gives the full details of the publication and is placed in number order in the list of references.

References for the above extract

1. HM Government. *Working Together to Safeguard Children – A guide to Inter-agency working to safeguard and promote the welfare of children.* 2006. Available at: www.everychildmatters.gov.uk/socialcare/safeguarding/workingtogether/

2. Department of Health and Home Office. *The Victoria Climbié Inquiry. Report of an Inquiry by Lord Laming.* London: HMSO, 2003.

3. Department of Health. *Safeguarding Children. A Joint Chief Inspectors' Report on Arrangements to Safeguard Children.* London: DH, 2002.

4. Commission for Social Care Inspection et al. *Safeguarding Children. The second joint Chief Inspectors' Report on Arrangements to Safeguard Children.* London: Commission for Social Care Inspection, 2005.

5. DfES. *Every Child Matters.* London: The Sationery Office, 2005.

6. The Stationery Office. *Children Act 2004.* London: The Stationery Office, 2004.

The sequence of information for books is: author, title, edition (if not the first), place, publisher, date. Books containing the work of several authors put together by an editor need details of the author cited as well as the editor, so lists: author, title of his/her chapter, editor, title of the book, place, publisher, date, relevant pages. Journal references are slightly different: author, title of article, title of journal, date, volume/issue or part number, relevant pages. See also examples below of news-papers, Internet sites etc.

Here are some additional examples that show the details of the Vancouver (numeric) system in different cases. Take particular care to be consistent with the punctuation, spaces, use of capitals and italics. Instead of italics you can use underlining or bold, as long as you are consistent.

1. *Children Act 2004.* London: The Stationery Office, 2004. **[Act of parliament]**

2. Appleton JV. Safeguarding Children. *Community Practitioner* 2006; 79 (6): 176–177. **[Journal article]**

3. Munro E. *Effective Child Protection.* London: Sage Publications, 2002.**[Book]**

4. Reder P, Duncan S, From Colwell to Climbié: Inquiring into fatal child abuse. In: Stanley N, Manthorpe J, editors. *The Age of the Inquiry. Learning and blaming in health and social care.* London: Routledge, 2004. p92-115. **[Chapter in a book]**

5. Wilson K, James AL, editors. *The Child Protection Handbook,* 3rd ed. London: Baillière Tindall, 2007. **[Edited book]**

6. Carvel J. NHS greatly improved – but not for all. *The Guardian* 2007 Dec 5. p12. **[Newspaper article]**

Harvard (author–date) system

This referencing system is also used internationally. It has the advantage that brief details of the publication are given in the citation in the text and the list of references is arranged alphabetically. This eliminates the need to synchronize the order of citations and references, so easily disturbed if you rearrange the text. Another advantage is that the basic information supplied by the citation remains with the relevant text wherever you might move it. It is therefore ideal for using in extended texts, such as dissertations, theses and books, subject to several drafts and revisions. Note that 'et al.' is used when there are more than two authors.

Below is the same text as in the example above, but using the Harvard system:

> The revised guidance for England, *Working Together to Safeguard Children – A guide to Inter-agency working to safeguard and promote the welfare of children* (HM Government, 2006) was launched in April 2006 and replaces the 1999 edition ... The new guidance reflects major developments in legislation, policy and practice which followed Lord Laming's Inquiry into the death of Victoria Climbié (DH and Home Office, 2003) and the Chief Inspectors' Reports on Safeguarding Children (Department of Health, 2002; Commission for Social Care Inspection et al, 2005). The Government's response to these reports informed the Green Paper *Every Child Matters* (DfES, 2005) and the Children Act (2004), with plans to integrate services around the needs of children.... Safeguarding and promoting the welfare of children is defined as: 'protecting children from maltreatment; preventing impairment of children's health or development; and ensuring that they are growing up in circumstances consistent with the provision of safe and effective care; and undertaking that role so as to enable those children to have optimum life chances and to enter adulthood successfully'. (HM Government, 2006, p.5)

The references are given in alphabetical order in the list of references. Note the different order of the items and use of punctuation. The date is given in brackets after the name of the author, rather than near the end. This is quite useful, as there might be several works by one author but of different dates. List these in date order. If there is more than one reference of the same date, then letter them, e.g. (2008a), (2008b), (2008c). Use the same lettered date in the citation. Below is a final reference list formatted using the Harvard system.

References

Appleton, J.V. (2006) Safeguarding Children. *Community Practitioner*, 79 (6), pp. 176–177. **[Journal article]**

Carvel, J. (2007) NHS greatly improved – but not for all. *The Guardian,* 5 December, p. 12. **[Newspaper article]**

Children Act 2004. London: The Stationery Office. **[Act of parliament]**

Department of Health (DH) and Home Office (2003) *The Victoria Climbié Inquiry. Report of an Inquiry by Lord Laming.* London: HMSO. **[Report]**

HM Government (2006) *Working Together to Safeguard Children – A guide to Inter-agency working to safeguard and promote the welfare of children.* Retrieved on 20 August 2006 from: http://**www.every childmatters. gov. uk/socialcare/safeguarding/workingtogether/** [Report in electronic format]

Munro, E. (2002) *Effective Child Protection.* London: Sage Publications.**[Book]**

Reder, P. and Duncan, S. (2004) From Colwell to Climbié: Inquiring into fatal child abuse. In Stanley, N. and Manthorpe, J. (Eds) *The Age of the Inquiry. Learning and blaming in health and social care.* London: Routledge, pp.92–115. **[Chapter in a book]**

Wilson, K. and James, A.L. (Eds) (2007*) The Child Protection Handbook.* 3rd ed. London: Baillière Tindall. **[Edited book]**

Other reference systems differ in detail. If you use bibliographic or reference management software such as Endnote, Procite or Reference Manager the program will automatically draw up reference lists correctly in a choice of many referencing systems on the basis of the details you enter on the database.

How many references do I need?

There is no simple answer to this question. It all depends on the type of dissertation you are writing. Also, some sections of the dissertation will have many more references than others. So where and when should these references appear? Here is a list of these instances, some more obvious than others:

- In a general description of the background to your chosen subject. This will appear in your proposal and in the introduction to your dissertation. What are the main factors, ideas, approaches in the subject?

- In a literature review of the particular issues raised by your research question or problem. Just about every dissertation will have one of these reviews. Who wrote what – up-to-date evidence and comparisons?

- In the description of the methodology you have used to do your research. Again, every dissertation should contain some of these. What are the sources of your information on research methods?

- Appealing to higher authorities as a way of justifying your arguments. The opinion of an expert usually carries more weight than that of an under-graduate student. Who said it, where?

- Using secondary data sources. You might use government or other statistics. Where do they come from?

- Inserting quotations, diagrams and illustrations. Always a useful and attrac-tive feature. You must acknowledge the sources. Where did they come from?

You will see from the above that the type of dissertation that will be full of references is one that reviews the work of others, for example in a crit-ical analysis of parenting programmes, an evaluation of health economic theories, or a review of different self-care practices. Where most of the writing describes your actions and your own collected information, for example in carrying out an experiment or survey, then fewer references will be required. But every dissertation will need to refer to ideas, infor-mation, methods and material produced by others: nothing is new, every-thing comes from somewhere.

Given that some dissertation subjects will automatically require more references than others, how can you judge for yourself, apart from the mate-rial you have collected anyway, how many references will be enough, or even too many? The latter is easier to answer. Do not bolster your list for the sake of trying to impress. Adding spurious or irrelevant references will actually count against you.

As to the question of how many is enough, this is a matter of both knowledge and judgement. If you are a particularly keen and effective sleuth you will unearth more relevant secondary material than if you are a reluctant searcher. What you must ensure is that you have included the essential references to the most important work in your subject. You will not know what these are unless you find out! After having done your searches, if you can, check with your supervisor or a specialist in your sub-ject whether you have missed anything important. Swapping information with your fellow students can also help at this stage.

Assuming you have included the basic minimum of references, your method of enquiry and style of writing will influence how you use refer-ences. Be alert to making unsubstantiated statements: always add a ref-erence or give some supporting information. In the end, you will have to judge what you are comfortable with.

What should I do next?

If you have not been systematic in recording your references in your notes, now is the best time to go back and do it. The later you leave it, the more likely you will have forgotten the sources of your information and quotations.

If you have been meticulous in keeping the references with the notes, then whatever note taking and storing system you have used, you will manage the referencing without problem. When you prepare a draft of a chapter or section, include the citations and references straight away. We know that it is tedious and tends to break up your flow of thought, but if you do not do it immediately it will take much longer to go back and do it later.

Do check through your drafts to spot any assertions, quotations, descriptions or other material that are not purely based on your own individual work.

Further reading

First, consult your own library or department to find any guidance or handouts they might produce. These should be ideally suited to your needs. If you really need more information, then here are some books:

Bosworth, D. (2004) *Citing Your References: A Guide for Authors of Journal Articles and Students Writing Theses or Dissertations*. Thirsk: Underhill.

British Standards Institution (1990) *Recommendations for Citing and Referencing Published Materials*. BS 5605. London: BSI.

Pears, R. and Shields, G. (2005) *Cite them Right: The Essential Guide to Referencing and Plagiarism*. Newcastle upon Tyne: Pear Tree Books.

Chapter 18

How Can I Manage a Long Piece of Writing?

Chapter contents

- When to start writing up
- Frame and fill
- Marshalling your notes and drafting your text
- Revisions
- Tops and tails
- How do I come to conclusions?
- Do not forget your grammar, spelling and punctuation!
- What should I do next?
- Further reading

When to start writing up

To sit down in front of a blank computer monitor with the task of writing a 10,000- or 20,000-word dissertation is a daunting prospect and one to be avoided. It is easy to ensure that you will not be faced with this situation. The trick is to gradually amass a collection of notes, observations and data on the issues relevant to your study, which you can then use as a basis for your first draft. This way, you will have started writing your dissertation without even realizing it. If you have followed the advice in Chapter 9 about organizing your note-taking system, you should have little problem in retrieving the notes in an orderly fashion.

To lessen the anguish of starting to write up later on in the programme, it helps to build up your first draft from an early stage. To be able to do this you will need to prepare a structure for the dissertation as soon as you are clear what you will be doing. You can devise this in outline after you have done some background reading and completed your proposal. The structure will then provide a framework into which you can insert your text. Do not expect either the framework or the text to be the final version. Both will need refining and revising as your work and understanding progress. Luckily, word processors make revision very quick and easy.

The issue of writing style should be considered at this point. As a dissertation is an academic piece of work, generally a more formal style is adopted. At its extreme, this avoids use of the first person and therefore the personal pronoun 'I' altogether. It is a good idea to raise the issue of style when you discuss your work with your tutor or dissertation supervisor. There may be some indications given in the assignment details: you should read these carefully anyway for instructions on what is expected of you.

Frame and fill

The framework for your dissertation is most easily created by making a list of possible chapter or section headings. Consult your proposal and plan of work for indications of what these may be. At the very simplest level the divisions may be like this:

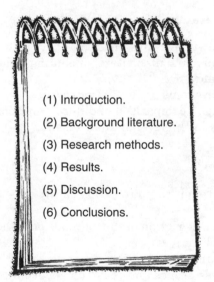

(1) Introduction.

(2) Background literature.

(3) Research methods.

(4) Results.

(5) Discussion.

(6) Conclusions.

This assumes that you will use the background reading to clarify the main issues of your research; that you will use one or several research methods to delve more deeply into these issues; that this will produce some data or results that you will present and analyse; and that you will be able to draw some conclusions from this analysis in relation to the main issues. This is a conventional format and can be applied to a study in almost any subject. There are other, unconventional, ways of organizing a dissertation. If you do want to use an unusual structure or even want to develop your own, it is best to discuss this with your supervisor to check that it will be acceptable. The main thing is that you can set up a convincing overall argument that leads from your intentions to your conclusions.

Once you have the main framework, you can elaborate on the contents of each section by inserting subheadings indicating the aspects that you want to cover in each. Just use your current knowledge and a bit of imagination at first to suggest relevant subheadings. This will help to establish the thread of your argument as discussed in Chapter 10. You will be able to reorder, expand or change these as you progress.

An example of subheadings is given in the box below.

Introduction

- Outline the main focus of your dissertation and the research question.
- A short summary of the context of the study.
- The main problems or issues to be investigated.
- The overall approach to the project.
- A short description of the structure of the dissertation.

Background literature

- Aspects of the subject investigated.
- Historical and current context, including relevant health and social care policy.
- Evidence of problems or contentious issues.
- Current debate – comparison of different opinions or approaches.
- Shortcomings in the level of knowledge.

Research methods

- General approach to your research study – brief mention of philosophy.
- Selection and description of the methods of data collection related to the study objectives.
- Selection of sample and pilot work.
- Issues of access, ethics and research governance.
- Issues of validity and reliability and/or rigour.
- Analytical methods used (e.g. statistical tests – specify which ones, comparisons, coding, thematic analysis).
- Methods of presentation of results.

Results

- Results of your data collection and analysis, illustrated using charts, graphs, diagrams, spreadsheets, statistics, quotes from interviews.

Discussion

- A discussion of the results and what they mean in relation to the research question and study objectives.
- What are the implications for practice?
- Recommendations arising from the study.
- Any study limitations or problems and how these were addressed or overcome.
- Personal reflections on the research process.

Conclusions

- Overall conclusions of the dissertation, drawing together your discussions on the main issues investigated.
- Implications of the study for health and/or social care practice, education and research.

The subheadings outlined above are fairly general so that you can possibly apply these or something equivalent in the context of your subject. You will have to use your imagination and judgement to assess if this arrangement actually suits what you want to do. Devise your own sequence if you like, but note the overall pattern of identifying issues from background study, the definition of how you will investigate these, and how you will present the information gained and how this will be analysed to enable you to come to conclusions.

You do not have to start writing your text at the beginning and continue to the end. Use what notes you have got so far and insert them where they are relevant in order to fill in the framework. If you have the notes already written on computer, then you can simply copy and paste them in a rough order under the appropriate headings and subheadings. If you have recorded them on paper, now is the time to transfer them into the word processor. You will thus quickly have several pages of (very) rough draft.

However, be warned. Even though it might look pretty impressive, the text will be no more than a series of raw notes, completely unedited, disjointed and incomplete. But it will provide a solid basis for working on to produce a first draft.

Marshalling your notes and drafting your text

You will probably be told what the overall length of your dissertation is required to be. If not, find out by asking your supervisor, or consult your module or course handbook. You need to know this in order to determine how long each section should be to get a balanced result. As a guide, 5,000 words are equivalent to about 25 pages of double-space type. Taking the above six-chapter arrangement as a guide, a balanced proportion of content might be as follows.

- **Introduction 5%.** This serves as a guide to the dissertation for the reader.
- **Background 20%.** A review of the literature and information about the context of the study, and a description of the specific research problems or questions that have emerged and that you will tackle in the rest of the dissertation.
- **Research methods 20%.** A description of the steps you will take and techniques you will use to actually investigate the main issues. Reasons for using these methods must also be included.
- **Results 20%.** A record of what you did and what results came out of your investigations. You might split this into two or three sections if you are investigating two or three different issues.
- **Discussion 20%.** A discussion of the results and how they relate to the research question and study objectives.
- **Conclusions 10%.** An interpretation of the results in light of the main issues.
- **The remaining 5%** will be ancillary matter such as the abstract or summary, list of contents, bibliography, etc.

Now you will be ready to start inserting your notes into your structure. How do you get the right notes in the right place? This is where your retrieval techniques will be put to the test. Assuming that your framework gives you enough indication of what you are looking for, search through your notes by key word or subject. If you do this on the computer, you will be shown a selection of relevant notes, from which you can choose what you think is suitable for that section. You can do this manually with notes on paper. Other useful search parameters may be date or author.

For the introduction, just insert your proposal for now. You will be able to use this, suitably edited, when you have finished the rest of the writing, to explain the nature of the dissertation. More will be added later to explain the structure of the dissertation.

Your proposal will indicate the sort of areas that your background study will need to cover. There are likely to be several aspects of the subject that need looking at, for example, health and social care policy, national statistics, current evidence, conflicting opinions, political, financial, organizational and social aspects. At this stage you will need to clearly define the limits of your study: you only have a short time to complete it, so keep it manageable.

Revisions

The nice thing about using a word processor is that you can easily change things after you have written them. This takes off the pressure of getting everything right first time – something that is impossible to do anyway. Once your work is on paper, then you can review it, get a second opinion on it, and discuss it. You cannot do these if it is still all in your head; hence the importance of getting on with writing as soon as possible. Regard the making of revisions as an integral part of the process of doing a dissertation. You will of course have to include some time for this in your time plan.

You do not have to finish the dissertation or even a section of it before you revise it. You can use the process to accumulate your written material, adding to the latest version as the information comes in or as you get the writing bug. Regularly reviewing what you have done so far and to what quality will keep you aware of how far you have progressed and what still needs to be done. It also enables you to break down the work into small sections, revising, altering and expanding sections as your understanding develops. The text will thus evolve as a series of small steps that should need no drastic revision at the last moment.

Revising can be done at different levels. The more general levels are concerned with getting the structure and sequence right. Revision might entail moving around headings and blocks of text. Apart from the content of the text, you may want to try out different page layouts and formatting. At a more detailed level, you might look at the sequence of paragraphs: does each concentrate on one point, do they follow each other in the right sequence? At the most detailed level you will be looking at grammar, punctuation, vocabulary and spelling.

We find that it is much easier to review what we have written when it is printed out on paper rather than still on screen, one can get a better overview of the layout, length of sections, and line of the argument. If your eyesight is good, change the font to really small (perhaps eight point) before printing, both to save paper and to make it easier to have an overall view of the work. You will quickly spot gaps, dislocations in the sequence and imbalances in the length of sections. Alternatively, reduce the line spacing instead of the font size in order to maintain the line justification and familiar appearance of the script. Do remember though, that you are only doing these adjustments to make it easier to review your draft. Normally, the final version must not be submitted in less than 12-point font size (check the submission details for your dissertation, see Chapter 19).

It is important to keep track of your revisions: make sure you know what the latest one is! The best way is to save each revision as a new file, clearly labelled with a revision number (e.g. Chapter_3_version_1, Chapter_3_version_2, etc.). You will thus be able to go back to a previous revision if you change your mind or want to check on some detail. Most word processing programs also provide a facility for keeping track of revisions.

Tops and tails

Particularly if you write your dissertation over a longish period and produce sections based on your notes, thoughts and blocks of data, it is difficult to get smooth continuity in the text. This is really needed in order to make the dissertation clear and easy to read. You cannot usually do this completely as you are building up the text, so one aspect of your revisions should be to check this. As is usual with most things, continuity can be considered at different scales. You can check on the following aspects in descending order.

Scale of the whole dissertation

- Introduction – gives a brief guide to the reader about the content and structure of the whole work. It should be a separate chapter or section at the beginning of the dissertation.
- Conclusions – the finale of your dissertation. One should be able to read this section separately as a full account of the results of your investigations.
- Links and cross-referencing – the issues studied should arise out of the background; the methods used in the investigation should relate to the research question(s)/issue(s) studied; data collection (the actual fieldwork or personal research work) should follow the methods described; the data should arise from the fieldwork or personal research; the conclusions should be produced from the data and encapsulate the answers to the question(s) or issue(s) raised at the beginning of the work. In this way you will complete the circle: problems raised, answers found.

Scale of the chapters or sections

- Introduction – a few paragraphs provide a lead-in to the subject of the chapter.
- Conclusion or summary – draws together the main results of the discussion in the chapter.
- Links and cross-referencing – the introduction might usefully refer to the main issues/problems dealt with in the chapter; a final sentence or two form a bridge to the next chapter; sometimes cross-references are usefully added to linked information in other chapters.

> **Scale of the paragraphs and sentences**
>
> - Paragraphs – make one overall point or deal with one topic. First sentence introduces this, subsequent sentences develop this, the final sentence possibly forms a conclusion and leads to the next paragraph.
> - Sentences – best to keep short and clear.
> - Links and cross-referencing – consistent use of terminology. Define terms and abbreviations the first time they are used.

How do I come to conclusions?

The whole point of collecting data and analysing them is so that you can come to some conclusions that answer your research questions and achieve the aims of your dissertation project. The trouble with this part of the dissertation is that it inevitably comes near the end of your project, when you are probably tired from all the work you have already done, when your time is running out, when you have pressures from other commitments such as revision and exams or clinical practice placement assessments – let alone all the other things you want to get in before your undergraduate days are over.

To compound it all, the coming to conclusions is a quite demanding and creative process that requires a lot of clear thinking, perception and meticulous care. All the previous work will be devalued if you do not sufficiently draw out the implications of your analysis and capitalize on the insights that it affords. You cannot rely on the reader to make inferences from your results. It really is up to you to vividly explain how the results of your analysis provide evidence for new insight into your chosen subject, and to give answers to the particular research questions that you posed at the beginning of the dissertation. The main point we want to make is that you should programme some time for this process, and not underestimate its importance.

Ideally, you will have the research questions at the forefront of your mind throughout your time working on your dissertation. However, this is not always possible as you grapple with learning new techniques and methods and the problems of organizing your data collection and analysis. But you must come back to them regularly in order to ensure that you are keeping to the intentions of the project, and will end up with relevant material in order to be able to suggest answers to the questions.

Coming to conclusions is a cumulative process. It is unlikely that the problem you have chosen is simple, with questions raised that can be answered with a simple yes or no. Even if they can, you will be required to describe why it is one or the other and make an argument to support your case. Normally, you will find that the questions have several subquestions, and even these can be broken down into components requiring separate investigation. Throughout the analysis part of your work you will be able to make conclusions about these fragments of the main issues. The skill is to gather these up at the end in the concluding chapter to fit them together into a 'mosaic' that will present the complete picture of the conclusion to the entire dissertation.

Just as you should be able to summarize the main problem that your dissertation addresses in one or two sentences, so you should be able to state the conclusion equally briefly. This belies the complexities that lie in between. You can picture your dissertation as having a continuous thread of argument running through it. The beginning and end of the argument are fat and tightly woven. But in between, the separate strands fan out, become twisted and frayed as different aspects are investigated, but manage to rejoin before reaching the end. The secret to success lies in the sound construction of your argument.

Do not forget your grammar, spelling and punctuation!

Grammar

The principles of English grammar are too complicated to outline here. If you have forgotten the principles of grammar, or never learned them, do not worry. Use your own 'voice' as you write, and explain everything as clearly as you would if you were talking to someone. However, do make sure about any particular requirements of academic writing style. Generally, as long as you are consistent in developing your argument by using straightforward sentences to build up well-formed paragraphs (as explained above) you will be able to communicate effectively. If you are writing in a foreign language, it is worth getting a native speaking colleague to check through a section of your work to see if you are making any recurring mistakes.

Your word-processor program (in this case Microsoft® Word) will indicate any gross grammatical errors if you use the grammar check facility in the tools menu. Check the settings of the spelling and grammar options in the tools menu to see what is actually being checked: you can tick the option boxes for different features. Similar features will be available in most word processing programs.

Spelling

Spelling is also easily checked with the spell check facility. Make sure that the language is correctly stipulated (again, find this in the tools menu). Because of the ease of use of this facility, it is no longer acceptable to submit work with typographical errors. Spell checkers are not infallible. They will not detect a typing mistake that forms a recognizable – albeit a wrong – word e.g. their or there; bowel or bowl. If, for reasons of presentation, you are handwriting some parts of your work, after checking the spelling yourself, get someone else to read the text. It is surprising how blind one gets to one's own mistakes.

Punctuation

Punctuation can also be checked automatically. There is some flexibility here. A good guide to the use of punctuation is to read the text aloud, and fit the punctuation in where the natural pauses occur in speech, for example: commas for short pauses [,], semicolons for greater divisions [;], colons preceding lists [:]. Commas or spaced dashes (often typed as spaced hyphens) should be used both before and after an aside or additional piece of information within a sentence, just as you would with brackets. Direct quotations must always be within quotation marks (now usually only single inverted commas), unless they are lengthy (in excess of 40 words), in which case they are best presented as indented paragraphs. Page numbers should be included in the main text for all direct quotes used.

One of the most common punctuation errors concerns the apostrophe with 's' when noting possession, e.g. 'the animal's face'. With 'it', only use the apostrophe when you can read 'it's' as 'it is'; for the possessive, e.g. 'its face', no apostrophe is needed. As the style of writing a dissertation should not be too conversational, it is better anyway to avoid using abbreviations such as 'it's', 'don't', 'couldn't'.

What should I do next?

Get started, is the simple message. If you have not yet formulated an outline of your dissertation, then this is probably the best place to start. This framework will allow you to painlessly insert any notes you have, thus providing a first body of written work.

It is worth checking your word processing program (or software/ application) for the spelling and grammar features mentioned above. They may need to be activated in order to work.

If you feel that there is not enough information or prompts in the text above, read other books that are more specialized on aspects of dissertation production, such as the process of writing, specific subject-oriented dissertation guides and study guides. See the list below for some suggestions.

Further reading

Here are two books that deal exhaustively with the art of writing, both the technique and practice.

Woods, P. (2005) *Successful Writing for Qualitative Researchers*, 2nd edn. London: Routledge. Really thorough on all aspects of writing – getting started and keeping going, organization, alternative forms of writing, style and editing.

Mounsey, C. (2002) *Essays and Dissertations*. Oxford: Oxford University Press. A compact, easy-to-read guide to writing; in the 'One Step Ahead' series. Other titles in the same series might also be useful: *Editing and Revising* by Jo Billingham, *Punctuation* and *Spelling* by Robert Allen, and *Words* and *Writing Reports* by John Seely.

Also have a look at Chapter 10 in the following book:

Rudestam, K.E. and Newton, R. (2007) *Surviving your Dissertation: A Comprehensive Guide to Content and Process*, 3rd edn. Thousand Oaks, CA: Sage Publications.

And here are three books to help you sort out the finer points of writing in English:

Evans, H. (2000) *Essential English: For Journalists, Editors and Writers*. London: Pimlico. Get your spelling and grammar and construction right with this.

Peck, J. and Coyle, M. (2005) *The Student's Guide to Writing: Grammar, Punctuation and Spelling. Palgrave Study Guides*. Basingstoke: Palgrave Macmillan.

Trask, R.L. (2001) *Mind the Gaffe: The Penguin Guide to Common Errors in English*. London: Penguin. See whether you make common mistakes.

Chapter 19

How Can I Make My Work Look Interesting and Easy to Read?

Chapter contents

- Presentation ideas
- Cover design and binding
- Title
- Acknowledgements
- Abstract
- Contents list
- Introduction
- References and bibliography
- Appendices
- Internal layout and design
- Advanced tips and tricks with the computer
- Avoid the production blues
- What should I do next?
- Further reading

Presentation ideas

Unless you are particularly design oriented, you have probably not spent much time thinking about just what your dissertation will look like. After all, there are many more important things to occupy your time while trying to get it finished. However, a dissertation is as much an exercise in communication as one in research, so time spent in production design pays good dividends. When your examiner is faced with a pile of dissertations to mark, it is obviously those that are attractive, clear and easy to read that will be the most welcomed. Although there are many possible styles of presentation, a few basic guidelines should be followed. These relate to the actual design of the thesis as well as the organization of the material contained within it. The best way to success is to devote some time in forethought and preparation, as it is very frustrating, time consuming and risky to work by trial and error.

As you will be only one of many students at the university or college with the same deadline for submission, the pressure on printing and binding facilities will become greater as the date approaches. Delays will increase just as you are running out of time. We know it is easy to say 'get your work finished early' but you will be doing yourself a favour not to have to join in the last minute scramble. In fact, giving yourself enough time can result in you actually enjoying putting the finishing touches to your 'masterpiece'.

Cover design and binding

Let us start with the first impressions from the outside. You should keep the whole work in one volume, in an A4-sized paper format, which makes it is easy to photocopy. There are several ways of binding your work. However, it is important to ensure that pages cannot become separated, so a folder of loose sheets or slide-on plastic holders will not do. Even the clip-type ring binders are vulnerable to coming undone or the pages being pulled out, with disastrous results. Ring binding with plastic 'comb' rings can cope with almost any number of pages, and also allows the pages to be opened right up so that they lay flat. You need to have access to a special machine for slotting your paper and inserting the binder; these should be available to you somewhere in your university or department, so it is worth finding out in good time.

The cover should have the title of the dissertation, your name, a date and details of the module or course number. Check with the official module instruction for any stipulations on this. Get some good quality coloured card for the front and back covers. You can print on these to good effect. For an even more glossy finish, you can add a piece of transparent plastic front and back. Even if you keep it very simple, ensure that the typography is well arranged and easy to read.

What does 'well-arranged' mean? There are no hard and fast rules on this: you will need to rely on your aesthetic sense and on any ideas gleaned from the layout of other publications that you admire. You should aim to get a certain logic and consistency in the layout, so that it expresses a distinct style. Decide whether you want to centre the text, or if you want to align it to the left or right. Usually, it is wise to keep to the same typeface, altering the size to suit the importance of the text. Using a large font for the main title aids legibility, as does leaving plenty of empty space around the lettering. Avoid having a strong picture as a background to the text.

Title

The title of your dissertation has undoubtedly been the focus of your work for many weeks or even months, but now that you have virtually completed the dissertation, it is worth reviewing it in the light of what you have actually done. Does it still accurately and succinctly sum up the nature of your study? As briefly stated in Chapter 3, the title must contain the crucial terms related to the work; after all, this is what will be listed in any reference to it. Keep it as short as possible.

A useful way to review your title is to check the following points:

- Are the one, two, or perhaps three main concepts or issues mentioned? For example: sport and fitness; learning difficulties; reflection on clinical practice; corporate working, caseload management and health visiting practice.

- Are these then located into a context to focus and limit the study? The context might be a sector of society, time period or location, for example, sport and fitness for disabled people; learning difficulties in first-generation ethnic minorities; reflection on clinical practice with third year student nurses; corporate working, caseload management and health visiting practice in the 21st century.

- An indication of the main methodology or philosophical stance might also be usefully added, for example, whether it is a qualitative study, a case study, a feminist perspective or a literature review.

A common way of forming the title is to state the main concepts, then add the detail as a subsidiary phrase, for example, 'Involving older people in NHS service redesign: a critical review of the literature'. Beginning phrases like 'A study of' or 'A comparison between' can generally be omitted.

On the title page, you should also add your name and the date. You might also add a description of what course or module the dissertation is set to fulfil. Check the module or assignment details for any specific instructions.

Acknowledgements

These are short expressions of thanks to people or organizations that have been particularly helpful in your work. The relatively small scale of an undergraduate dissertation makes this an optional feature, but you may feel particular gratitude that you want to express to someone. If you have been funded by an organization, it is good practice to acknowledge the funding body and this may also be part of the agreement.

Abstract

You have probably realized by now that you do not have time to read whole books or even journal articles in order to find out if they are of interest to you. You have also probably noticed how useful the abstract, list of contents and introduction are as shortcuts to finding out the content of the text. The index is also useful in this respect. In order to provide a guide to the reader of your dissertation, you should also provide these features. Seeing it from the point of view of the reader will help you to make these features really useful.

The abstract (or résumé, often called the executive summary in reports) is a compact summary of the whole dissertation, usually not more than 150–200 words long. It is placed right at the beginning of the dissertation, usually after the acknowledgements (if any) and before the list of contents. Despite it being at the beginning of your document, you can only write it, for obvious reasons, when you have completed the rest. This will be at a time when you are under stress to complete, so it is worth allotting some time for its production in your dissertation work timetable. It should not take too long, but is really worth the effort from the point of view of impressing your marker. Because it is a précis of your work, it must be short and may not be so very easy to write: you will need all your skills in summation to make it read well (this paragraph is already more than 150 words long).

Start with a statement of the main aims of the project. Then add a bit of background to give the context in which it was carried out. Follow with the specific questions or problems that you posed, and then with the principal methods you used to investigate them. End with the main conclusions and perhaps a note about their significance.

For examples of abstracts, see any thesis, journal papers published in both academic and professional journals, conference abstracts, or a journal of abstracts.

Contents list

The list of contents is much easier to devise. All you have to do is make a list of all your chapter headings, subheadings, and even sub-subheadings, together with their page numbers. Put this just before the main text. You can automatically generate the list of contents with your word processing software if you do not want to do it manually (see below for how it is done). To be really professional, you can also add lists of figures, charts and illustrations, either separately or all together on one list. Just make a list of the titles and page numbers in order of appearance. Insert this after the list of contents, starting on a separate page. A list of appendices, if you have any, should also be added.

Introduction

The subject matter of the introduction has been mentioned in the previous chapter. Just to remind you, here it is again: the main aims of the dissertation, a short summary of the context of the study, the main problems or issues to be investigated, the overall approach to the project, and a short description of the structure of the dissertation. This lead-in to the main body of the work will be just a short chapter, the main function of which is to provide a guide to the reader about the subject and structure of the dissertation, and to point out its main features. It should whet the reader's appetite to read on, but not give away the conclusions – just as a detective novel will create a certain suspense from the start but not say 'whodunnit'. As your work is unlikely to go exactly as originally planned, it is not feasible to complete the introduction before the main part of the study is completed. Hence, allow yourself some time near the end of your dissertation programme for finishing this writing.

References and bibliography

What is the difference between these two? A list of references mentions all the publications that have been referred to in the text, but nothing else. A bibliography lists also other publications that are useful or related to the subjects covered.

You definitely need to include a list of references. Normally, and most conveniently, the list is put at the end of the dissertation. Alternative locations, which are more difficult for your marker to review, are at the end of each chapter, or as footnotes to the relevant pages. If you are using the British Standard (numeric) system (see Chapter 17), make sure that the numbers follow correctly in sequence and tally with the references. These may have been shifted when you made revisions to the text. If you are using the Harvard (author–date) system, check that the references are in alphabetical order. You should also scan through all the citations in the text to ensure that they are detailed on the reference list – a tedious task, but one that can save you losing marks.

The order and punctuation in each reference should accord with the standard requirements and be consistent throughout. Mistakes are easily made here, so a thorough check is required. You will save yourself time and trouble if you have used a bibliographic or reference management software package, as the list can be generated automatically. Even if you have not, you have probably made a list of references as you went along, so paste this in and revise it rather than attempt to type it all out again from scratch.

If you want to indicate that you have read more widely than just those publications cited, it is best to add a bibliography as a separate list. The intention might be to show that you have consulted supplementary information, for example, on writing skills, research methods or project organization. Do not overdo it though; it is obviously easy to list whole sections of the library catalogue, but this will convince no one of your extraordinary diligence.

Appendices

These are additional sections added at the end to supplement the main text, and are generally to be avoided. The main argument for this is that either the information is relevant to the subject and therefore should be included in the main text, or it is not directly relevant and should therefore not be added at all.

There are certain exceptions to this though. If you have sought ethical review from a research ethics committee, the ethics committee application form and a copy of the approval letter should be included as an appendix. Copies of letters of permission or other crucial correspondence might also be included. If you have done a survey, a copy of the questionnaire or interview questions should be added as an appendix, perhaps also with a copy of a typical response (anonymized of course). Similarly, a typical data sheet of observations could be shown. For those undertaking a literature review, it is usual to include a copy of the critical appraisal form used in the study and one worked example of an appraisal of a research paper. Other bits of information that will illustrate how you did the work might also be usefully added, if these are really informative but would disrupt the flow of the main text. You should refer to the appendices where appropriate in the main text and they should be numbered sequentially.

To be avoided is inclusion of lengthy articles on related subjects, full survey responses, elaboration or discussion of important issues. What is certain is that you will not get extra marks by padding out your dissertation with sundry additional information added as appendices.

Internal layout and design

Typographic design and layout is a profession of its own. But even without the help of an expert, it is possible to produce really smart results with a computer. Unless you are a student in publishing or a related subject, it is probably not worth the time and effort to learn a specialized publishing program. It will take you some time just to exploit all the features provided by a normal word processor.

There will probably be stipulations about font choice, minimum font size, line spacing and margins in the module instructions for your dissertation, so it is worth checking before you spend much time experimenting.

We will explain first the design issues that you need to address, then afterwards go into details on how you may achieve these using the computer (based on Microsoft® Word).

Page layout and margins

A bit of design input should be used here. The page layout and margins determine the overall appearance of the content of the dissertation. You only have to look at a few books of different types – novels, textbooks, non-fiction – to see what a range of options there are. Once you have set up a page layout style, make sure that you are consistent in its application. One choice is whether to mirror the layout of left and right pages, or to keep the design the same orientation on all pages. If you are only allowed to print on one side of the paper, which is normally the case, this problem does not occur. As with most issues of design, a few experiments to try out and compare different options will help you to make decisions.

A balance should be achieved between white paper and printed areas; very full pages are tedious to read. Wide margins, as well as being left blank, can be used as an area to place key words, and small illustrations or diagrams. Leave plenty of space at the hinge side of the pages (called 'gutter' in some software), especially if the pages cannot be folded flat when opened.

Word processor tips

- Go to 'File' drop down menu and select 'Page Setup' – start here to determine how the layout of all the pages will look.

- Adjust the margins, paper size, paper source, page layout as desired.

- Go to 'View' drop down menu and select 'Print Layout' – to see the appearance of your page while writing.

- Try also 'File' drop down menu and select 'Print Preview' to see how it will look when printed.

- Go to 'Format' drop down menu and select 'Columns' – to set out your text in columns.

Typography

Here you have a range of choices to make. First, you should decide on the typeface (font). There is a wide choice of these with a range of fanciful names, most used only for billboards or advertising copy. However, even among the 'standard' fonts there is quite a choice. The main distinction is between 'serif' and 'sans serif' designs. Serif designs have the little tails at the ends of the lines, derived from the stonemasons having to start the incision when carving the letters. Times New Roman is one of these. Sans-serif fonts, without these tails, look more modern. Arial is one of these. Funnily enough, it is not always the simplest font that is easiest to read – perhaps because the lack of subtlety makes letters and words less instantly recognizable. The choice of font will determine the overall stylistic appearance of your text. It is easy to try out different ones to see what they look like. Do check though whether your dissertation assignment guidance has any specific requirements about the font and size to be used.

Word processor tips

- Go to 'Format' drop down menu and select 'Font' to determine what font will be used from where you have the cursor onwards. For altering the font in all the text, go first to 'Edit' drop down menu and select 'Select All' to highlight the entire document. You can see in the window what the different fonts on the list look like. Normally you should keep to regular style. For size, see below. You should not need to alter the character spacing. The animations in 'Text Effects', though fun, are not really suitable for use in an academic work: they do not print out well anyway.

- 'Format' drop down menu and select 'Reveal Formatting' is a useful short-cut to formatting features. If it is not visible then go to 'View' drop down menu and select 'Toolbars' and tick the 'Formatting' box.

Font sizes

For easy legibility use a font size of 11 point or more for the general text. Large fonts make reading slower and take up lots of room (this can be used to your advantage if your content is rather meagre). Normally, keep to one font for the text. Exceptions can be for quotations, headings, labelling of diagrams and tables. If the text is divided to serve two different purposes, for example as an extract from the literature and as a commentary on that extract, then you could use two different fonts to make this obvious. Remember to check whether your dissertation assignment guidance has any specific requirements about the font size to be used.

Word processor tips

- 'Format' drop down menu and select 'Font' and then 'Size'.

Line spacing

A normal requirement for work that is marked is that the lines should be double-spaced. This provides room for the marker to add comments and corrections. Check on any official requirement in this respect. If you need to stretch your work a bit, then increase the spacing marginally. Quotations, if in a separate paragraph, are normally single-spaced (i.e. should not need correcting).

Word processor tips

- 'Format' drop down menu and select 'Paragraph' then 'Line Spacing' controls only the appearance of the current and subsequent paragraphs.

Highlight the whole text (Edit/Select All) in order to adjust the whole document.

Paragraphs

You have the choice of indenting the first line to show the beginning of each paragraph. However this is not necessary if you leave a blank line between paragraphs (which we personally prefer).

Word processor tips

- Go to 'Format' drop down menu and select 'Paragraph' then 'Indentation' – note the previous tip about what this controls.

Bold, italics and underlining

These should be used sparingly within the text. They can be used to good effect to accentuate particular words when they are used for the first time (for example, specialist terminology) and to highlight crucial sentences (for example, statement of the main research problem). Be consistent in their use, and it is best not to combine styles (underlined italics). Another common use of a style change is italicized quotations within the text, and within the references in the list of references and bibliography.

Word processor tips

- Go to 'Format' drop down menu and select 'Font' then 'Font Style', or use the 'buttons' on the Format Toolbar.

Headings

This is where a change of font, size and/or style can be used to emphasize the different levels of heading. The most important thing is not to get too complicated and to be consistent – not always easy in a very long document. The placing of headings on the page can be varied. Normal is to keep them aligned to the left. Centred headings tend to look very formal, and headings aligned to the right are rather modern. Indenting sub-headings is common.

Word processor tips

- Go to 'Format' drop down menu and select 'Font' or use the Format Toolbar to do this manually.

- The Format Toolbar also has a Style section with a dropdown menu of automatic headings and other styles. Click on the desired heading level.

You can alter these to your desire in Format/Style/Modify/Format.

Section numbering

Section numbering helps the reader to navigate the dissertation, so it should be consistent and easy to follow. The features that need numbering are: chapters, sections, possibly subsections, figures, diagrams, charts, tables, graphs, appendices and, most important of all, pages (see below).

There are several styles of numbering of chapters and sections, all of which you can generate automatically using the word-processing program. However, these formatting aids are not foolproof and sometimes come up with unexpected results, so checking is always necessary. Consistency is what is looked for. The simplest form of numbering and the most commonly used for lengthy reports is that each chapter is numbered in succession (1, 2, 3, etc.), each main section of the chapters is numbered within that chapter (1.1, 1.2, 1.3, etc.). Subsequent subsections follow the same pattern within the main sections (1.1.1, 1.1.2, 1.1.3, etc.). Three levels of numbering are usually quite sufficient; you may find that two is enough. Make sure that the table of contents corresponds with the actual numbering in the text.

Bullets can be used when you are providing a list where the sequence of items is not significant. Bullets can be generated automatically.

Numbering of illustrations is a normal feature of academic writing. You will have to decide whether to make no differentiation between your different graphical additions, or to categorize them, with each category numbered separately. The simplest is to label them all as figures and number them consecutively in each chapter (Figure 1.1, Figure 1.2, etc.). If there are many illustrations you could divide them into figures (pictures, drawings, cartoons, maps, etc.), charts (graphs, bar charts, pie charts, diagrams, etc.) and tables (tables and matrices). There are no established rules about this categorization; however, each type should be numbered separately in each chapter (Diagram 1.1, Diagram 1.2, Table 1.1, Table 1.2, etc.). An index of the illustrations at the beginning of the dissertation is a useful feature. In all cases, use your judgement to provide maximum clarity and ease in navigation.

Word processor tips

- Select Numbering or Bullets on the Format Toolbar. To format these select the 'Format' drop down menu and select 'Bullets and Numbering'.

Page numbering

This is an essential feature. If you have saved your text as several different files, you will have to ensure that, once combined, the page numbers follow through correctly from beginning to end. There is a choice about the location and style of page numbers that will be dictated by your overall presentation. Choose what you think is the best position for your page layout (top, bottom; centre, left or right), making the numbers easy to find when flicking through the pages. To aid easy finding, keep the numbers near the outside edge of the pages rather than in the centre. Automatic page numbering is a standard feature of word processors.

Word processor tips

- Go to 'Insert' drop down menu and select 'Page Numbers'. To format these go to 'Format' in this last window. If the numbers appear on the Print View but do not print, it might be because the header or footer margins are not big enough. Go to 'File' drop down menu and select 'Page Setup' and 'Margins' to alter these.

Headers and footers

These are the zones at the top and bottom of the page that are repeated on every page, often containing the page number, chapter heading, dissertation title, etc. The headers and footers should be generated using the tool in the word processor; do not try to type them out on each page. The program will ensure that any changes to the length of the text on the page or an increase in page numbers will automatically be catered for. You can use different text in the left and right page headers, for example, the dissertation title on the left, and the current chapter title on the right. You can insert a line to separate the headers and footers from the main text.

Word processor tips

- Go to 'View' drop down menu and select 'Header and Footer'. Write in the box whatever text you want. Use the normal text Align Left/Centre/Right tools from the Format Toolbar to position the chosen headings. If the Header/Footer margins are not big enough to contain your text, increase the margins in 'File' drop down menu and select 'Page Setup' and then 'Margins'.

Illustrations

These can vary so much in size, shape and complexity that you need to make your own judgements as to how you will present them. Colour illustrations require lots of memory, and, of course, colour printing. Scanning in the pictures requires a bit of practice to get the best results. Ensure that you select a compressed file format (e.g. .tif for black and white, .jpg for colour) to ensure the file sizes do not become unwieldy. Do not forget to acknowledge the source of the illustrations.

Word processor tips

- Go to 'Insert' drop down menu and select 'Picture' and 'From File'. You can then locate the file of your illustration. Some clip art illustrations are also provided; most are rather banal, but they might be useful to highlight a point (see example below). Once inserted, you can change the size and position as required.

Graphical work

Graphs, charts and tables can easily be inserted, especially from associated programs (such as Microsoft® Excel® and Access® in the case of Word). Most programs are interlinked through Microsoft® Windows®.

Word processor tips

- Go to 'Insert' drop down menu and select 'Object' or 'File'. If you want to set up a table or worksheet from scratch, use the tools on the Standard Toolbar.

Text boxes

These can be used to separate sections of text in the form of vignettes, excerpts and lists.

Word processor tips

- Go to 'Insert' drop down menu and select 'Text Box', then click on the place where you want it in your script. It can be sized to your requirements, and the font and layout of the text can be determined separately from the normal text. You can also fill the box with colour or shading, alter the frame lines etc. and determine how the surrounding text reacts to it, all by clicking on the box and then from the 'Format' drop down menu, select 'Text Box'.

Advanced tips and tricks with the computer

Word-processing programs bristle with features to help you write and compile reports (and dissertations) so that they are clear and easy to read. We will be referring to the Microsoft® Word program in this section. However, similar features are provided by other word-processing programs.

Spelling, grammar and language

Not really advanced, as checking spelling and grammar is a pretty basic task. You can set the program to check as you go along and alert you to any mistakes. If it does not do this, go to 'Tools' drop down menu and select 'Options' then 'Spelling and Grammar' to alter the settings. But do remember to check what language is set (go to 'Tools' drop down menu and select 'Language' and then 'Set Language'), as there are several types of English available. Highlight the whole document before you reset this (in 'Edit' drop down menu and select 'Select All').

Find and change

Sometimes you want to find a particular word in your document, or need to change a word whenever it appears. To save time go to 'Edit' drop down menu and select 'Find', which will help you do both. Even bits of words, punctuation and other features can be found (look under 'More' and then 'Special').

Auto formatting

The 'Styles and Formatting' tool in the 'Format' menu gives a choice of instantly formatted styles. These arrange the margins, fonts, heading styles and indents to suit a wide range of different types of documents. If you apply one of the options to text that is already written, it shows you instantly in a window just what it will look like. The 'AutoFormat' tool gives you the full range of options on all aspects of formatting, and will apply your choices throughout the document.

Table of contents

This can be generated automatically if you have used the 'Style' facility when setting your text. The 'Styles and Formatting' is on the Format toolbar and gives a range of choices of text style, for example, normal, heading 1, heading 2, etc. These will be picked up when you use the 'Insert' drop down menu and select 'Reference', 'Index and Tables' then 'Table of Contents' facility. You will see that an Index, a Table of Figures and a Table of Authorities can also be generated this way. Consult the Help advice for details of how to mark the text correctly for these.

Readability

Readability scores can give an indication of how easy your style of writing is to read. When you finish checking spelling and grammar, information about the reading level of the document, including the following read-ability scores, is displayed. Each readability score bases its rating on the average number of syllables per word and words per sentence. The Flesch Reading Ease score rates text on a 100-point scale: the higher the score, the easier it is to understand the document. For most stan-dard documents, aim for a score of approximately 60 to 70. The Flesch–Kincaid Grade Level score rates text on a US grade-school level. For example, a score of 8.0 means that an eighth grader can understand the document. For most standard documents, aim for a score of approxi-mately 7.0 to 8.0.

Other word processing programs are likely have a similar readabil-ity check, and there are also other programs that are entirely dedi-cated to evaluating writing styles. Check on your university intranet for these.

Despite this kind of technological wizardry, it is difficult to beat personal judgement. Try to get one of your colleagues or relatives to read a section (or all, if you can persuade them) of your text and ask them whether it is easy to read, is clear and informative, and provides a convincing argument. Take a practical approach to any comments made; ask for suggestions on how any shortcomings could be remedied.

Avoid the production blues

Take some good advice on organizing your computer-based work.

Saving and backing up

You will need to store months of your work, which is so easily corrupted or damaged beyond repair. Ensure against disaster by saving your work regularly and by making backups. Copy your work to two, or better, three different media, for example, USB memory stick, CD-ROM, computer hard drives, and your university intranet home directory (if available to you). There are inexpensive backup programs available that will auto-matically copy or mirror your files on to an external/removal hard drive. It is also a good idea to print out what you have done so far; if all else fails, you can scan this with a character/text recognition program. While you are writing, make a habit of saving your work every 10 or 15 minutes so you do not lose too much if the computer crashes. You can instruct your program to make recovery and backup saves itself automatically, at regular intervals (in the 'Tools' drop down menu, select 'Options', then 'Save', then 'Save Autorecover' every x minutes).

Large files

Your entire dissertation could, no doubt, be saved as one file. However it is a good idea to split it up into sections, perhaps as chapters, and create a file for each. Keeping the files reasonably small can help to speed up the computer and makes it easier to navigate your work. More importantly, if one file becomes corrupted, at least the other ones are safe.

Printing

Dissertations can be quite complicated to print. It may take some time to get what you see on the screen to print correctly. Different printers have different printable areas, so your carefully arranged pages may not appear as desired. Before printing, check all the pages on the Print Preview (in the 'File' drop down menu and select 'Print Preview', or 'button' on the Format Toolbar). Colour illustrations and other graphic work may need colour printing, perhaps on different size paper. Tables and diagrams might need to be in landscape format, or perhaps you might want to print certain pages on acetate. This all needs some thought and time in order to get it right.

Timing

Remember that you will be one of many who want to use the computers and printers before the submission date, so try to avoid the rush of the last few days. Other equipment, such as scanners and binders, will also be in great demand during this time. If you have problems, even the help desk is likely to be subject to long queues.

What should I do next?

Make sure that all your work is adequately backed up. One way to preserve your text against all disasters is to print it out. To do this economically, temporarily reduce the font to eight point, single-line spacing, when you print it. Not only do you save paper, but it is much easier to swiftly review what you have written, and to check the sequence of subheadings and numberings.

See what others have done in the past. You have surely by now looked at examples of successful dissertations from previous years. Now compare a few, looking at the presentation. You will soon see what is attractive, easy to read and professional looking. Consider the cover design, type of binding, and size of paper. Then look at the internal layout and design, use of illustrations and figures. What about the typeface and font size? You will have to make notes and even perhaps sketches of what you think is the most attractive and effective.

This is a good time to check with the official requirements. Is the minimum font size stipulated? Are there instructions concerning margins, paper size, line spacing, binding? If you cannot find the requirements, ask your supervisor or module leader for another copy. Better be safe than sorry.

Play a formatting game. Save one of your chapter drafts to a new file and give it a new label (safest for playing around with) and, with the cursor at the beginning, try out different styles in the style gallery in the format menu. You can also see examples of reports etc. with full formatting. This not only will give you ideas on presentation but can provide a shortcut to the whole formatting process. Do check through afterwards to make sure that the formatting is as you wish throughout.

You can also experiment with generating the contents, fixing the headers and footers, aligning text around illustrations and text boxes, and all the other word processing tricks. Once you have decided what you want and determined how it works, then you can apply it to your proper text.

Further reading

The first port of call for questions about any aspect of word processing is the help facility in your software program. This should answer questions about how to do things, and perhaps suggest things that you had not thought about or did not know. Although time consuming, just exploring all the menus of any computer program is a good way of learning how they work. As you probably will be short of time at this stage of the project, using an explanatory handbook about the program is another option that might be useful. See what is available in your library and your university or college computer centre.

There is no point, we think, in our recommending here lots of books about typography, publishing design, layouts and so forth, as you are unlikely to want to spend the time now in learning about these subjects in detail. However, here are a few books that might be useful:

Allison, B. and Race, P. (2004) *The Student's Guide to Preparing Dissertations and Theses*, 2nd edn. Milton Park: RoutledgeFalmer.

Hudson, D. (1998) *Designing for Desktop Publishing: How to Create Clear and Effective Documents*. Oxford: How To Books.

Lumgair, C. (2000) *Desktop Publishing*. London: Teach Yourself.

Parker, R.C. (2006) *Looking Good in Print*, 6th edn. Phoenix, Paraglyph.

Chapter 20

Who Else Might Be Interested in My Writing?

Chapter contents

- Do not waste all your hard work: make it work for you
- Feedback to participants
- Publishing an article
- Conference papers and poster presentations
- Radio and television
- Grants, awards and prizes
- Publishing on the Internet
- Setting up your own business
- Ethics reminder
- What should I do next?
- Further reading

Do not waste all your hardwork: make it work for you

As soon as you have submitted your dissertation, you will undoubtedly sigh with relief and be keen to get on with doing other things. But do not forget, your submission has been the result of a great deal of hard work and has taken up lots of your time. Perhaps you can wring more use out of it than just a mark from the examiners. It is therefore a very good idea to make a copy of your dissertation for your own use, as in most courses you will not receive it back. It will go into the dissertation collection that you consulted so many weeks ago (well, that is a good start to widening its readership). Anyway, you will probably (and should) have saved an electronic version onto a CD-ROM or USB memory stick.

So what can you do with it so that it produces some more advantages for you? Most people do not bother to do anything, so you will be an exception.

Obviously, whatever you do will take time and effort, so it is only worth doing if you get some benefits. Having some sort of dissemination strategy is important if you want to increase the likelihood of your study having an impact on practice. Consider the following possibilities. You could:

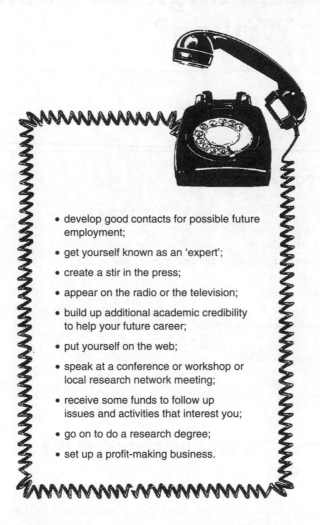

- develop good contacts for possible future employment;

- get yourself known as an 'expert';

- create a stir in the press;

- appear on the radio or the television;

- build up additional academic credibility to help your future career;

- put yourself on the web;

- speak at a conference or workshop or local research network meeting;

- receive some funds to follow up issues and activities that interest you;

- go on to do a research degree;

- set up a profit-making business.

It is pretty obvious that you might get several benefits at once if you work things out in the right way. So, how can you go about it? For a start, in order to be motivated and successful, you need to remain really interested in the subject of your dissertation, as you will have to spend some time revising the length and format of what you have written. If you chose your title wisely right at the beginning, you might have developed even more interest now that you know so much more about your subject.

Listed below are a variety of ways to disseminate your work suitable for the different beneficial goals listed above.

Feedback to participants

If you have used a real-life situation for your dissertation research, for example, in case studies or surveys, you have probably received plenty of help from several people. These may be managers, clinicians or specialists. If you were finding out about aspects of their organization, they may be very interested to know about your findings. They are unlikely to want to read your whole dissertation, but the parts that deal particularly with their organization, perhaps in comparison with others, and the conclusions you have drawn, will certainly be of interest to them. Indeed it is certainly good practice, and often a requirement for being given permission to do research in the first place, that you provide feedback to the participating individuals and/or organization. To disseminate your study findings, you could cut and paste sections of your work to provide them with a short report, tailored to their particular interests. You could also investigate whether they have an in-house or R&D newsletter to which you could contribute a short article, or you could produce a leaflet. Developing a leaflet is a particularly effective way of disseminating the key messages from research to a lay audience and to those who have participated in your study (Neale, 2008).

Providing this type of feedback will certainly get you noticed. People appreciate receiving feedback and this is often one of the key reasons for them agreeing to get involved in a research project in the first place. Offering feedback also provides a nice 'thank you' for their help, it might also be a good step towards getting some work in their organization, if that is what interests you. Even if you are not angling for a job, having contact with the movers and shakers in your particular field of interest is an asset that may be useful in the future.

It is more difficult, and probably not worth your effort, to provide feedback to a large number of interviewees or respondents to questionnaires. However, if you were investigating a community of practitioners, that is, school nurses, or a special interest group, their leaders might appreciate it if you gave a short presentation of your study at one of their meetings. You might be treading on delicate ground, so make sure that the leaders are aware of the contents of your presentation in advance. Assess how this exercise might be useful to you. It will certainly be a plus for your CV, and might also lead to useful contacts and recommendations. It also might be a stimulating experience and end up in a lively discussion – or worse! If a face-to-face session rather daunts you, see if they produce a newsletter or discussion board (many NHS Trusts, R&D departments and social care organizations have these), perhaps even a website to which you could contribute.

Publishing an article

Getting into print is always a good idea, though quite a challenge. You will be well aware of the huge variety of daily, weekly and monthly papers and journals available. Every one of them must fill their publication with articles and advertisements, so they are always looking for material. However, they must be selective – and therefore so must you! How do you target the right publication? It depends on what you write about. Consider the nature of the report you could submit. If you feel it's too ambitious to write an article at this stage of your career, consider writing a letter or an opinion piece instead. Opinion pieces are usually 200–400 words in length, can be written relatively swiftly, yet can contribute significantly to debates on health and social care practices (Cook, 2000).

If your research has come up with really surprising results, that could have a serious or wide significance, that is, something that could be considered newsworthy in a general sense, either locally or nationally, then you could devise a press release and submit it to a local paper or the national press. A press release is only two or three paragraphs long, and provides the essential details of the 'story', the what, where, how, when, who information. Address it to the editor and do not forget to add the date and your contact details. If someone on the editorial team is interested, they will contact you for more information. Obviously, local newspapers are easier to get into, particularly if the story is based in their area. Something along the lines of 'A study at our local university has recently revealed that …' might be a good way to start. The national press will be most interested in sensational (and bad) news – but do not get carried away. You could land yourself in hot water if you exaggerate or falsify your report.

If your research is of interest to a specialist health and social care readership because of its particular subject, then you should look for publications that are focused on this subject and cater for the people with this interest. Academic journals are really aimed at publishing the work of academics and professional researchers. However, niche market professional papers and journals in all aspects of health and social care have proliferated in recent years. You will probably be already aware of those catering for your particular area of interest. If there are several publications focusing on the same topic area, note that each will have its own character, and aim at a particular level of understanding and target readership.

Get to know the journals that focus on your topic of health or social care, you can do this by scanning the journals and obtaining their 'Guidelines for Contributors' (Cook, 2000). Then gauge the level at which you will be most comfortable writing: will it be a clinical article aimed as an educational piece, or a research paper to disseminate information to social workers? Make your choice, keeping in mind the motivation for writing the article in the first place. You normally have to write the whole article first and then submit it to the editor of the chosen publication for consideration. Even so, before you start to write your article it is a very good idea to speak to the journal's editor first. Make a preliminary enquiry by telephone to find out the style of article they prefer and what your chances are of being accepted.

Conference papers and poster presentations

There are numerous conferences that are organized for information, training and debate on virtually every aspect of health and social care practice and at every level of sophistication. There are some that are specifically aimed at the student level, while others sometimes have a student section in them. Find out from your university department and other student friends what is on offer. Some conferences are an annual event and it is likely that previous students have contributed a paper or poster presentation at one of them. One thing is certain, you will not be paid for doing these.

A paper is presented as a short talk of about 15–20 minutes, usually supported by some visual aids such as slides. A poster is an information panel about your work, containing text, graphs, tables, and illustrations, that is displayed in the conference area. You will normally have to respond to a call for papers by sending in a short summary (abstract) of your intended paper or poster several months before the planned event. If accepted, you may have to submit the full paper or poster shortly before. If the conference is far away, perhaps even abroad, see if you can get some financial support for travel and accommodation from your university, your future employer or local R&D department, or your professional organization – they may have some funds for this. Your presentation at a conference will be a good addition to your CV particulars.

Radio and television

Some people will do anything to get on to television. You will not need to, as you have already chosen your own reason for appearing on the radio or television. How you persuade the programme makers is another question. And what advantages you will get from being successful you will have to ask yourself. Let us consider radio first.

The advantage of radio is that there is a multiplicity of stations ranging from the local hospital radio to national networks. Our local area has at least three radio stations that feature all sorts of local news, characters and events. Listen in on the programmes for a few days, if you have not already, and you should soon see whether you could compile something that would interest one of them. Obviously, if your work has revealed some attention-grabbing information about the locality you will have a good chance of being asked to make an appearance – vocally, that is. National radio is a different matter. Apart from taking part in a phone-in discussion, many of which are of questionable quality and will definitely not get you any kudos, you will probably struggle to find acceptance. Only if your dissertation has produced really important or surprising information on a topic of national concern will you have a chance of interesting programme makers on national radio. Again, you need to be familiar with the format of the station output to spot the chance of getting on. Some stations do rely on audience input in some of their programmes.

Local television, apart from the regional news, is virtually non-existent, so you need to try a different approach. You are far more likely to appear on the television if you have committed 'an 'orrible murder' and got caught than if you have done sterling work to help your community. Nicholas Walliman has been invited several times to appear in top entertainment programmes just because he featured in a small book about weird hobbies as someone who played the Swiss alphorn. No one ever asked him to talk about his research projects though. So unless your findings are shocking, amazing, amusing or damning, you will have difficulty in making your break on the small screen. Look out for feature programmes that draw on local knowledge or specialist expertise. One problem is that most serious programmes are planned well in advance, so you do not know what is being looked for. Personal contacts in the television world will be an invaluable asset in this respect.

Grants, awards and prizes

There are several schemes and competitions that give awards on the basis of undergraduate and postgraduate dissertations. If you have done particularly well you might have a chance to cash in on your work. Again, you will have to find out what is offered in your particular subject. Ask your supervisor, your department and your university information centre. The scheme may be awarded by your university, a professional body, a commercial company or another institution. You could win a grant to travel and widen your studies (perhaps registering for a higher degree), win a cash award or prize, or win a place for work experience at a specialist institution or a foreign university. Whatever it is, it will be another good addition to your list of achievements on your CV, as well as an enjoyable reward for all your hard work.

Publishing on the Internet

Anyone can put a web page or add to information on the Internet. What good it will do is another question. This may sound cynical, but it really depends on just how you design and locate your presence on the web. Make a search to see what there is on your subject interest; you have probably done this already during your background research. The main question to ask, whatever you do, is: how will it benefit you?

Having a personal website has advantages if you have something to sell or you need to provide information about yourself and your activities. The contents of your dissertation are unlikely to be an important element of this. However, you might be able to use your newfound knowledge and skills to contribute to existing sites on your subject, or if you are particularly impassioned, to set up a new site dedicated to your interest. The main advantage of doing either of these is that you will be able to network with others with similar interests. Make sure there is a facility to contact you or contribute to a discussion forum on your site. There is plenty of advice available about how to set up and design web pages: see in your university library and magazines in your newsagents. You will also be able to use software programs at your college or university to do the work whilst you are still there.

Setting up your own business

This is probably a long shot in this context. But setting up a business does not necessarily mean hiring a suite of offices and getting yourself a PA. You may be able to exploit your acquired knowledge or skills to earn a bit of money in a more informal way. It is pointless for us to offer loads of advice about what kinds of business you could start and how it is done; the possible options are too wide. But do spend some time considering whether you could offer some kind of a service that you could charge for. Has your added knowledge and skills in research and writing provided you with something other people need? If so, is there a way that you can convince them it is worth hiring you to do the work? Using personal contacts will inevitably be the easiest way to find work of this kind. You will probably have made quite a few during your dissertation work and will also have found out what their needs are. All it needs is some thought and imagination, then some skills of presentation and persuasion, and then some sound work to deliver the goods in order to earn perhaps a very useful addition to your income.

Ethics reminder

It is particularly important when you publicize your research work in any form, that you carefully follow the ethical guidelines. Make sure that where confidentiality has been assured, it is strictly adhered to. The last thing you will want is to cause damage to people or organizations, or get yourself landed in legal troubles.

The two main aspects you should consider are privacy and organizational sensitivity. Just because people have been willing to provide you with personal and organizational information for your university study, it does not mean that they would be happy to see that information in the public domain. Get specific written permission from the sources of information to ensure probity and adhere to the ethical principles outlined in Chapter 13. If you are at all uncertain about any aspect of this, get advice from your supervisor, your university school or department research ethics officer or the chairperson of your local research ethics committee.

Watch out too for copyright issues on illustrations and copies of newspaper articles or headlines. Any pictures, diagrams, graphs and tables copied from published sources are covered by copyright. You need to have written permission from the copyright holder to reproduce them, and they sometimes charge for this. Look at the publishing details at the beginning of the book or journal to find out whom to apply to. Alternatively, only use your own figures and illustrations.

You should also be careful not to make claims that you cannot back up with sufficient evidence. You might not automatically get enough feedback from when your dissertation is marked to see if your arguments were really convincingly based on the supporting data. If in any doubt, you should consult with your supervisor, and even better, the internal examiner who marked your dissertation, and raise the relevant issues to gain his/her opinion.

If you sought ethical approval for your research from a formal research ethics committee, it is likely that you will be required to submit a final summary report form outlining your key study findings to the ethics committee. Any study gaining research governance approval must also provide a final report to the relevant NHS Trust as this is a requirement of the Research Governance Framework (Department of Health, 2005).

What should I do next?

Only go back to exploiting your dissertation work when you feel ready and motivated. But do ensure that you provide any study participants and/or participating organizations with feedback on your research. We hope that this chapter has given you some interesting ideas of what you can do. As any of these options requires quite a bit of time and effort, make sure that you have clear reasons for doing what you have chosen and that you will reap sufficient benefits.

Most research work gets quickly out of date, so the longer you leave it the more difficult it will be to successfully exploit your work. Also, you will quickly lose contact with people you have consulted during the process and you yourself will have moved onto doing other things. So, strike while the iron is hot, make hay when the sun shines, and ... well, you can probably think of a few more proverbs in this vein.

Further reading

Probably the last thing you want to do now is to read more books. However, you may need to get some advice on writing press releases, articles and papers or designing a website. Here are some suggestions on different aspects of getting published – the titles speak for themselves:

Bartram, P. (1999) *Writing a Press Release: How to Get the Right Kind of Publicity and News Coverage*. Oxford: How To Books.

Baverstock, A. (2002) *One Step Ahead: Publicity, Newspapers and Press Releases.* Oxford: Oxford University Press.

Cook, R. (2000) *The Writer's Manual. A Step-by-Step Guide for Nurses and other Health Professionals.* Oxford: Radcliffe Medical Press.

Day, R.A. and Gastell, B. (2006) *How to Write and Publish a Scientific Paper*, 6th edn. Cambridge: Cambridge University Press.

Kogan (1998) *500 Tips for Getting Published: A Guide for Educators, Researchers and Professionals.* London: Kogan.

Lengel, J.G. (2002) *The Web Wizard's Guide to Web Design.* Boston, MA: Addison Wesley.

Lynch, P.J. (2008) *Web Style Guide: Basic Design Principles for Creating Web Sites,* 3rd edn. New Haven, CT: Yale University Press.

Sheridan, D.R. and Dowdney, D.L. (1997) *How to Write and Publish Articles in Nursing*, 2nd edn. New York: Springer.

References

Abidin, R.R. (1995) *Parenting Stress Index*, 3rd edn. Odessa, FL: Psychological Assessment resources.

Appleton, J.V. (2002) 'An examination of health visitors' professional judgments and use of formal guidelines to identify health needs and prioritise families requiring extra health visiting support', PhD thesis, King's College London, University of London.

Appleton, J.V. (2006) 'Safeguarding children', *Community Practitioner*, 79 (6): 176–77.

Appleton, J.V. and Cowley S. (2003) 'Valuing professional judgement in health visiting practice', *Community Practitioner*, 76 (6): 215–20.

Appleton, J.V., De St Paer, A. and Williams J. (2001) 'Community nurse referrals of children in need: an analysis of focus group interviews', RCN International Nursing Research Conference, 5 April, Glasgow.

Appleton, J.V. and King, L. (2002) 'Journeying from the philosophical contemplation of constructivism to the methodological pragmatics of health service research', *Journal of Advanced Nursing*, 40 (6): 641–48.

Avis, M. (1994) 'Reading research critically I. an introduction to appraisal: designs and objectives', *Journal of Clinical Nursing*, 3: 227–34.

Aveyard, H. (2007) *Doing a Literature Review in Health and Social Care: A Practical Guide*. Maidenhead: Open University Press.

Baldwin, M.A. (2008) 'Concept analysis as a method of inquiry', *Nurse Researcher*, 15 (2): 49–58.

Banerjee, A. (2005) *Medical Statistics Made Clear: An Introduction to Basic Concepts*. London: The Royal Society of Medicine Press Ltd.

Bromley, D.B. (1986) *The Case-Study Method in Psychology and Related Disciplines*. Chichester: Wiley.

Burns, N. and Grove, S. (2004) *The Practice of Nursing Research: Conduct, Critique, and Utilization*, Elsevier Philadelphia/London: Saunders Company.

Bury, T. and Jerosch-Herold, C. (1998) 'Chapter 7. Reading and critical appraisal of the literature', in T. Bury and J. Mead (eds), *Evidence-based Healthcare: A Practical Guide for Therapists*. Oxford: Butterworth Heinemann.

Cave, E. and Nicholls, C. (2007) 'Clinical audit and reform of the UK research ethics review system', *Theoretical Medicine and Bioethics*, 28 (3): 181–203.

Campbell, D.T. and Stanley, J.C. (1963) 'Experimental and quasi-experimental designs for research on teaching', in N.L. Gage (ed.), *Handbook of Research on Teaching*. Chicago: Rand McNally.

Chinn, P.L. and Kramer, M.K. (2008) Integrated Theory and Knowledge Development in Nursing, 7th edn. St Louis, Mosby.

Clare Taylor, M. (2000) *Evidence-Based Practice for Occupational Therapists*. Oxford: Blackwell Science.

Cluett, E. (2000) 'Chapter 5. An introduction to statistics', in E.R. Cluett and R. Bluff (eds), *Principles and Practice of Research in Midwifery*. Edinburgh: Ballière Tindall.

Cohen, L., Manion, L. and Morrison, K. (2007) *Research Methods in Education*, 6th edn. Abingdon, Oxon: Routledge.

Coles, L. (2008) 'Prevention of physical child abuse: concept, evidence and practice', *Community Practitioner*, 81 (6): 18–22.

Collier, A. (1994) *Critical Realism: An Introduction to Roy Bhaskhar's Philosophy*. London: Verso.

Cook, R. (2000) *The Writer's Manual: A Step-by-Step Guide for Nurses and Other Health Professionals*. Oxford: Radcliffe Medical Press.

Copi, I.M. and Cohen, C. (2005) *Introduction to Logic*, 12th edn. Upper Saddle River, N.J: Pearson/Prentice Hall.

CRD (2009) *Systematic Reviews. CRD's Guidance for Undertaking Reviews in Health Care*. York: Centre for Reviews and Dissemination, University of York.

Davies, P. (2001) *Get Up and Grow: How to Motivate Yourself and Everybody Else Too*. London: Hodder and Stoughton.

Dawes, M.(1999) Chapter 18: 'Evaluating Change', in M. Dawes, P. Davies, A. Gray, J. Mant, K. Seers and R. Snowball (eds), *Evidence-Based Practice: A Primare for Health Care Professionals*. Edinburgh: Churchill Livinsgtone.

Deeks, J.J. (1998) 'Systematic reviews of published evidence: miracles or minefields?', *Annals of Oncology*, 9: 703–9.

Department of Health (2001) *Governance Arrangements for NHS Research Ethics Committees*. London: Department of Health. (Available from NRES website http://www.nres.npsa.nhs.uk/)

Department of Health (2005) *Research Governance Framework for Health and Social Care*, 2nd edn. London: Department of Health.

Diggle, L., Deeks, J.J. and Pollard, A.J. (2006) 'Effect of needle size on immunogenicity and reactogenicity of vaccines in infants: randomised controlled trial', *BMJ*, 333: 571.

Diggle, L.E. (2006) 'The effect of needle size on the immunogenicity and reactogenicity of vaccines in infancy: a randomised controlled trial', PhD thesis, Oxford Brookes University.

Dixon-Woods, M., Fitzpatrick R. and Roberts K. (2001) 'Including qualitative research in systematic reviews: problems and opportunities', *J Eval Clin Pract*, 7: 125–33.

Dixon-Woods, M. and Fitzpatrick, R. (2001) 'Editorial qualitative research in systematic reviews: has established a place for itself, *BMJ*, 323: 765–66.

Dixon-Woods, M. and Fitzpatrick, R. (2001) 'Including qualitative research in systematic reviews: problems and opportunities', in M. Dixon-Woods, R. Fitzpatrick, K. Roberts (eds), *J Eval Clin Pract*; 7: 125–33.

Earl-Slater, A. (2001) 'Critical appraisal of clinical trials critical appraisal and hierarchies of the evidence', *British Journal of Clinical Governance*, 6 (1): 59–63.

Freeman, R. and Meed, J. (1993) *How to Study Effectively*. London: Collins Educational.

Goodman, R. (1997) 'The strengths and difficulties questionnaire a research note', *Journal of Child Psychology and Psychiatry*, 38: 581–86.

Greenhalgh, T. (1997) 'How to read a paper. Papers that summarise other papers (systematic reviews and meta-analyses)', *British Medical Journal*, 315: 672–5.

Greenhalgh, T. (2006) *How to Read a Paper: The Basics of Evidence-based Medicine*, 3rd edn. Malden, Mass: Blackwell Publishing.

Greenhalgh, T. and Peacock, R. (2005) 'Effectiveness and efficiency of search methods in systematic reviews of complex evidence: audit of primary sources', *British Medical Journal*, 331: 1064–5.

Guba, E.G. (1990) *The Paradigm Dialog*. London: Sage Publications.

HM Government (2006) *Working Together to Safeguard Children – A Guide to Inter-agency Working to Safeguard and Promote the Welfare of Children*. Available at: http://www.everychildmatters.gov.uk/socialcare/safeguarding/working together/(accessed 19 May 2009).

Hewitt, M. (2000) Chapter 2: 'Carrying out a literature review', in M. Saks, M. Williams and B. Hancock (eds), *Developing Research in Primary Care*. Abingdon: Radcliffe Medical Press.

Hewson, C., Yule, P., Laurent, D. and Vogel, C. (2003) *Internet Research Methods: A Practical Guide for the Social and Behavioural Sciences.* London: Sage Publications.

Hek, G. and Langton, H. (2000) 'Systematically searching and reviewing literature', *Nurse Researcher,* 7 (3): 41–57.

Husserl, E. (1964) *The Idea of Phenomenology,* trans. W. Alston and G. Nakhnikian. The Hague: Martinus Nijhoff.

Kane G.A., Wood V.A. and Barlow J. (2007) 'Parenting programmes: a systematic review and synthesis of qualitative research', *Child: Care, Health and Development,* 33 (6): 784–93.

Kemp, V.H. (1985) 'Concept analysis as a strategy for promoting critical thinking', *Journal of Nursing Education,* 24 (9): 382–84.

Kerlinger, F.N. (2000) *Foundations of Behavioral Research,* 4th edn. New York: Holt, Rinehart and Winston.

Krueger, R.A. and Casey, M.A. (2008) *Focus Groups: A Practical Guide for Applied Research.* London: Sage Publications.

Kübler-Ross, E. (1973) *On Death and Dying.* London: Tavistock/Routledge Publications.

Leedy, P. (1997) *Practical Research: Planning and Design,* 6th edn. Upper Saddle River, New Jersey: Pearson, Merrill Prentice Hall.

Leedy, P. and Ormrod, J.E. (2005) *Practical Research: Planning and Design,* 8th edn. Upper Saddle River, New Jersey: Pearson, Merrill Prentice Hall.

Le May, A. (1999) *Evidence-based Practice.* Nursing Times Clinical Monographs No 1. London: Emap Healthcare Ltd.

Lofland, J. (1971) *Analysing Social Settings: A Guide to Qualitative Observation and Analysis.* Belmont, CA: Wadsworth Publishing Company.

Lofland, J. and Lofland, L.H. (1995) *Analyzing Social Settings: A Guide to Qualiative Observation and Analysis.* Belmont, CA: Wadsworth Publishing Company.

McGovern, D.P.B. (2001) 'Meta-analyses', in D.P.B. McGoverns, R. M. Valori, W. S. M., Summerkill and M. Levi (eds), *Key Topics in Evidence-Based Medicine.* Oxford: BIOS Scientific Publishers Ltd.

Miles, M.B. and Huberman, A.M. (1994) *Qualitative Data Analysis: An Expanded Sourcebook.* London: Sage Publications.

Muir Gray, J.A. (2001) *Evidence-based Healthcare: How to Make Health Policy and Management Decisions,* 2nd edn. Edinburgh: Churchill Livingstone.

Muir Gray, J.A. (2008) *Evidence-Based Health Care and Public Health: How to Make Decisions About Health Services and Public Health,* 3rd edn. Edinburgh: Churchill Livingstone.

Mulrow, C.D., Cook, D.J., and Davidoff, F. (1997) 'Editorial: systematic reviews: critical links in the great chain of evidence', *Annals of Internal Medicine,* 126 (5): 389–91.

Mulrow, C.D. (1994) 'Rationale for systematic reviews', *BMJ,* 309: 597–99.

Munhall, P. (1988) 'Ethical considerations in qualitative research', *Western Journal of Nursing Research,* 10 (2): 150–62.

NICE (2002) *Principles for Best Practice in Clinical Audit.* Abingdon: Radcliffe Medical Press.

Neale, J. (ed.) (2008) *Research Methods for Health and Social Care.* Basingstoke: Palgrave Macmillan.

NHS Executive (1996) *Clinical Effectiveness for Nurses, Midwives and Health Visitors.* London: Department of Health.

Nursing Times (2003) 'Clinical audit', *Nursing Times,* 99 (13): 31.

Oppenheim, A.N. (1992) *Questionnaire Design, Interviewing and Attitude Measurement,* 2nd edn. London: Pinter Publishers.

Osgood, C.E., Suci, C.J. and Tannenbaum, P.H. (1957) *The Measurement of Meaning.* Urbana, Illinois: University of Illinois Press.

Oxford Brookes University (2007) *Regulations for Students Taking Assessments.* Oxford: Oxford Brookes Academic Board, Student Conduct Regulations.

Pawson, R. and Tilley, N. (1997) *Realistic Evaluation*. London: Sage Publications.

Pinter, H. (1998) *Various Voices: Prose, Poetry Politics 1948–1998*. London: Faber and Faber.

Polit, D.F. and Tatano Beck, C. (2004) *Nursing Research: Principles and Methods*, 7th edn. Philadelphia; London: Lippincott Williams & Wilkins.

Polit, D.F. and Tatano Beck, C.T. (2005) *Essentials of Nursing Research: Methods, Appraisal, and Utilization*, 6th edn. London: Lippincott Williams & Wilkins.

Preece, R. (1994) *Starting Research: An Introduction to Academic Research and Dissertation Writing*. London: Pinter.

Reason, P. (1994a) 'Three approaches to participative inquiry', in N.K. Denzin, and Y.S. Lincoln (eds), *Handbook of Qualitative Research*, 1st edn. London: Sage Publications. pp. 324–39.

Reason, P. (1994b) *Participation in Human Inquiry*. London: Sage Publications.

Reason, P. (1998) *Human Inquiry in Action: Developments in New Paradigm Research*. London: Sage Publications.

Renoir, J. (1952) 'Filmed interview about his 1930s film', *Une Partie de Campagne*. BBC.

Reynolds, P.D. (2006) *A Primer in Theory Construction*. An Allyn and Bacon Classics, edn. Pearson Education.

Robson, C. (1993) *Real World Research: A Resource for Social Scientists and Practitioner-Researchers*, 2nd edn. Oxford: Blackwell.

Rodgers, B.L. (1989) 'Concepts, analysis and the development of nursing knowledge: the evolutionary cycle', *Journal of Advanced Nursing*, 14: 330–35.

Smith, R. (1992) 'Audit and research', *British Medical Journal*, 305: 905–6.

Snaith, R.P. (2003) 'The hospital anxiety and depression scale', *Health and Quality of Life Outcomes*, 1 (29): 1–4.

Straus, S.E., Scott Richardson, W., Glasziou, P. and Brian Haynes, R. (2005) *Evidence-based Medicine: How to Practice and Teach EBM*, 3rd edn. Edinburgh: Churchill Livingstone.

Summerskill, W.S.M. (2001) 'Hierarchy of Evidence', in D.P.B McGovern, R.M. Valori, W.S.M. Summerskill and M.Levi (eds), *Key Topics in Evidence-Based Medicine*. Oxford: BIOS Scientific Publishers Ltd.

Taylor, M.C. (2000) *Evidence-Based Practice for Occupational Therapists*. Oxford: Blackwell Science.

Taylor, G. (1989) *The Student's Writing Guide for the Arts and Social Sciences*. Cambridge: Cambridge University Press.

The Shorter Oxford English Dictionary (2002) (5th edn.) Oxford: Oxford University Press.

Wainwright, S.P. (1997) 'A new paradigm for nursing: the potential of realism', *Journal of Advanced Nursing*, 26 (3): 1262–71.

Walker, L.O. and Avant, K.C. (2005) *Strategies for Theory Construction in Nursing*, 4th edn. Upper Saddle River, New Jersey: Pearson Education Inc, Prentice Hall.

Whittemore, R. and Knafl, K. (2005) 'The integrative review: updated methodology', *Journal of Advanced Nursing*, 52 (5): 546–53.

Wilson, J. (1969) *Thinking with Concepts*. New York: Cambridge University Press.

Woods, P. (2006) *Successful Writing for Qualitative Researchers*, 2nd edn. London: Routledge.

Zigmond, A.S. and Snaith, R.P. (1983) 'The hospital anxiety and depression scale', *Acta Psychiatr Scand*, 67: 361–70.

Index